British Progressive Pop 1970–1980

British Progressive Pop
1970–1980

Andy Bennett

BLOOMSBURY ACADEMIC
NEW YORK • LONDON • OXFORD • NEW DELHI • SYDNEY

BLOOMSBURY ACADEMIC
Bloomsbury Publishing Inc
1385 Broadway, New York, NY 10018, USA
50 Bedford Square, London, WC1B 3DP, UK
29 Earlsfort Terrace, Dublin 2, Ireland

BLOOMSBURY, BLOOMSBURY ACADEMIC and the Diana logo
are trademarks of Bloomsbury Publishing Plc

First published in United States of America 2020
Paperback edition first published 2021

Copyright © Andy Bennett, 2020

For legal purposes the Acknowledgments on p. viii constitute
an extension of this copyright page.

Cover design: Louise Dugdale
Photo of 10CC by David Warner Ellis/Redferns/Getty images

All rights reserved. No part of this publication may be reproduced or
transmitted in any form or by any means, electronic or mechanical,
including photocopying, recording, or any information storage or retrieval
system, without prior permission in writing from the publishers.

Bloomsbury Publishing Inc does not have any control over, or responsibility for,
any third-party websites referred to or in this book. All internet addresses given
in this book were correct at the time of going to press. The author and publisher
regret any inconvenience caused if addresses have changed or sites have
ceased to exist, but can accept no responsibility for any such changes.

Library of Congress Cataloging-in-Publication Data
Names: Bennett, Andy, 1963-author.
Title: British progressive pop 1970-1980 / Andy Bennett.
Description: [1.] | New York: Bloomsbury Academic, 2020. |
Includes bibliographical references and index. |
Summary: "Considers the often overlooked significance of early
1970s British pop-rock as a period during which the boundaries between pop and rock
uniquely overlapped"–Provided by publisher.
Identifiers: LCCN 2019035763 (print) | LCCN 2019035764 (ebook) |
ISBN 9781501336638 (hardback) | ISBN 9781501336645 (epub) | ISBN 9781501336652 (pdf)
Subjects: LCSH: Popular music–Great Britain–1971-1980–History and criticism.
Classification: LCC ML3492.B46 2020 (print) | LCC ML3492 (ebook) |
DDC 781.660941/09047–dc23
LC record available at https://lccn.loc.gov/2019035763
LC ebook record available at https://lccn.loc.gov/2019035764

ISBN: HB: 978-1-5013-3663-8
PB: 978-1-5013-8599-5
ePDF: 978-1-5013-3665-2
eBook: 978-1-5013-3664-5

Typeset by Integra Software Services Pvt Ltd.

To find out more about our authors and books visit
www.bloomsbury.com and sign up for our newsletters.

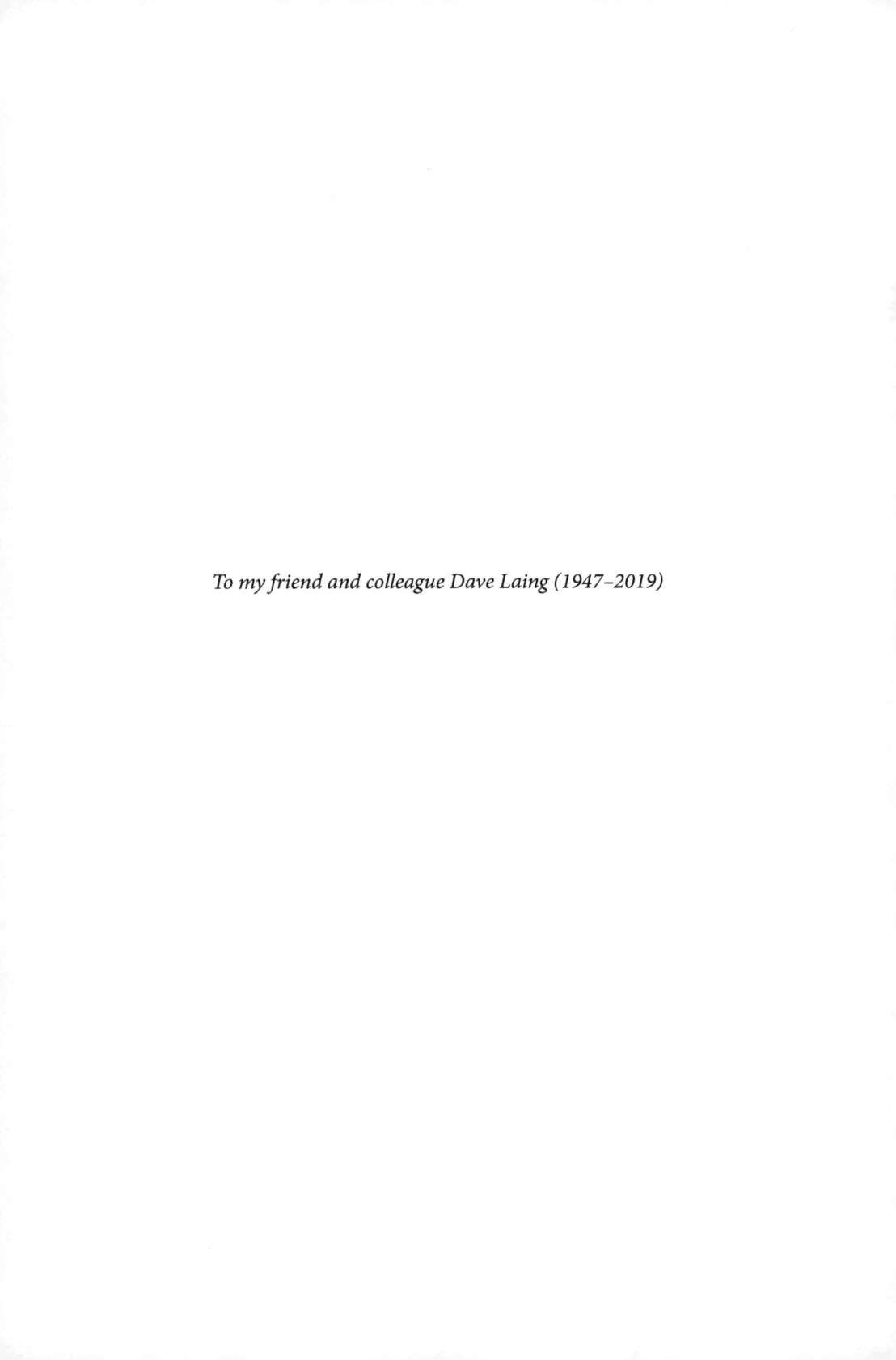

To my friend and colleague Dave Laing (1947–2019)

Contents

Acknowledgements		viii
Introduction		1
1	Progressive pop in context	11
2	New sounds for a new decade	35
3	Progressives in the world of pop	57
4	Big songs and generational soundtracks	79
5	Small 'p' politics	101
6	The end of an era	121
References		145
Index		154

Acknowledgements

The ideas for this book took shape over a number of years during which I steadily compiled a series of notes and musings while working on other academic projects. An early indication that there might be merit in writing a book such as this came from my late and beloved friend and colleague Dave Laing with whom I had many conversations about British popular music of the 1970s over drinks and food during our regular catch-ups in London. Little did I realize at the time that when I actually got down to the business of writing this book, it would be on the other side of the world, and in quite a remote place. Thus, the first draft of the book took shape during a period of study leave in the second half of 2017 down at my family's little hideaway beach house on Kangaroo Island in South Australia. The peace and tranquillity there provided its own unique inspiration. I am also sincerely grateful to all of the islanders I have met to date who have helped me get the house into shape and provided invaluable tips on island living. I would also like to acknowledge the support of the School of Humanities, Languages and Social Science at Griffith University for granting me that important period of study leave to work on the book and the Griffith Centre for Social and Cultural Research for their ongoing generous support of my research and publication endeavours. During my career to date, I have been privileged to meet so many wonderful colleagues, a number of whom have also become very good friends. That would be quite a long list to write down here so I would just like to acknowledge a few of them, including some of those who have given me important ideas and insights for this book: Jon Stratton, Mark Percival, Ben Green, Asya Draganova, Richard Frenneaux, Ross Haenfler, Raphaël Nowak, Helena Huhta, Tim Dowd, Paul Hodkinson, David Baker, Ernesta Sofija, Ian Rogers, Zoe Armour, Andy Linehan, Sara Cohen, Bill Osgerby, Matt Worley, Mikko Salasuo, Paula Guerra, Gordon Thompson, Catherine Strong, Sam Bennett and Mel Bateson. Very late in the writing of the book, I was given a marvellous opportunity to interview Graham Gouldman of 10cc. I'm indebted to Graham for his generosity in answering my various questions and the insights he gave me regarding the career of 10cc. A special word of thanks also needs to go to Leah Babb-Rosenfeld at Bloomsbury Publishing for her interest and ongoing enthusiasm for this book project. Finally, my eternal thanks and gratitude go to my wife Monika and son Daniel for their never ending love and support.

Introduction

The popular music scene in early 1970s Britain is frequently represented as lacking in terms of innovation and distinctiveness. Spanning the years between the break-up of the Beatles in 1970 and the first stirrings of punk in 1976, the British popular music that emerged during this time is often couched in terms of its growing effeteness. This feature of the music is also said to be characterized by a common detachment among popular music artists of the time from the sociopolitical status quo and a drawing on the styles from the previous two decades for inspiration. The purpose of this book is to rethink this premise with reference to six British artists who experienced their creative peak during the early to mid-1970s: David Bowie, Roxy Music, Queen, 10cc, the Electric Light Orchestra (ELO) and Cockney Rebel. Each of these artists contributed majorly to the sound of British rock and pop during the 1970s, producing songs that in some cases became indelibly inscribed in the musical soundscape of the decade. All of these artists were featured regularly on the weekly British television chart show *Top of the Pops* and enjoyed a string of top 20 hits that gave them frequent exposure on mainstream daytime radio, something that could not be said for British hard rock and progressive rock artists who were conspicuously absent from UK television and radio during this period. Like their hard rock and progressive rock peers, however, Bowie, Roxy Music, Queen, 10cc, ELO and Cockney Rebel also built highly credible reputations as album artists. Influenced by the popular music of the late 1960s, and notably the Beatles, they each extended the experimental spirit of much sixties rock, using this to frame their own musical aspirations.

David Bowie's critical breakthrough came in 1972, when his album *The Rise and Fall of Ziggy Stardust and the Spiders from Mars* climbed to number 5 in the UK album charts and spawned the top 10 single 'Starman'. Backed at this point by Mick Ronson (guitar), Trevor Bolder (bass) and Mick 'Woody' Woodmansey (drums), Bowie's musical output during his 'Ziggy' era established the artist's reputation in Britain and subsequently worldwide. It was not merely Bowie's music but also his image that critically connected with audiences, and particularly youth audiences, at this time. With his highly flamboyant and androgynous look, Bowie's Ziggy Stardust persona became a new youth icon of the early 1970s, challenging then established conventions of gender and sexuality and also creating new benchmarks for visual and musical innovation. Throughout the 1970s, Bowie was to remake himself, visually and musically, several times, dynamically manipulating the plasticity and ephemerality of pop.

Roxy Music was formed in London in late 1970 by singer, musician and songwriter Bryan Ferry. A former art teacher, Ferry had initially auditioned for the vocalist spot in progressive rock band King Crimson but was not offered the role as it was felt that his voice was not suited to the band's music. Throughout its early years, Roxy Music went through a number of line-up changes although Ferry (vocals and keyboards), Phil Manzanera (guitar) and Andy Mackay (saxophone, oboe and keyboards) remained in the band throughout its career. During the early 1970s Roxy Music produced what has since become their most critically acclaimed music, an eclectic mix of styles accentuated by the often abstract lyrics of Ferry, whose baritone voice was an unmistakable trademark of Roxy Music's sound. Roxy Music's first two albums, *Roxy Music* (1972) and *For Your Pleasure* (1973), also benefitted significantly from the input of Brian Eno. Although Eno was not a musician in the then conventional sense of the term, his skill in using the VCS3 synthesizer, and in particular its sound manipulation qualities, brought an added depth to the early material of Roxy Music. Eno left Roxy Music in mid-1973 to pursue solo projects, the band carrying on to make a further six albums between 1973 and 1982.

Queen was also formed in London in 1970 by drummer Roger Taylor, guitarist Brian May and vocalist Freddie Mercury (real name Farrokh Bulsara). Taylor and May had previously been part of the late 1960s heavy rock trio Smile together with bassist and vocalist Tim Staffell (see Hodkinson, 1995). Following Staffell's departure from Smile, Mercury was drafted in and plans for the formation of a new band set in motion. Having worked with a number of bass players, the ultimate Queen line-up was completed in early 1971, when bassist John Deacon joined the band. This line-up was to remain together for the next twenty years until Mercury's death in November 1991 from an AIDS-related illness (see, Gunn and Jenkins, 1992). Following the release of their debut album in 1973, Queen quickly established themselves as one of the most successful new British bands of the 1970s, an achievement benchmarked by the 1975 hit 'Bohemian Rhapsody', which remained at the top of the British charts for nine weeks. During their early years, Queen's sound was characterized by an eclectic mix of musical influences, topped with intricately layered vocals and guitars.

The evolution of British progressive pop, however, was not confined to London with contributions also emerging from the British midlands and the north-west of England in the shape of ELO and 10cc. ELO was founded in 1970 in Birmingham by Roy Wood, Jeff Lynne and Bev Bevan, all former members of late sixties British rock band The Move (Herman, 1983). Having already scored a series of hits with The Move, including 'Flowers in the Rain' (1967), 'Fire Brigade' (1968) and 'Blackberry Way' (1968), with ELO Wood, Lynne and Bevan embarked on a radically different kind of musical project. Heavily influenced by the Beatles, and particularly the band's later, more studio-orientated material (see Spicer, 2018), ELO's earliest work extended the Beatles' use of orchestral instruments (most of these being played by Roy Wood using overdubbing techniques in the recording studio). Such influence was highly evident in ELO's debut single '10538 Overture', which climbed to number 9 in the British charts in July 1972. From the opening guitar riff to the overdubbed cellos and other orchestral instruments, the song is firmly positioned in the mode of later Beatles' work, such as 'Sgt. Pepper's Lonely Hearts Club Band' and 'I am the Walrus' (both released in 1967). Wood left ELO in June 1972 citing musical differences between him and the rest of the band as the reason for his departure.[1] With Lynne taking over as the creative driving force behind ELO, the band then pared back the more elaborate orchestral experiments of their first two albums, but maintained the use of strings in a fusion that brought together rock and classically trained musicians to create one of the most commercially successful British popular music acts of the 1970s.

Manchester-based quartet 10cc took their name in 1972 when they signed their first recording contract, with Jonathan King's UK Records. Prior to that, they had been writing and recording together for several years. As a group, 10cc had an interesting pedigree comprising Eric Stewart, who had initially found success as a member of 1960s band Wayne Fontana and the Mindbenders, and Graham Gouldman, already an established and highly prolific songwriter who during the mid-1960s had composed hit songs for the Yardbirds ('For Your Love' and 'Heart Full of Soul'), the Hollies ('Look Through Any Window' and 'Bus Stop') and Herman's Hermits ('No Milk Today') (see Logan and Woffinden, 1977). Completing the line-up of the original version of 10cc (which was active from

1972 to 1976) were Kevin Godley and Lol Creme. Godley and Creme had played with various bands in the Manchester area during the late 1960s before teaming up with Eric Stewart in an impromptu band named Hotlegs, whose novelty song 'Neanderthal Man' was a surprise worldwide hit in 1970 (see Charlesworth, 1983). The song had come about when Eric Stewart enlisted Kevin Godley to play drums in the newly established Strawberry Studios (which had been built and were partly owned by Stewart along with Peter Tattersal and Graham Gouldman, who was an investor in the project) in order to test out drum sounds on the studio's recording and playback equipment. Strawberry Studios would subsequently become a base for the original line-up of 10cc, who between 1972 and 1976 recorded each of their four most critically acclaimed albums there – *10cc* (1973), *Sheet Music* (1974), *The Original Soundtrack* (1975) and *How Dare You!* (1976). A key ingredient of 10cc's success was the strong songwriting ability of all four members of the band. Although often pairing into two songwriting teams, comprising Godley and Creme and Stewart and Gouldman, respectively, this was not a set-in-stone approach as seen, for example, in Creme and Stewart's collaboration on the hit song 'Life Is a Minestrone', which reached number 7 in the UK singles chart in 1975. Another notable quality of 10cc was the strong vocal ability of all four members of the band, with each providing lead vocals on specific tracks and contributing to the richly layered backing vocals that became a trademark of the 10cc sound and a critical aspect of their appeal during the band's heyday of the early to mid-1970s. Quickly achieving high reverence as both an album and a singles band, 10cc are perhaps a primary example of pop – rock crossover in the early 1970s. While their singles regularly topped the British charts, 10cc were also located in the AOR camp by music journalists who regularly interviewed the band about their songwriting craft, including the inspiration for and meaning of their songs.

London-based band Cockney Rebel, formed in 1972 and later renamed Steve Harley and Cockney Rebel, also made notable contributions to the British popular music soundscape of the early 1970s. Although less commercially successful than the artists discussed above and with a shorter span of hit singles, songs such as 'Judy Teen' (1973), 'Mr Soft' (1974) and the band's most famous track, 'Make Me Smile (Come Up and See Me)' (1975), provided Cockney Rebel with top 10 chart prominence in the early 1970s, while their 1974 album *The Psychomodo* was also well received, attaining a position of eight in the UK album charts that year. Cockney Rebel was also a more localized act than the other artists discussed in this book, the band's biggest commercial success, and thus main fan base, being in Britain. A likely reason for this is the more overtly 'British' nature of Cockney Rebel's music, something indelibly stamped on their songs through the highly pronounced English accent of lead singer Steve Harley. During the early 1970s, the American market had become discernibly harder for British bands to break into due the growth in number of home-grown bands at that point and the faded novelty of the so-called 'British invasion' (see Wells, 1987). And yet, in the context of Britain, the band's 'Britishness' was undoubtedly one of the key qualities that set Cockney Rebel apart from other British artists at this time. Indeed, when Britpop (see Bennett and Stratton, 2010) emerged in Britain some twenty years after the demise of the original Cockney Rebel,[2] the influence of Harley was clearly evident. Thus, as Bennett observes:

> Singer and songwriter Steve Harley was in many ways a proto-Britpopper on several accounts. Noted by the British music press for his arrogance, and something of an enigma in the British pop world due to an image which drew heavily on Stanley Kubrick's highly controversial film about English gang culture *A Clockwork Orange*, Harley was a highly distinctive artist, and musical force ... The songs of Cockney Rebel were deeply accentuated by Harley's 'mockney' vocal style. In terms of its association with Britpop, many consider the 'mockney' style of artists such as Damon Albarn, lead vocalist with Blur, to have evolved directly from 1960s groups, notably the Small Faces. In the context of the English pop soundscape, however, it seems likely that, whether explicitly stated or not, Harley's own mockney-take may have also been influential on the 1990s Britpop scene. (2010: 77)

As both a singles and albums band, Cockney Rebel found the same rock-pop crossover appeal as the other British artists discussed in this book. Similarly, a debt to the legacy of the Beatles is evident in the band's work. This was consolidated when, in 1976, the band under their new name of Steve Harley and Cockney Rebel released a cover version of George Harrison's song 'Here Comes the Sun'. This was the second single from their then current album *Love's a Prima Donna* and provided the band with their fourth and last top 10 hit in Britain.

Several of the artists discussed in this book have already been located by scholars within specific genres, or subgenres, of popular music. For example, in the context of their early 1970s music output and stylistic appearance, David Bowie and Roxy Music have been identified as exponents of glam (Auslander, 2006). Queen have been described as a rock band (Moore, 1993) and 10cc as art rock, while ELO have variously been described rock, pop and even symphonic rock (Spicer, 2018). And yet it is arguable that none of these terms, and the often quite specific parameters of musical field and associated audience or 'scene' they suggest, is effective in capturing how these artists operated musically or the appeal they found across different audience segments.

At the same time, it is also true to say that, with the exception of David Bowie, none of the artists discussed in this book have received much in the way of sustained critical attention in scholarly work to date. What follows, then, is an attempt to begin redressing these oversights through an in-depth examination of Bowie, Roxy Music, ELO, 10cc, Queen and Cockney Rebel not as single artists but as acts that contributed to a particular moment in British popular music. Specifically, the book focuses on the contributions of these artists to what is referred to as a progressive pop aesthetic evident in British popular music between 1970 and 1976. The intention is not to attempt to define progressive pop as a genre – although an in-depth discussion is offered in Chapter 1 concerning the specific properties of progressive pop as they are identified in this book. Rather, the aim is to consider how the artists referred to here as progressive pop effectively straddled the British album and singles markets of the early to mid-1970s, crossing an aesthetic divide and appealing to a broad audience with music that appropriated aspects of art rock, progressive rock and pop.

Chapter 1 focuses on the influence of what could be described as the 'long musical sixties' on the emergence of British progressive pop in the early 1970s. The most strident point of reference for many progressive pop artists was the legacy of the Beatles, whose musical and technological innovations from the mid-1960s onwards provided strong platforms on which their successors were able to build. As the chapter discusses, even before the break-up of the Beatles, their creative legacy was being felt in landmark British pop singles such as the Small Faces 'Itchycoo Park', Procul Harem's 'A Whiter Shade of Pale' and the Moody Blues 'Nights in White Satin', each of these songs pushing the parameters of mainstream popular music and what could pass muster as a top 20 single. The chapter also considers additional contributing factors to the emergence of British progressive pop artists during the early 1970s, notably the willingness of certain record labels at this time to allow artists to retain creative control over their music and receptiveness of the music press to artists whom they identified as possessing bona fide 'rock' credentials.

Chapter 2 examines the specific conditions of British popular music during the early 1970s and how this contributed to the ongoing evolution and consolidation of a progressive pop aesthetic. In order to properly situate this progressive pop aesthetic, a broad range of musical developments in Britain is considered. As the chapter notes, in the aftermath of the 1960s, rock British rock music during the early 1970s became noticeably less political, the anthemic call to arms of songs such as 'Street Fighting Man' being replaced by more world-weary commentaries such as The Who's 'Won't Get Fooled Again'. On the pop front, glam rock became the new music of youth, its musical and lyrical references often celebrating the rock and roll era of the 1950s and what was increasingly coming to be regarded as a 'golden age' of youth and music. At the other extreme, progressive rock retained a spirit of 1960s musical innovation but in a context of album-oriented-rock (AOR) that, due to its absence from mainstream music television and radio in Britain during the early 1970s, assumed an essentially underground status at a national level. Such a mainstream-underground bifurcation in British popular music during the early 1970s became a catalyst for the emergence of progressive pop among artists who proved an ability to successfully draw upon both progressive and mainstream musical influences and, in doing so, appeal to each of these markets.

Chapter 3 offers a more in-depth analysis of the progressive pop aesthetic, its evolution in the context of early 1970s British popular music and the specific contributions of David Bowie, Roxy Music, Queen, 10cc, ELO and Cockney Rebel in the consolidation of this aesthetic. It is suggested that the year 1973 in particular was a watershed moment in the development of progressive sounding music in Britain as evidenced by the release of a number of highly distinctive albums that year, including Pink Floyd's *Dark Side of the Moon* and Mike Oldfield's *Tubular Bells*. Additionally, 1973 also saw the release of David Bowie's *Aladdin Sane* and Roxy Music's *For Your Pleasure*, albums that continue to be rated as landmark recordings for these respective artists. In July of 1973 the debut albums of 10cc and Queen were also released, these albums similarly serving to expand the currency of progressive traits in British popular music during the early 1970s. Having considered these albums and other associated recordings in depth, the chapter then goes on to examine their broad-based appeal and how the artists responsible for them simultaneously asserted themselves with mainstream pop audiences through significant singles chart placings and a consistent presence in teen-pop magazines of the era.

Chapter 4 examines how progressive pop contributed to the musical soundscape of early 1970s Britain and its continuing influence on generational memories of the decade. As part of this analysis, consideration is made of mainstream popular music radio and television in Britain during the early 1970s with particular reference to shows such as *Solid Gold Sixty* and *Top of the Pops*. As the chapter explains, each of these shows played a significant part in the production of the popular music soundscape of the 1970s, maintaining a strong weekly presence throughout the decade. The chapter then goes on to focus on two particular songs, 10cc's 'I'm Not in Love' and Queen's 'Bohemian Rhapsody'. Both of these songs were number 1 hits in Britain during the 1975, with 'Bohemian Rhapsody' also producing a promotional film that ushered in a new age of pop video. Through their conceptualization, arrangement and production, each of these songs challenged the conventional format of the pop single, consolidating along the way a progressive pop aesthetic that bridged AOR and the pop singles market in Britain at this time.

Chapter 5 considers the relationship between progressive pop and politics. As the chapter explains, popular music in the early 1970s was often criticized for what was considered a lack of engagement with political issues, something that came to a head with the emergence of punk in late 1976. An argument is presented in this chapter suggesting that while post-1960s, pre-punk popular music in Britain could by and large not be badged political as such, at the same time it would be erroneous to say that the music in a broad sense possessed no critical voice at all. At its most obvious some of those music artists discussed in the book took to task dominant notions of sexuality, creating androgynous images that challenged the hegemonic masculinity of early 1970s Britain. In their lyrics too, however, progressive pop artists often examined particular aspects of the social pathology becoming increasingly evident in the early 1970s as the optimism and liberation of the 1960s gave way to reveal an underbelly of social and psychological frustrations, neo-liberal obsessions with self-benefit and the first stirrings of what would become known as 'therapy culture'.

Chapter 6 focuses on the challenges issued to the progressive pop aesthetic in Britain through the emergence of punk. Although the antagonism of punk is often held to have been primarily directed at progressive and stadium rock bands such as Yes, Genesis, Pink Floyd and Led Zeppelin, several of those artists discussed in this book also found themselves the object of punk's critical derision. The chapter considers in detail the, often uneven, impact of punk on progressive pop and the attempts of various artists to reposition themselves as the British AOR era came to an end and the emphasis was increasingly placed on shorter, more musically stripped back and accessible songs. One surprising development occurring in 1977, just as punk became more dominant in Britain, was a sudden and unprecedented spike of singles by British progressive rock bands such as Emerson, Lake and Palmer and Yes in the UK top 10. This, along with the success of bands such as ELO, with their single 'Mr Blue Sky' and accompanying album *Out of the Blue*, respectively, topping the UK singles and albums charts, problematizes the popularly accepted notion that punk dominated British popular music at this time. Ultimately, however, punk forced British progressive pop artists to evolve, as did the burgeoning pop music video industry. The chapter concludes by considering how artists such as David Bowie, Peter Gabriel and late 1970s newcomer Kate Bush preserved a progressive pop aesthetic in the post-punk and video-friendly era of 1980s popular music.

Notes

1 Wood then went on to form Wizzard, trading on the then fashionable glam rock style (see Auslander, 2006) and scoring six top 10 hits in the UK between 1972 and 1975, when Wizzard disbanded.
2 Following the rediscovery of Cockney Rebel when 'Make Me Smile' was included in the films *The Full Monty* (1997) and *Velvet Goldmine* (1998), the latter a tribute to the British glam rock scene of the early 1970s, Steve Harley formed a new version of the band, which has remained active to date with various line-up changes.

1

Progressive pop in context

The progressive pop era of early 1970s Britain, like other popular music eras before it and since, is inextricably bound up with the cultural, socio-economic and technological factors that surrounded its emergence. Britain was still, at the very beginning of the 1970s, a country buoyed up by the optimism of the 1960s. Although this confidence would begin to falter early in the new decade due to a slowing of the economy, on a popular culture footing, the nation's music, sports and film icons provided Britain with an aura of kudos that rivalled that of the United States. In that respect at least, Britain in the early 1970s imbibed the spirit of the 'long sixties' even as a wariness concerning some aspects of the 1960s was evident. With the failed promises of the late 1960s counter-culture still a recent memory, popular music and its audience in Britain were looking to express themselves in different ways. The music described in this book as progressive pop retained an aesthetic of 'seriousness' borrowed from the rock world of the late 1960s, but its creative ethos was grounded less in the revolutionary fervour of the 1960s rock ethic and erred more towards the new creative pathways suggested by the Beatles and others as the 1960s drew to a close. Riding a wave of rapid development and expansion of recording studio technology, progressive pop artists were thus beneficiaries of a 'best of both worlds' moment in the history of British popular music, when 'rock' credentials could still earn an artist artistic capital while a seemingly endless supply of new technological aids assisted artists in realizing their creative ambitions in ways that allowed for increasing levels of complexity and accomplishment that enjoyed a broad appeal across different segments of the British music-buying public. The purpose of this chapter is to examine the early roots of 1970s British progressive pop through considering the musical and technological transitions that took place between the mid-1960s and the early 1970s.

Reconstructing a popular music past

Grossberg (1994) has suggested that particular generations are often transfixed around the music and associated popular culture of their own youth so as to become in many cases dismissive in a wholesale sense of subsequent generational eras and epochs, which they consider as culturally vacuous. In offering this observation, Grossberg focuses on the baby boomer generation of the 1960s, but his 'warning' seems equally pertinent in the case of other post-war generations who are now actively revisiting and re-evaluating their musical and cultural pasts. To the extent that this book is an academic exploration of what the author identifies as an era of progressive pop in the early 1970s, it is also a book written on the basis of much personal knowledge, together with lived memories, of that particular period of British popular cultural history. This is displayed, for example, through references to more obscure British music television programmes of the early 1970s such as *Lift Off with Ayshea* and *Shang-a-Lang* (see also Chapter 2), references such as these being familiar to music fans and television viewers who grew up in Britain during the 1970s but often far less meaningful in an immediate sense to anyone else.

Since the beginning of the new millennium, a fascination with the British popular culture of the 1970s has rapidly come to rival the 1960s as an in-vogue decade for retrospective scrutiny in the British media. This began in earnest with the BBC television mini-series, *I Love the '70s*, which premiered in July 2000, with each of the ten episodes focusing on a consecutive year of the 1970s decade. Although the series was not exclusively focused on music, perhaps inevitably musical references were a signature part of the appeal of the series, reconnecting a significant cross section of the audience with the music and pop icons of their youth. Although not all of the featured artists were British, a significant proportion of them were. There is a direct correlation between this trend in media production and consumption and the identification of a phenomenon referred to as cultural memory (Assmann, 2011). This refers to a process whereby individual reflections on the recent past are seen to converge as collective remembering clustered around particular representations, including those produced by the media and cultural industries (see also Bennett and Rogers, 2016). Cultural memory can also be, and indeed typically is, a nationally or locally inscribed form of remembering. More recently, the public appetite in the UK for music retrospectives specifically focusing on British artists has led to a veritable rush of documentaries. Largely produced by the BBC, these include

Mr Blue Sky – The Story of Jeff Lynne and ELO (2012), *I'm Not in Love: The Story of 10cc* (2015) and *Queen: Rock the World* (2017). Similarly, a slightly earlier BBC documentary *The Old Grey Whistle Test Story* (2007) relates the history of the iconic BBC2 music programme which, during the first half of the 1970s, offered British music fans their only option for a regular television viewing of AOR (album-orientated-rock) artists (Fryer, 1997; Mills, 2010; see also Chapter 2). On the surface, this trend for music and pop culture retrospectives is patently a representation of the British seventies generation coming of (middle) age and beginning to engage in a collective re-evaluation of their youth and its sociocultural context. It is also illustrative of the fact that some members of that same generation, now invested with power to make creative decisions at a mainstream media level, are harnessing that power to re-present the seventies era and its popular music icons back to those for whom the musical output of this era signified the soundtrack of their youth (Bennett, 2013). Viewed through the conceptual lens of cultural memory, it can be seen how the producers and consumers of these products are connected through common patterns of taste in music and associated cultural trends of the popular past. As such, resources such as music documentaries with a historical focus can be seen to serve to form a kind of memory feedback loop, whereby a shared and mutually preferred version of the past is continually reproduced in the present (Bal et al., 1999).

It is an inevitable admission that aspects of these same visual and material culture resources have been drawn upon in the writing of this book. At the same time, however, it is not the intention of the author to simply re-map what are already well-defined contours of media-framed cultural memories and thus create yet another object of memory or nostalgia. Rather, a key objective of this book is to critically investigate a period of British popular music which, despite its obvious cultural resonance at a generational level, constitutes a missing moment academically speaking in the history and heritage of contemporary British popular music. Indeed, when embarking on the study of popular music in Britain during the 1970s, and particularly the music that featured during the first half of the decade, what becomes quickly apparent is the overall lack of attention that has been given to this period of British popular music in academic scholarship in a wholesale sense. There are, of course, some exceptions here, notably work on the British glam rock era (see Auslander, 2006) and British progressive rock bands such as Yes, Genesis and Pink Floyd (Macan, 1997; Martin, 1998). Similarly, rock group Led Zeppelin have received a significant level of academic attention over the years (see, for example, Waksman, 1996; Fast, 2001; Brackett,

2008). However, and as will be further considered in Chapter 2, even with these genres, the picture painted of their specific significance in a British context is far from complete, particularly in relation to those glam rock and progressive rock artists, whose fan base and appeal were primarily localized, that is to say British (and with an occasionally smaller footprint in continental Europe) rather than 'trans-Atlantic'. Moreover, in the case of almost all other British popular music artists, the years spanning 1970 to 1976 barely register, if at all, in academic scholarship (with only slightly better representation in the trade press it must be said). Only with the advent of punk, and to a lesser degree reggae (see, for example, Hebdige, 1979; Jones, 1988; Laing, 1985), does popular music in Britain during the 1970s begin to garner more sustained attention in academic work (see Bennett, 2007). In essence then, from an academic perspective, British popular music during the early 1970s has been glossed over in a broader sense.

Getting to grips with why this proves to be the case is difficult to say the least. One salient clue, however, appears in some of the early academic work on popular music, now more commonly positioned under the broad banner of popular music studies. While popular music studies, in Britain and elsewhere, was gaining momentum during the late 1970s and the early 1980s, much of the scholarship at this time appeared to be focused on popular music prior to 1970s or, as noted above, on musical developments later in the decade such as punk and reggae (see, for example, Frith, 1983; Middleton, 1990). Driven by a critical agenda embedded in the cultural Marxism underpinning much popular music studies output, and indeed other aspects of the humanities, arts and social sciences in Britain at this time, the post-1960s/pre-punk era of British popular music seemed perhaps unworthy of serious academic scrutiny due to its ostensibly non-political and more overtly 'commercial' nature. Certainly, and as discussed in detail in Chapter 5, there was a notable turn in British popular music of the early 1970s away from music with a more hard-edged political message. As this book illustrates, however, this is by no means the whole story. Another clue is evident in the links present during the 1970s between academic studies of popular music and music journalism, where similar critical lenses were being applied to provide a definition of 'worthy' popular music (see, for example, Laing, 1994). In that sense, a dismissive discourse is often evident in academically attuned journalistic accounts of some new British popular music artists of the early 1970s, notably Queen, whose work was often portrayed in the British music press as naïve, self-indulgent, derivative and lacking in the artistic integrity of British artists who rose to prominence during 1960s, notably the Beatles, the Rolling Stones and the Who (see Jones, 2018). However, even artists such as David Bowie and Roxy Music, who escaped the scathing criticism directed at some other early 1970s artists, also failed to attract more sustained academic attention until much later in the evolution of popular music studies (see, for example, Frith and Horne, 1987). Furthermore, while many popular music scholars have become more focused on the history and heritage of rock and pop since the 1950s (see, for example, Cohen et al., 2015), the lack of attention given to British popular music in a broader sense during the early 1970s has continued. In this and the following chapter, the intention is to re-focus attention on this period and the contribution of specific artists whose music characterized what is in many ways a unique era of British popular music – one in which genre distinctions were often less clear-cut and a trend for musical experimentation was tolerated by the music industry and music audiences alike.

The long musical sixties

The ultimate aim of this book, then, is to bring more fully into relief an era of British popular music that is essentially overlooked in existing academic scholarship. This, however, cannot be effectively achieved without first considering events and developments in the world of British popular music that preceded the early 1970s, thus providing the background context for the evolution of progressive pop. In that sense, the impact of what many have referred to as the 'long sixties' is a highly pertinent point of reference. While this term is more readily used with reference to the longevity of the cultural politics and protest that emerged during the 1960s under the broad banner of the counter-culture (see, for example, Marwick, 2005; Whiteley and Sklower, 2014), musically too it can be argued that the 1960s, and particularly the mid to late 1960s, continued to have a significant influence on the popular music of the decade that followed. In Britain this is evidenced by the fact that many musicians who (re)emerged in the early 1970s as progressive pop artists had served important musical apprenticeships during the 1960s (as detailed in the Introduction to this book).

A further point of commonality between many of these new British popular music artists and their sixties peers was the prevalence of an art school education. The British art school tradition, which began to flourish as a breeding ground for future rock and pop artists during the 1950s and early 1960s (see Frith and Horne, 1987), had served an important role in shaping the creative talents of many prominent British musicians, among them John Lennon, Keith Richards and Pete Townshend. This trend continued in the late 1960s and early 1970s with a new generation of aspiring rock musicians being introduced to experimental and provocative expressions of creativity via an art school education. These included Bryan Ferry, Brian Eno and Andy McKay of Roxy Music and Kevin Godley and Lol Creme of 10cc. Similarly, Freddie Mercury of Queen and David Bowie also benefited from an art school education and the added scope this afforded them in the development of the creative skills necessary to their future success as songwriters and performers (see Hodkinson, 1995; Trynka, 2011). Frith and Horne (1987) suggest that the influence of the British art school has been key to the international impact of British popular musicians since the Beatles. While there is certainly merit in Frith and Horne's observation, it seems equally the case that art schools have been responsible for the highly diverse range of music and artists to have emerged from Britain since the 1960s, supplying a desire for experimentation and the testing of musical boundaries.

Such trends in British popular music deepened during the early 1970s as the creative opportunities for musicians expanded drastically due to the improving music technology at their disposal. In particular, the advances made in studio recording during mid-late 1960s and the continuation of such advances in the early 1970s had a critical bearing on the kind of music made by many British music artists during this period. Indeed, and as will be examined in more depth in subsequent chapters, the importance of the recording studio was pivotal in the ability of several bands, notably 10cc and Queen, to create defining songs of the early 1970s era – songs that were instantly recognizable to audiences due to their literally 'big' sound (an effect achieved in large part with the aid of studio multi-tracking, which had moved on considerably in the few short years since the pioneering four-track recordings of artists such as the Beatles and the Beach Boys during the mid-1960s). Similarly, the license enjoyed by these and other artists to draw eclectically on a range of musical styles and influences, producing albums where each song was distinctive from the next, owes much to the creative freedom afforded to recording artists in the wake of the commercial success enjoyed by the Beatles. Although ultimately short-lived, the fact that this music industry ethos spanned the late 1960s and early 1970s created the conditions whereby a number of post-Beatles popular music artists were also given scope to take creative ownership of their music and its production (see Harron, 1990). Indeed, in an overall sense the legacy of the Beatles, including the band's break-up in April 1970 while still at their creative peak, had a significant influence on many of the new British bands that began to emerge soon thereafter. While the Beatles' 1967 release *Sgt. Pepper's Lonely Hearts Club Band* is still regarded as the band's seminal creative masterpiece (see Martin, 1979) or, to use current parlance, their 'classic album' (see Bennett, 2009), the combined output of the Beatles from 1965's *Rubber Soul* through to *Abbey Road*, the Beatles' last official studio album, in 1969 sowed the seeds of much home-grown musical innovation in Britain that would come to be a trademark of British progressive pop in the early 1970s. Indeed, Spicer has gone as far as to suggest that:

> [T]he Beatles sheer fluency and innovation as songwriters and performers, along with their constant pushing of the boundaries of what could be achieved technically in the recording studio, set the bar so high that all subsequent pop and rock musicians striving for originality have had to navigate the huge creative space that they carved within the landscape of popular music. (2018: 107)

There are obvious caveats in Spicer's account, not least of all punk whose musical aesthetic, if not dismissive of the Beatles legacy in a wholesale sense, took a consciously back-to-basics approach in direct response to the more 'ambitious' musical styles and genres inspired in whole or in part by the Beatles' later output. In the pre-punk 1970s, however, Spicer's observations do indeed carry critical weight, particularly in relation to the evolution of progressive pop. And in that context, the clearest connection to be made in terms of a Beatles' influence with much of the British popular music that immediately followed the band's demise is the emphasis placed on the recording studio as a 'creative' tool. Indeed, as Théberge, observes:

> Whereas, in the early 1960s, a band would not ordinarily enter a studio without having a selection of material rehearsed and ready to record, less than a decade later it was normal for bands to compose in the studio, spending weeks and months experimenting with various creative possibilities inherent in the multitrack process. (2001: 11)

As seminally inspirational artists in the creative appropriation of the recording studio, the Beatles had begun to hone this craft early in their recording career. Paul McCartney's song 'Yesterday', released as a non-album single in the United States in September 1965 (and as part of an EP release in the UK the following year), had tested the waters with its incorporation of strings in a studio-produced version of the song which at that stage was beyond the reach of live performance. The album *Rubber Soul* released at the end of 1965 saw the Beatles exploring more fully the capacity of the recording studio, using the available technology to create music that surpassed the limitations of live performance. In this respect, *Rubber Soul* established the pattern of what was to follow in subsequent Beatles' releases and would eventually see the band abandoning live performance to focus exclusively on making studio recordings. According to many commentators, the *Rubber Soul* album marked the first recording by a rock band not only to focus wider attention on the creative possibilities of the recording studio but to redefine the album format as a 'creative work' rather than merely a collection of songs of varying quality and often including filler tracks (see Howard, 2004). Thus, as O'Grady observes:

> most of the songs contained on [*Rubber Soul*] are unified in their demonstration of a new approach to rock and roll – an approach that focuses on musical detail rather than on the massive, ear catching sound gestures of the [Beatles'] earlier pop-rock songs. (1979: 93)

The musical eclecticism of *Rubber Soul*, combining blues, soul and folk styles while at the same time introducing new and, at the time, novel sounds into the world of pop – as heard for example in George Harrison's use of a sitar on the track 'Norwegian Wood', was also a highly influential point of departure. The following Beatles' albums *Revolver*, released in 1966, and *Sgt. Pepper*, released the year after, followed this pattern of musical innovation and diversity in songwriting that made increasing demands on the technological capacity of the recording studio. Indeed, according to Beatles' producer George Martin, such was the ambitious nature of the music written for *Sgt. Pepper's Lonely Hearts Club Band* that it pushed the limits of the at that time state-of-the-art four-track recording technology, necessitating that many tracks were bounced[1] once completed to make way for the addition of new tracks (Martin, 1979).

Apart from the musical achievements and influence of the Beatles themselves, particularly during the mid- to late 1960s, it is important to understand the broader musical milieu inspired by the band. In that context, new sensibilities of popular music as a quasi high-brow form of art and cultural expression rapidly emerged and were absorbed by many other popular music artists of the time. Indeed, the musical possibilities being explored by the Beatles on their later albums, together with their demonstration of how special effects and studio overdubs could be used to create recordings comprising 'ideal not real events' (Frith, 1988: 21–2), became a wide source of inspiration among British contemporaries, including the Rolling Stones, the Who and the Kinks. Perhaps most strident here was the Who, whose 1969 album *Tommy* drew on key aesthetic properties of *Sgt. Pepper's Lonely Hearts Club Band* to create a new point of departure in rock music, the 'rock opera'. In addition to such major names in British popular music, however, the Beatles' creative footprint extended further, also helping to produce some of the most memorable 'pop' hits of the late 1960s and ensuring a deeper penetration of the Beatles' progressive influence in the national pop landscape. A salient example of this is Procul Harem's debut single, and the band's most remembered song, 'A Whiter Shade of Pale', which reached number 1 in the British charts on 8 June 1967, remaining there for six weeks. The song's signature musical motif, played on a Hammond organ and inspired by the style of Baroque-era German composer Johan Sebastian Bach, gave the song an instantly recognizable character as did the poetic and slightly abstract nature of the song's lyrics, which make reference among other things to 'The Miller's Tale' from Chaucer's literary classic, *The Canterbury Tales*. Such abstract pop lyrics and classical music influences had earlier been evident on the Beatles' album *Revolver* and on the band's non-album double A side 'Strawberry Fields Forever'/'Penny Lane', released in February 1967.

Another top-selling single from a British band in 1967 displays the psychedelic influence of *Sgt. Pepper's Lonely Hearts Club Band*, both in its musical content and also in its production. 'Itchycoo Park', written and recorded by London-based band the Small Faces, reached number three in the UK singles chart in August 1967 and was instantly recognizable due to its featuring of a new electronic effect that would later become known as *flanging*.[2] The Beatles had employed a similar effect on the album track 'Lucy in the Sky with Diamonds' (from *Sgt. Pepper's*) to accentuate the psychedelic feel of the song's lyrics. In 'Itchycoo Park', however, this production concept was taken and re-prescribed for a pop chart audience, the song's infectious chorus and syncopated tom tom roll back into the verse being bathed in the pioneering flanging effect. This startling new sound had been added after the recording of the song was complete and created through the manual manipulation of two synced recordings of the finished track to produce an out-of-phase effect, the alleged intention being to sonically re-create the drug experience suggested by the lyrics of the chorus. Even with the relatively primitive radio speaker quality of the late 1960s, the special studio-crafted effects used on 'Itchycoo Park' gave the song a distinctive sound that set it apart from other popular music being played on the radio at this time. In this sense, even for those listeners for whom a homological connection (Willis, 1978) between drugs and music was not a feature of the way that they understood and appreciated music, the introduction of such innovative techniques in British chart music certainly helped to broaden pop's musical vocabulary and with it the taste of popular music audiences for chart music that extended the boundaries of their usual daily listening.

A further example of an early 'progressive pop' single appeared in the same year in the form of the Moody Blues' 'Nights in White Satin', written by the band's lead singer and guitarist Justin Hayward. Although a lesser hit on its initial release, in November 1967 the song's high production standards, orchestral backing and distinctive instrumental section, featuring a flute solo played by Ray Thomas, set a new standard for highly polished pop songs with dramatic contrasts of light and shade. Just over two years after the release of 'Nights in White Satin', in January 1970 the Moody Blues released the song 'Question'. Also written and sung by Justin Hayward, this was a track that further pushed the boundaries of the then accepted format for a pop single, being almost five minutes in length and split into three distinct sections marked by tempo changes at different stages in the song. Rather than comprising a conventional verse-chorus-verse-chorus format, 'Question' opens with an up-tempo section written in a rock style, followed by a slower middle part with the feel of a ballad before returning to the up-tempo rock style of the beginning before the fadeout. The song also makes use of orchestral backing, adding to its dramatic light and shade dynamics. Indeed, 'Question' has often been described as an early example of progressive rock (Hegarty and Halliwell, 2011), yet through its novel delivery of a slightly unorthodox style of songwriting into the pop singles market. 'Question' could equally be described as a blueprint for a new progressive pop sensibility that would quickly evolve as the 1970s got underway.

Technical ecstasy

It the Beatles had set a new benchmark for studio production and had, in their day, pushed the limits of the then available technology, progressive pop was propelled by a new era of technological expansion, in which the creative possibilities afforded by multitrack recording increased exponentially. While multitrack recording was reshaping the creative process across various genres of popular music in the early 1970s, it was through the medium of progressive pop that the fruits of such labour typically reached a mainstream audience. This was certainly the case in Britain, where more avant-garde genres of music, such as progressive rock and jazz rock, were far less frequently featured on radio and television than music with a presence in the top 40. Although all of the progressive pop artists discussed in this book were by definition both live *and* recording acts, the individual reputations of these artists and the creative benchmarks they established in the early 1970s were firmly built on the high quality of their studio output. Indeed, it is fair to say that some artists, notably ELO and Queen, initially struggled with live performance given the limited technology at their disposal to re-produce their richly layered sound in a live context. As recording artists, however, their popularity was assured through a string of successful singles and albums sales, which kept them squarely in the public eye.

By the early 1970s studio technology had advanced in such a way that even the technology used to make the innovative late 1960s pop albums and singles referred to earlier in this chapter had begun to look decidedly primitive by comparison. By this time albums and singles were being routinely recorded and mastered in stereo, giving tracks a far wider sound than had often been the case with the mono recordings of the 1960s. Similarly, the amount of tracks available for use in the recording of music had increased significantly. The first sixteen-track tape recorders were introduced in 1968 in the United States, with Trident Studios in London being the first British recording studio to acquire a sixteen-track machine in late 1969 (Massey, 2015). Among the first British artists to use these new recording facilities at Trident were Genesis, David Bowie and Queen (with Queen recording their first three albums, *Queen*, *Queen II* and *Sheer Heart Attack*, at Trident between 1972 and 1974, Hodkinson, 1995; see also Chapter 3). As Massey observes: 'By the end of 1971 there were some two dozen studios in London offering 16-track capacity ... In a few short years, even 16-track would become obsolete as most British studios made the transition to 24-track recording' (2015: 14). The rapid transition from sixteen to twenty-four track recording allowed producers, engineers and artists far greater flexibility in the recording studio. And yet, the technology-pushing trend set in motion by the Beatles a decade earlier remained very much alive in the minds of a new generation of British popular music artists. This was apparent in songs such as 10cc's 'I'm Not in Love' and Queen's 'Bohemian Rhapsody', both of which were number 1 hits in Britain in 1975. During the recording of these songs, the possibilities of multitrack recording were stretched to the limit, even with many more tracks available to achieve the richly layered and complex sound tapestries that characterize each of these tracks. In addition to these two groundbreaking hit singles, the newly expanded technological capacity of British recording studios at this time also resulted in progressive pop artists making some of the most iconic albums in the history of British popular music. These include David Bowie's (1972) *The Rise and Fall of Ziggy Stardust*, Roxy Music's (1973) *For Your Pleasure*, 10cc's (1974) *Sheet Music*, Queen's (1975) *A Night at the Opera* and ELO's *Out of the Blue* (1977).

The dawning of the 'album' bands

Another important musical and indeed cultural segue from the late 1960s to the early 1970s was the emergence of what came to be referred to as AOR (album-orientated-rock), an early attempt at rock branding albeit one that erred on the side of a more intellectual categorization of a somewhat loose affiliation of artists. Again, albums such as *Sgt. Pepper's Lonely Hearts Club Band* (together with the Beach Boys' album *Pet Sounds* released in 1966) can be regarded as cornerstone recordings in the grounding of AOR in that such recordings did much to facilitate the cultural reclassification (Janssen, et al.: 2008) of the vinyl 33 LP (Long Player) as a body of work rather than (in rock and pop terms) simply a collection of songs used in the promotion of hit singles (Stratton, 1983). As pertinent in the currency of the AOR label, however, was the way that the redefinition of the album as a *cultural* artefact simultaneously began to feed a new discourse of musical artistry and 'authenticity'. This discourse positioned those artists who, in the style of the Beatles, proved themselves capable of using the album format as a more cohesive, and in many cases conceptual, framing for their music as 'distinct' from chart artists, whose reputation and livelihood were very much tied to the commercial success of each consecutive single release. Indeed, by the beginning of the 1970s something of a two-tier situation had evolved in popular music, whereby an increasing number of artists were able to live a creative life free from the need to continually release chart singles due to the commercial success of their albums, while others – essentially designated by the music industry as chart 'fodder' – were subject to the ever-changing musical fads and fashions of pop. In the case of Britain, this situation was most aptly characterized by progressive rock and glam (or at least the majority of those associated with British glam). Thus, glam artists such as Alvin Stardust, Mud and the Rubettes traded heavily on adopted musical styles from the 1950s, creating a string of largely interchangeable top 10 singles (see Stratton, 1986). Progressive rock, on the other hand, incorporated influences from classical music and featured often extended song structures and heavily abstract lyrics. Such centrally defining characteristics of progressive rock were deemed to render it unsuitable for radio airplay, at least in Britain, but found it a new kind of audience who aesthetically positioned themselves as 'non-mainstream' music consumers (Macan, 1997). This aesthetic and marketing divide in early 1970s British popular music and how it set the scene for the emergence of progressive pop is discussed in depth in Chapter 2.

The critical weight placed upon the album as a musical statement had become significantly more marked between 1968 and 1970, an important factor here being the emergence of what was loosely termed political or counter-cultural rock (Bennett, 2001). At this point the cultural meaning of popular music was seen to shift as a new counter-hegemonic movement, commonly referred to as the counterculture (see Whiteley and Skower, 2014), established itself. Although typically perceived to connote the 'hippie' scene, as Clecac (1983) observes, in point of fact the term 'counterculture' encompassed a far broader range of counter-hegemonic interests and factions. Key to most of these, however, was a shared belief in the significance of music, and in particular rock music, as a vehicle for social change. Thus, as Frith (1981) observes, through its intimation of a new era of community based on shared musical taste and associated cultural values, rock music in the late 1960s came to be regarded by many of its followers as a political force that could literally change the world through supporting a new level of consciousness (Reich, 1971). This, it was argued by many at the time, could ultimately succeed in overthrowing the existing sociopolitical order of Western(ized) society and its technocratic obsessions (Roszak, 1969). Although often identified with American bands such as The Grateful Dead, Jefferson Airplane and Country Joe and the Fish, all of whom were closely associated with the countercultural scene of San Francisco's Haight Ashbury district (Hill, 2016), British artists including the Beatles and the Rolling Stones importantly contributed to the political rock scene of the later 1960s as well. Songs such as the Rolling Stones' 'Street Fighting Man' and the Beatles' 'Revolution' quickly became interwoven into the musical soundtrack of the late 1960s and were embraced as countercultural anthems (Platoff, 2005). Musically speaking, the rock music that provided the soundtrack for the counterculture also continued to push the boundaries of rock and pop in often radically new directions. For example, the Beatles' *White Album* released in 1968 contained the song 'Revolution No. 9', which extended the band's earlier use of tape loops on *Revolver* and *Sgt. Pepper's Lonely Hearts Club Band* to a new expressive level by adding speech, overdubbed vocals and sound effects. Inspired by the avant-garde art of his partner Yoko Ono, John Lennon initially claimed that in 'Revolution no. 9' he was attempting to portray a revolution using sound but later revised this comment, stating the piece was actually an anti-revolution statement (Guesdon and Margottin, 2013).

This kind of 'broad canvass' approach to music making in the recording studio remained critically influential during the early 1970s. While it was not generally the case that post-Beatles artists, including those documented in this book, took their music-making craft to the same avant-garde extremes pursued by Lennon in 'Revolution No. 9', the new creative freedoms expressed in such work made an impact upon many of those British bands who came after the Beatles and who shaped the progressive pop landscape of the early 1970s. Key here was the idea that a song or piece of music could be built from scratch using studio technology to create it. While, as noted earlier, progressive pop would continue to figure as a live medium, the objective would be to frame the studio work as a primary text (Moore, 1993), with the live version of a song either working to emulate as far as possible what had been achieved in the studio or adopting a new arrangement better suited to the conditions of live performance. Thus, for example, in the case of 10cc, backing tapes were used to reproduce the looped and richly layered backing vocals of 'I'm Not in Love' in live performance while Queen opted initially to perform parts of 'Bohemian Rhapsody' as part of medley in concert, later featuring the song in its entirety but with the album version of the song's mini opera section (see Chapter 4) segued into the band's stage performance at the appropriate point in the music. David Bowie, whose originally acoustic version of 'Space Oddity' was transformed by producer Gus Dudgeon into a lavish production number including the use of a mellotron (played by Rick Wakeman, who would later go on to join British progressive rock band Yes) (see Trynka, 2011), initially continued to play the acoustic version of the song in live performance, introducing a band version of the song in the early 1970s but then coming full circle in 1979 with a minimalist studio version of the song that took it back to its acoustic roots.

Pop, rock and music journalism

A further contributing factor in the setting apart of albums and singles artists during the early 1970s was the discursive distinctions made between *pop* and *rock* in 'quality' music journalism. Again, such distinctions began to proliferate during the later years of the 1960s. The dramatic increase in critical music journalism from 1966 onwards and the coining of the term 'rock' as a form of music distinct from pop provided a platform for the (re)appraisal of given popular musicians as 'artists' (see Shuker, 2001). Applying a quasi-high art discourse, the new journalism gave credence and legitimacy to subjective notions such as 'authenticity' and 'credibility'. A key player in this respect was *Rolling Stone Magazine*. Founded by Jann Wenner and Ralph J. Gleason, this publication established a new trope for critically informed writing about popular music and, specifically at this point, rock music. Based in San Francisco, *Rolling Stone* was importantly influenced by the hippie counterculture and its deep investment in rock music as a generational mouthpiece for social, cultural and political change. The magazine's rapid influence on the world of music journalism was to create a new way of presenting popular music artists and their songs. A large part of this related to how the artists themselves were depicted in the writing. Thus, as Kutulas observes:

> Magazines and newspapers illuminated musicians' life-styles, and professional critics offered authoritative opinions about the relative value of different singers and songs. Founded in 1967, *Rolling Stone* would become, its editor promised, a forum for music and 'the things and attitudes that the music embraces'. (2010: 685)

In Britain, established weekly music newspapers such as *New Musical Express* and *Melody Maker*, together with newer publications such as *Sounds* (which was first published in October 1970), assumed a critical role as mediators of rock journalism to British audiences. These publications were also important tastemakers when it came to creating awareness of new emerging British artists in the early 1970s (see, Toynbee, 1993).

The impact of these new journalistic trends on the perceptions of readers regarding the cultural currency of music was unequivocal. For the first time, popular music artists of the post-war era, and particularly those positioned within the AOR canon, were being discussed using a form or quasi high-art discourse. Up until this point all popular music had been discussed in two main ways. Either it was squarely dismissed by *serious* critics as little more than throwaway entertainment aimed at an undiscerning youth audience and transforming them into cultural dupes (see, for example, Johnson, 1964) or it was implicated in inciting acts of antisocial behaviour among and often between young people (Cohen, 1987). Through the emergence of the new music journalism of the late 1960s, youth culture and its music (or at least a particular segment of it) were radically empowered as writers from within, rather than outside, youth culture offered their own interpretation of popular music, its cultural significance and value as art. Popular music, it was argued, was there to be taken 'seriously' rather than dismissed as ephemeral youth entertainment. As part of this aesthetic shift, popular music artists such as the Beatles, the Rolling Stones and the Who were elevated beyond the status of mere pop performers to the new status of 'rock' artists (Jones, 2008). The music and lyrics of these and other critically acclaimed artists placed in the rock canon were judged to reflect a particular outlook on the world around them. Interviews with these artists were conducted and written up in such a way as to allow the artists scope to discuss their views and opinions on things such as war, politics, art and culture and how such themes had provided them with inspiration for their music. This development in critical writing about particular music and artists of the time was achieved in the knowledge that there was a new, more discerning audience who would welcome the opportunity to read such first-hand accounts from the artists whose music they bought and whom they went to see in concert and at festivals (the rock festival also becoming an increasingly prominent forum at this point for countercultural gatherings; see Bennett, 2004; Anderton, 2011).

The intellectualization of popular music through the prism of rock journalism was also instrumental in creating the new binary distinction, in aesthetic terms, between rock and pop. Although in reality both genres were entirely reliant on the forms of industrial mass production integral to the music industry as a primary institution of leisure capitalism (Stratton, 1983), rock journalism helped create and maintain a form of aesthetic discourse around rock that supplied it with an aura of authenticity and worthiness considered by many to be lacking in more 'mainstream' pop (Shuker, 2001). The discourse of rock artistry and *authenticity* kick-started by music journalists in the late 1960s was to survive well into the 1970s. Indeed, by this point the assumed differences between rock and pop had become well entrenched. Certainly the political fervour around rock had diminished with the collapse of the counterculture and the reduction of music as a vehicle for social change to a romantic myth (Frith, 1981). Artistically speaking, however, the notion of rock as a 'superior' music made for a more discerning audience steadfastly remained a part of the rock ideology during the first half of the 1970s. Only with the emergence of punk did this perception of rock begin to unravel (see Chapter 6).

Among other aspects of the oversight that persists in academic scholarship relating to early 1970s popular music in Britain and elsewhere, the ongoing intellectual and artistic currency of the rock discourse between 1970 and 1975 has been largely ignored. Indeed, as noted earlier in this chapter, there appears to have been an assumed belief on the part of many scholars that the apparent de-politicization of rock during this period rendered it unworthy of intellectual scrutiny. It has also been noted earlier in this chapter how early 1970s British rock artists who have received the most attention, academically speaking, tend to be those who achieved significant success in the United States. Such a selection denotes a reading of these artists in the context of their status as high demand exponents of early North American stadium rock.[3] Indeed, it can be observed that for British rock artists, whose music failed to translate into larger auditoriums and stadiums in the United States, their chances of a commercial breakthrough in that country remained somewhat limited. Such was the fate of British bands such as Status Quo and 10cc, acts who were 'household names' of rock and pop in Britain during the early 1970s but failed to find a significant American audience (although 10cc did enjoy a brief period of chart success in the United States with 'I'm Not in Love', a number 2 hit in 1975, and 'The Things We Do for Love', which went to number 5 in 1976 and earned the band a Gold disc). The same is true of glam rock band Slade, who, following their huge commercial success in Britain, relocated to the United States in 1975 with the hope of breaking the much bigger market there. However, despite appearing as the opening act for some of the most well-known American rock bands of the day, including Aerosmith and ZZ Top, Slade were unable to achieve anything near the success they had enjoyed in the UK during the early 1970s. In Britain, however, there was an openness and indeed desire for 'home-grown' bands during this period. Detached from the political and ideological discourses that had defined a significant part of the rock field during the late 1960s and existing in a moment before the critical onslaught of punk and the subsequent often quite clinical branding of popular music that would characterize the video age, British popular in the early 1970s was a musically rich and diverse arena.

In the British music media, the new generation of progressive pop bands with an album-singles crossover capacity was largely lauded by the British music press, with David Bowie, Roxy Music and 10cc receiving particularly positive reviews for their early work. While Queen endured a more negative response from the music press, they were, nevertheless, championed by other taste makers in the British rock media, notably Bob Harris, presenter of late-night British AOR television programme the *Old Grey Whistle Test* (*OGWT*), on which the band were featured a number of times during the 1970s. Indeed, and as will be further discussed in Chapter 2, the persistence of *OGWT* during the early 1970s in providing exposure for AOR artists to British audiences was a salient factor in the survival of AOR in the British context well into the decade. In the pre-punk 1970s, the British popular music artists focused on in this book continued to thrive on the late 1960s legacy of creative freedom. Indeed these artists, bestowed with the moniker of authentic *rock* credentials, were afforded a seemingly quarantined space, beyond the pop-factory logic applied elsewhere in the music industry, to nurture their craft. In an era where rock and AOR had yet to be challenged by punk and new wave, early 1970s British progressive pop artists lived two lives and served two different audiences, the singles buying teen audience and the album buying fans of AOR.

Why progressive pop?

Some readers of this book will no doubt want to question why the category of progressive pop is being applied as a conceptual framing – and in particular why it is being applied to such a diverse range of artists. Certainly in purely musical terms, and indeed stylistically as well, there is nothing to connect any of these artists. In a broad sense, the term 'rock' has been applied at one point or another to each of the artists discussed in this book. However, as the foregoing sections of this chapter illustrate, rock itself is a highly problematic and complex term, having been stretched discursively and operationally beyond its original sixties designation to encompass a very broad range of diverse music and artists. In that context, progressive pop is used in this book as a way of attempting to re-contextualize a small number of British popular music artists as having each in their own way channelled a range of musical influences (with one common influence having been the Beatles). In the context of the early 1970s, none of these artists could have been truly defined as either rock or pop as their musical output extended beyond the sonic boundaries commonly applied to each of these categories. At the same time, however, their music was more 'pop' in an aesthetic sense than other British bands of the era such as Led Zeppelin, Pink Floyd, Deep Purple and Yes as it frequently applied musical formulas borrowed from pop and designed to appeal to a mainstream pop audience. At the same time, however, straightforward comparisons between these artists and more pure examples of British pop in the 1970s are difficult to make given the more advanced level of musicianship and technical knowhow evident among them and clearly in evidence in the composition and sound of their music (with 10cc's 'I'm Not in Love' and Queen's 'Bohemian Rhapsody' being salient examples of this). As such, progressive pop presents as an effective way of describing these artists and their contributions to British popular music during the early 1970s – a series of contributions which, as noted earlier in this chapter, are now beginning to attract retrospective cultural consecration (Schumtz, 2005), during which aesthetic parallels are indeed often identified between artists such as Queen and 10cc or David Bowie and Roxy Music. In truth, however, progressive pop is not a newly coined term either, but its use has been rather more restricted in the past. Indeed, it would be fair to describe progressive pop as something of a 'ghost terminology' in that it has hovered around the edges of popular music classification for a number of years, often being used in a 'grey area' capacity to map particular moments in popular music when neither rock nor pop seemed to suffice as accurate descriptors for a band, an album or a song that appeared to blur these categories. As such, progressive pop is not a term that can be applied exclusively in relation to popular music during the early 1970s, in Britain or elsewhere. And yet, it is arguably the case that the popular music landscape emerging in Britain at this time created its own localized conditions for the priming of progressive pop, allowing the artists discussed in this book to cut new musical paths that were distinctive in themselves but each involving a particular blending of rock and pop territories, often with other musical elements fused into the mix as well. Frequently, this saw progressive pop artists incorporating the virtuosic traits of rock and progressive rock formats in songs that lent themselves to day-time radio playlists while at the same time achieving credibility among a more traditional rock audience. That such distinctions mattered so much in Britain during the early 1970s has much to do with the way that rock and pop continued to be separated out at the time in the media and, as a consequence, in the taste sensibilities of music audiences. What this situation gave rise to was a specific window in British popular music whereby a number of artists with a sufficiently broad musical approach were able to tap two markets, becoming simultaneously 'rock artists' and 'pop stars'. It has frequently been stated that genre categorization remains something of a blunt instrument in terms of mapping how audiences actually respond to music (Lena and Peterson, 2008), being more effective as a marketing device for hopefully capturing trends rather than anticipating them. In this context, the British progressive pop artists of the 1970s offer an interesting insight, tapping the taste agency of both the mainstream pop and AOR audiences through providing a body of cross-over work that both markets could claim ownership of.

Progressive pop in the context of this book then is used to describe a particular moment in the crossing of rock and pop sensibilities in the history of British popular music. Arriving at a particularly vibrant moment in the evolution of British pop, characterized at an extreme level by the emergence, and rapid crystallization, of progressive rock at one end of a musical and cultural continuum and glam at the other, progressive pop is used as a means of explaining and filling out a less well-understood middle territory. Taking David Bowie, Roxy Music, Queen, 10cc, ELO and Cockney Rebel out of the neat genre categories that are usually used to describe them, these artists are repositioned here as inextricably connected through a desire to experiment, drawing selectively and in quite different ways on disparate musical and cultural resources positioned across the rock-pop continuum.

A more pronounced emphasis on genre branding only began to emerge in earnest following the emergence of punk, which, despite its often stated anti-commercial rhetoric, was in its more mainstream capacity a critical commercial success (as demonstrated by the Sex Pistols' first, and as it turned out only original, album *Never Mind the Bollocks*, which generated 120,000 advance orders and debuted at number 1 in the British album charts). By the beginning of the 1980s and the launch of MTV, pop, rock and later rap and dance became musically and, quite literally, 'visually' segmented as popular music became as much about the production of promotional videos as about the music itself (see Kaplan, 1987). Pop video intensified the branding of popular music to the extent that this became one of the only ways of surviving in the hyper-commodified 1980s. In the case of British rock, for example, the fact that so many bands, among them UFO and Whitesnake, who had existed quite comfortably under the more amorphous hard rock banner during the late 1970s, were rebranded respectively as 'heavy metal' and 'soft metal' bands – aligning them with a new breed of MTV-ready artists such as Bon Jovi and Europe, is a clear indication of how much popular music became subject to more compartmentalized branding as the 1980s wore on. As a result of music video, pop too acquired new more clearly drawn parameters of definition, as seen for example with Michael Jackson's (1982) 'Thriller' and the supporting video directed by award-winning American film director John Landis (see Mercer, 1991). Similarly, Norwegian band Aha's debut single 'Take on Me' (originally released in 1984 but re-recorded and re-released in 1985) was promoted by a video that used a then completely new technique referred to as rotoscoping, involving a combination of pencil sketch animation and live action film.

The early 1970s, by contrast, was a period divest of such aggressive branding. Although the visual image of an artist was often an aspect of their success and appeal, at the same time it was by no means a prerequisite for gaining critical exposure to an audience. Thus, while artists such as David Bowie, Roxy Music and Queen (whose 'Bohemian Rhapsody' promotional video in late 1975 was an early sign of things to come, also Chapter 4) were tailor-made for the future video age, other artists including 10cc and ELO were visually unadventurous but musically successful nevertheless. In essence, however, what linked all of these artists was a will and a capacity to experiment musically and in a way that was successfully able to connect with a broad-ranging and eclectic audience. Absorbing both the influences of progressive rock and the pop sensibilities of the late 1960s and early 1970s, these artists were neither progressive rock nor mainstream pop. Musically, they brought an interesting dynamic to the popular music landscape of the early 1970s. In terms of their technical and creative abilities, easy comparisons could be made with the virtuoso fields of progressive and hard rock. For example, David Bowie likened the abilities of Mick Ronson, lead guitarist with his backing band the Spiders from Mars, to those of Jeff Beck (former guitarist with popular 1960s British band the Yardbirds, who then went on to form the Jeff Beck group before branching out to establish a highly successful solo career in the 1970s) (see Trynka, 2011). Similarly, Queen's lead guitarist Brian May cited influences including Jimi Hendrix, Eric Clapton and Who guitarist Pete Townshend, while both of Queen's first two albums displayed an obvious musical debt to Led Zeppelin. And yet, both Ronson and May, and the respective bands with which they were associated, were also operating in a pop idiom, giving them exposure to a far broader audience than many of their rock peers. A similar situation pertained in the case of 10cc, a band whose exceptionally well-honed musical skills put them well beyond the ambit of the majority of other British chart pop artists of the early 1970s. Nevertheless, 10cc quickly gained themselves a reputation as the 'first consistently entertaining [British] singles group since the 1960s' (Logan and Woffinden, 1977: 501) with regular comparisons to the Beatles also being made. As will be further explored in Chapter 2, what David Bowie, Queen, 10cc, ELO, Roxy Music and Cockney Rebel achieved during the early to mid-1970s was an ability to cross the discursively constructed boundaries between rock and pop. Indeed, through the diverse nature of their respective musical output, it was almost as if these progressive pop bands were consciously testing the boundaries of rock and pop, or at least throwing light on their extreme elasticity and bringing their audience along with them. With the emergence of what has been referred to as 'postmodern pop' (Hebdige, 1988) in the late 1980s, many popular music artists became quick to talk about the blurring and collapse of genre boundaries. It is difficult to make direct connections between the claims of these later artists, such as Talking Heads, Laurie Anderson and Thomas Dolby, and the popular music landscape of the early 1970s. And yet such connections are clearly there. Most pertinently, like their early 1970s counterparts, each of these artists are musically quite distinct but are connected by a common desire to experiment in a way that links the experimental and avant-garde with mainstream pop. Ultimately, then, it is possible to connect various eras of progressive pop over time, each era being set in its own sociocultural, temporal and technological context. Viewed in this light, it is also clear that in their challenge to the rock-pop distinction, and the increased eclecticism they introduced into rock and pop fields during the early 1970s, the six artists focused on in this book do define a significant moment of revision in British popular music, which was 'progressive' in its intent and 'popular' by nature.

Conclusion

The purpose of this chapter has been to examine the origins of British progressive pop and provide some definitional context in the transitional period between the late 1960s and early 1970s. A key contributor to the emergence of progressive pop traits among certain British popular artists of the early 1970s, it is argued, was the enduring influence of the Beatles. Both in terms of their songwriting and pioneering use of the recording studio, it has been suggested, the Beatles created a rich creative legacy on which a number of British artists who followed them were able to draw in the creation of their own music. The innovation associated with progressive pop, it has been further argued, was also facilitated by significant leaps forward in recording studio technology that occurred between the end of the 1960s and mid 1970s, which enabled artists to move from 8 to 16 to 24 track recording in a few short years. The impact of such a development on the character of progressive pop, it has been illustrated, was pivotal, allowing for the creation of richly produced songs, including some of the most enduring and remembered tracks of the 1970s. The willingness of the music industry at this point to allow many artists an opportunity to grow and develop their musical ability through a series of album and single releases was another important factor underpinning the emergence of British progressive pop. Again, this trend stemmed from the proven commercial success of the Beatles as a studio band during the late 1960s and continued into the early 1970s, where it proved particularly important in the success of David Bowie, Roxy Music, Queen, 10cc, ELO and Cockney Rebel. It has been further illustrated how the development of rock journalism during the later 1960s, and its role in shaping perceptions of popular music as something other than 'youth entertainment', was also instrumental in priming the conditions for the emergence of British progressive pop during the early 1970s. In Chapter 2, a closer analysis is offered of the development of British popular music during the early 1970s and the temporarily unique opportunities that this offered for the emergence of progressive pop, its cornering of the often quite distinct albums and singles markets and pervasive presence in the British popular music landscape of the time.

Notes

1. Bouncing refers to the clearing of track space on analogue tape by transferring a number of recorded tracks down onto a spare single track before erasing the bounced tracks so that new ones can be recorded. Such practices continued into the 1970s, when even as the technology had evolved to the extent that forty-eight and even seventy-two track recording was available, at the same time musical arrangements had become more ambitious, which thus increased demand for track space.
2. Flanging is a form of sound processing where two copies of the same signal are combined, with the second being very slightly delayed to create a swirling effect. Following early examples like that heard in 'Itchycoo Park' using two tape recorders, analogue and later digital flanging effects were developed for both studio production and live performance.
3. Although the term 'stadium rock' is often assumed to bespeak a particular genre of hard and/or progressive rock music, it can just as easily apply to any other group or artist whose popularity is sufficient for them to perform in stadium-style venues. For example, through the 1970s and into the 1980s, bands and artists such as the Eagles, Bruce Springsteen, U2, Dire Straits and David Bowie could all easily have been categorized under the stadium rock banner.

2
New sounds for a new decade

Although the British progressive pop bands documented in this book were eventually to have a reach that extended in most cases beyond the UK, it can be argued that their specific presence in that country as home-grown British acts, together with the rock-pop crossover music they became known for there, had a distinctly local flavour to it as well. While the creative legacy of the Beatles was felt worldwide, the emphasis in Britain on living up to that legacy and finding a successor to the Beatles to carry British popular music forward into the 1970s was arguably a factor leading to the emergence of progressive pop and its vibrancy in the British popular music soundscape of the early 1970s. At the same time, however, the new decade also brought with it a new generation of music fans in search of their own generational music icons. For these fans, it was often the case that the 1960s already marked something of a distant past, and the 1970s seemed wide open for the arrival of new talents on the British popular music scene. Politically too, the nature of Britain was beginning to change as the slowing of the national economy undermined the optimism of the 1960s, and along with it the countercultural investment in music as a vehicle for sociopolitical change. That said, if there was widespread opinion that the more overtly political rock music of the late 1960s had ultimately failed to install the change that many of its protagonists envisaged in their songs, there was also a sense that, artistically speaking, this music had opened the gates for more experimental and creatively ambitious music. Furthermore, for a brief period in the early 1970s, many of the major recording labels remained open to signing artists whose music did not fit comfortably into particular genre categories and who in some cases were more album orientated than chart focused. Indeed, a number of major record companies established new labels to facilitate the signing of such artists, as was the case with EMI's Harvest label. Established in 1969, Harvest signed a number of British progressive rock and more avant-garde artists, including Pink Floyd, Syd Barratt, Kevin Ayers, Barclay James Harvest and Bebop Deluxe. In Britain, the distinction that had emerged between album bands and more chart-orientated artists was further intensified during the early 1970s by the varying levels of access these artists had to radio airplay. For the most part UK radio was dominated by chart music, this being in the days when commercial radio in Britain was in its infancy and there was also no established college radio network to promote the work of more specialist and niche artists. A broadly similar situation applied to television in Britain, which at this point offered only a very limited number of regular programmes dedicated to popular music, with the majority of these also being focused on chart music (Fryer, 1997). Such a context provided a relatively well-defined space for the emergence of British progressive pop during this era. Indeed, a large part of what made such artists distinctive was their capacity to straddle the rock/pop and albums/singles markets, something they each managed to do with a high degree of success throughout the early to mid-1970s. To that extent, when considered retrospectively, British progressive pop artists can frequently lay claim to having produced what are now considered to be some of the most iconic albums of the early 1970s while at the same time maintaining a lofty presence in the British singles charts. As this chapter considers, such a situation provided the backdrop for the distinctive quality of progressive pop in a British context.

British popular music in the early 1970s

As noted in Chapter 1, following the 1960s, rock and pop music in Britain became on the whole less overtly political, until the emergence of punk in the mid-1970s (see Chambers, 1985; Hebdige, 1979). That said, British popular music of the early 1970s was characterized by several new directions, some of which built on and developed musical trends that had begun to take shape during the late 1960s. These included hard rock, whose late 1960s exponents included bands such as Cream, Led Zeppelin, Deep Purple, Humble Pie and Free (whose breakthrough song 'Alright Now' was a major worldwide hit in 1970). During the early to mid-1970s hard rock crystallized into a bona fide genre accompanied by the arrival of new acts such as Atomic Rooster, the Groundhogs and Bad Company, a hard rock 'super-group' that brought together ex-Mott the Hoople guitarist Mick Ralphs, vocalist Paul Rogers, drummer Simon Kirke (both formerly with Free) and bass player Raymond 'Boz' Burrell, who had previously been a member of progressive rock group King Crimson. Similarly, Led Zeppelin, founded by ex-Yardbirds guitarist Jimmy Page in 1968, consolidated their position as a premier hard rock band during the early 1970s with the release of their fourth album *Led Zeppelin IV* (also referred to as *Four Symbols*) in November 1971 (Fyfe, 2003). This became Led Zeppelin's biggest selling album, containing 'Stairway to Heaven', the song for which the band continues to be most well known internationally (Fast, 2001). Some commentators have suggested that the more straight-ahead direction of hard rock music in the early 1970s functioned as something of a (youth) cultural antidote to the failed promises of the sixties' counterculture. Indeed, several of the more established British bands that had begun in the 1960s and become pivotal figureheads in the counterculture also assumed a more identifiably hard rock direction in the early 1970s. These included the Who (one of a handful of British bands to have performed at the 1969 Woodstock festival, see Bennett, 2004) and the Rolling Stones, whose respective songs 'Won't Get Fooled Again' and 'Brown Sugar' were both top 10 hits in the UK during 1971 and became rock anthems of the new decade. Of these two songs, the former track in particular denotes a weariness and cynicism with countercultural ideology and the premise ingrained therein that music could provide a driving force for social and political change.

Rhythm and blues also experienced a significant resurgence in the early 1970s British music charts with bands such as Rod Stewart and the Faces (formerly the Small Faces), who scored major hits with 'Stay with Me' (1971) and 'Cindy Incidentally' (1973) (Morley, 1983). Similarly, Status Quo, who had had an initial moment of success in 1968 with the psychedelic pop hit 'Pictures of Matchstick Men', re-emerged in 1970 with 'Down the Dustpipe', a song that marked a major change in musical direction towards the twelve-bar boogie rock that would bring the band significant commercial success throughout the 1970s with songs such as 'Paper Plane' (1972) 'Caroline' (1973), 'Down Down' (1975) and 'Rockin' All over the World' (1977) (Wiggins, 1983), the last title being a cover version of a track written by ex-Creedence Clearwater Revival member John Fogarty and appearing on his second solo album, *John Fogarty*, released in 1975 (see Rossi and Parfitt, 2004). Other British bands adopting a boogie-rock style in the early 1970s included Foghat and Wishbone Ash (the latter diversifying slightly into more folk and progressive rock directions with the release of their 1972 album *Argus*, which contained the band's most well-known and enduring track 'Blowin' Free'; see Charone, 1983). In the case of these more rhythm and blues and boogie-orientated rock bands, the emphasis was very much on a back-to-basics approach typified by more simple chord structures and straightforward lyrics in stark contrast to the increasingly flamboyant and virtuoso playing styles that had become a trademark of much rock music in the late 1960s. A parallel, if more low-key, scene of blues and rhythm 'n' boogie-influenced music was also taking form in London during the early 1970s where a vibrant pub rock scene spawned bands such as Dr. Feelgood, Brinsley Schwartz, the Winkies (who would later record and perform with Brian Eno, see Pattie, 2016) and Kilburn and the Highroads (the first band to be formed by future punk and new wave legend Ian Dury). These and other pub rock artists would in their turn be highly influential on the emergence of British punk several years later, with many pub rockers fitting easily into the punk scene given its similar emphasis on shorter and more musically straightforward songs (see Laing, 1985).

This back-to-basics approach in British popular music was also reflected in the rise of glam rock, a highly popular genre associated with the early 1970s that embraced a full-on 1950s nostalgia in terms of its musical and to some extent stylistic influences. Stratton (1986) has argued that, more than any other British musical style of the early 1970s, glam represented a rejection of the overblown claims often made during the 1960s concerning the potential of rock music to change the world. Glam, suggests Stratton, was essentially intended as a 'feelgood' music, with celebrated glam artists such as Alvin Stardust rejecting the pretentiousness of the 'rock star' syndrome and trading instead on a consciously parodic image of throwaway pop plasticity. Indeed, Stardust had had a previous pop-singer alias during the 1960s as Shane Fenton (see Logan and Woffinden, 1977). Slightly older than many of his glam counterparts, as a recycled glam rocker, Stardust became the epitome of the tongue-in-cheek glam sensibility, at least as this manifested itself among many of those more chart-orientated glam artists who were a mainstay of popular music radio and television in Britain during the early 1970s. Glam's repertoire of lightweight, radio-friendly pop also produced a number of offshoots, including bands such as Mud and the Rubettes, each of whom took glam's penchant for fifties revivalism and perfected it to a fine art both musically and, in Mud's case, visually. At the other extreme, artists like Chicory Tip further exaggerated the spectacular parody of glam with costumes that conjured up images of the alien invaders from 1950s science fiction B movies. This futuristic image was also accentuated by the band's music, which, although intended as essentially lightweight chart material, offered the first commercial stirrings of electro-pop with two hit singles, 'Son of My Father' (1972) and 'Christina' (1973). The first of these songs was co-written and produced by Giorgio Moroder, who would later go on to work with Donna Summer on her 1977 disco hit 'I Feel Love' and Philip Oakey (lead vocalist of 1980s electro-pop band the Human League), with whom he collaborated on the 1985 hit single 'Together in Electric Dreams' and follow-up album *Philip Oakey and Giorgio Moroder*.

Glam represents a particularly significant moment in the history of British popular music, not only because of its proto-punk status (see Bennett, 2007) but also because of the way that, notwithstanding its aforementioned tongue-in-cheek status, it was seized on by a number of emerging artists in early 1970s Britain who arguably saw its potential as a vehicle for gaining early exposure (Bennett, 2017), acquiring at the same time a significant degree of critical acclaim. The music of these artists, which included David Bowie, Marc Bolan and Roxy Music, in many instances transcended the relatively narrow parameters of the classic glam sound of bands and artists such as Alvin Stardust and The Sweet. Indeed, in this respect there can be said to have existed in British glam a bifurcation of sorts between those artists who actively sought to exploit its creative possibilities and those whose 'glam careers' were to a large extent manufactured and handed down from above. Trynka, in his biography of David Bowie, provides an effective summary of this situation in noting how 'Bowie would later explain that he and Marc Bolan were high glam: conceptual. Brickies [British-English slang for bricklayers] in satin, like The Sweet, were low glam' (2011: 161). Predictably perhaps, in the field of popular music studies, it is the former category of British glam artists that has attracted the major attention. Auslander's (2006) *Performing Glam Rock*, the first academic book dedicated to British glam, is an illustrative case in point in that it focuses largely on more critically acclaimed artists of the glam era, including Marc Bolan, David Bowie, Roxy Music and Roy Wood's Wizzard.[1] That these artists are given preference over a range of other possible artists who could have been studied, notably, the aforementioned Sweet, or other commercially successful glam artists such as Slade, is problematic for a number of reasons. First, it can be legitimately argued that these latter bands, together with others in the more 'mainstream' British glam camp, such as Mud and Alvin Stardust, did as much (if not more) to define glam in the eyes of Britain's music-buying public as did the more critically acclaimed artists referred to by Auslander. Second, with the exception of Marc Bolan, whose untimely death in a car accident in September 1977 at the age of 29 curtailed an attempted post-glam comeback in Britain, each of the other artists referred to by Auslander were able to quickly reposition themselves following the demise of glam during 1974. The same is true of other British artists such as Queen and Cockney Rebel, who emerged towards the end of the glam era but also took advantage of the glam image as indicated by their early appearances on *Top of the Pops* (see also Chapter 4). The fact that Bowie, Roxy Music, Queen and Cockney Rebel were so quickly able to move beyond glam as its popularity waned, while other artists such as The Sweet later struggled with their glam legacy, begs the question as to whether such artists were as consistently glam in their early years as scholars have maintained or whether they merely used the glam label as a means of launching, or, in the case of Bowie re-launching, their musical careers. Likewise, it is arguable that music writers of the early 1970s who used the glam label with reference to artists such as David Bowie and Roxy Music did so largely out of convenience and typically with reference to the visual image of these artists, whose music was otherwise often quite difficult to categorize given its characteristically eclectic flavour. Indeed, a related distinction with David Bowie, Roxy Music, Queen and Cockney Rebel and their 'pop-glam' counterparts is that while they were highly visible in the singles charts, attracted significant radio airplay and appeared on prime-time music television programmes such as *Top of the Pops*, they were at the same building highly credible reputations as album artists, something that could not be said of Alvin Stardust, The Sweet and other more chart-focused glam artists whose albums were secondary to the hit singles that they contained.

As the above scenario suggests, the artistic weight carried by 'high glam' artists also reflected in the attention they received from the music industry. All were signed to record labels that had established track records of working with highly successful album artists. Queen and Cockney Rebel were quickly signed by premier British label EMI, who had also worked with the Beatles. Roxy Music were signed to Chris Blackwell's successful Island Records (see Hebdige, 1987) for their first five albums before moving to Polydor, who released the band's final three studio albums beginning with *Manifesto* in 1979. Similarly, ELO were initially signed to EMI's 'progressive rock label' Harvest (see Chapter 2) and then to Warner Bros., before moving to Jet records in 1975. The Jet label had been established by music manager, agent and businessman Don Arden, who also oversaw ELO's business affairs at this point in the band's career. In 1971 David Bowie's new manager Tony Defries managed to secure for Bowie a deal with American label RCA, who also had Elvis Presley and Lou Reed on their roster of artists (Trynka, 2011). By contrast, many of the more singles chart-focused British glam artists tended to be signed to labels that were less well established and/or were more orientated towards singles artists. An example of this was Bell Records, who signed artists such as the Glitter Band, Showaddywaddy and the Bay City Rollers. While some of the other more chart-orientated glam acts were signed to established labels, this did not always translate into album sales, a case in point being The Sweet, who, despite being with RCA and having significant singles success during the early 1970s, failed to make a significant impact on the album market in the UK or elsewhere even at the height of their popularity. The musically and lyrically more erudite quality of the 'high glam' artists indicated their awareness of broader musical trends emerging in Britain at this time, trends that had evolved from some of the more experimental and art rock aspects of late 1960s popular music. Similarly, when these artists did look back in time for musical inspiration, this was not limited to the 1950s parody-style that was a mainstay of much chart-orientated glam. Rather, Bowie, Roxy Music and Queen exercised a much deeper musical and cultural vocabulary that frequently saw them referencing musical styles and lyrical motifs from the 1920s and 1930s. Through their advanced levels of songwriting and musicianship, these artists were able to forge this broad range of musical influences into a compelling pastiche. Their songs were audibly recognizable and positioned in a pop and rock style, but the other sonic points of departure contained in them produced a novel quality that separated them out from the work of other more stereotypically glam artists. As with 10cc and ELO (artists whose careers did not converge with glam), the creative prowess of David Bowie, Roxy Music, Queen and Cockney Rebel enabled these artists to develop dual careers, as innovative pop singles artists who were simultaneously cast firmly within the orbit of album-orientated rock. As noted in Chapter 1, the foundations of AOR had begun to develop during the late 1960s. By the early years of the 1970s, however, AOR had become a fully fledged aspect of popular music production and consumption. Although AOR could not be described as a genre-specific label, one style of popular music in particular did much to define the parameters of AOR, particularly in Britain, during the early 1970s.

Overtures, symphonies … and progressive rock

In the same period when glam rock dominated the British singles charts, an altogether different chapter in British popular music was beginning to take shape in the form of what would ultimately come to be referred to as progressive rock (see Macan, 1997; Stump, 1997; Martin, 1998). The very antithesis of glam, but an equally 'British' genre, at least in its formative years, progressive rock's roots date back to the late 1960s when bands such as King Crimson, Procul Harem and the Moody Blues had begun to experiment with different sound textures, time signatures and song structures, moving beyond the conventional notion of the three-minute pop song to produce longer pieces of music that often had different sections or stages woven into them (see Holm-Hudson, 2002). As this brief description suggests, progressive rock was by definition predisposed to the album format, with single tracks sometimes taking up the whole side of an album and being tied together by thematic conceptual threads that demanded they be listened to as a whole (Willis, 1978). Taking some of their creative nourishment from psychedelic rock, as well as from the later work of the Beatles, progressive rock bands developed these influences further though utilizing the significant advances in recording technology that had been made since the late 1960s. A further hallmark of the progressive rock style was the emphasis placed on the technical ability of individual musicians who often attracted their own fans based on their reputations as virtuoso players. The earlier pioneers of the progressive rock movement in Britain were soon joined by new bands such as Yes, Jethro Tull, Genesis and Emerson Lake and Palmer (ELP). Similarly, Pink Floyd, having parted company with original singer, guitarist and songwriter Syd Barrett in 1968 (Watkinson and Anderson, 2007), had moved away from their psychedelic roots and adopted a style that leant itself more towards the evolving progressive rock scene of the early 1970s. This was in evidence on the band's 1970 album *Atom Heart Mother*, whose title track was twenty-three minutes long and included orchestral arrangements and sections where wordless vocals were provided by a sixteen-piece choir (led and conducted by John Alldis). Pink Floyd, together with the other bands referenced above, did much to define the musical and aesthetic parameters of progressive rock during the first half of the 1970s. While each of these artists were to a fair degree stylistically different from each other, what unified them was a desire to make more artistically ambitious music that often drew as much on classical and jazz influences as on rock and blues. Keyboard players with a background in classical music, such as Tony Banks (Genesis), Keith Emerson (ELP) and Rick Wakeman (Yes), the latter having studied for a time at the Royal College of Music in London, were often a feature of progressive rock bands as were other musicians whose style and influences often extended across genres not at that time conventionally associated with rock.[2] Yes, Jethro Tull, Genesis, ELP and Pink Floyd would all go on to achieve significant commercial success during the early 1970s, with Pink Floyd's 1973 LP release *Dark Side of the Moon* becoming one of the biggest selling albums of all time.

As somewhat pithily depicted in Alan Parker's 1982 film *Pink Floyd: The Wall* (a filmic adaptation of Pink Floyd's double album *The Wall* released three years earlier), during the early 1970s some British progressive rock bands had particularly significant success in the United States, where their popularity, alongside British hard rock and heavy metal bands such as Led Zeppelin, Deep Purple and Black Sabbath,[3] took them into increasingly larger venues (see, Rutherford, 2014). In that context, the growing reliance of these artists on large-scale public address (or PA) systems, elaborate stage lighting and special effects helped to establish the groundwork for what would later come to be termed 'stadium rock' (Denski and Scholle, 1992). In Britain, as in other parts of Europe, however, there was far less opportunity for such artists to perform in stadium-sized venues as it was not the custom at that point for sports stadiums to be used as venues for live rock music (see Chase and Healy, 1995). As a result, with the exception of rock festivals, such as those held annually at Glastonbury (see McKay, 2000) and Reading (Stone, 2009), British audiences for progressive rock concerts tended to be smaller than in the United States. As a consequence, in Britain progressive rock continued to have more of a niche and even 'underground' reputation and following, whereas in the United States, it quickly became to all intents and purposes a mainstream music enjoyed by a mass audience. Indeed, this perception of progressive rock and hard rock as fringe musics in Britain during the early 1970s is also captured in some academic literature on youth and music published at that time. This is seen, for example, in a study by Taylor and Wall (1976), where artists such as Pink Floyd and indeed Deep Purple are referred to as 'underground', denoting their lack of presence on mainstream British radio and television.

Progressive rock's more mainstream status in the United States was also significantly helped along by the much larger amount of airplay received by progressive rock artists on American radio as compared with Britain. Mike Rutherford, a founding member of British progressive rock band Genesis, who enjoyed increasing commercial success in the United States from the early stages of their career, alludes to this in his memoir when he observes how 'in America you'd hear rock on the radio all the time', further noting that the quality of radio playback in the United States was far superior to radio in Britain at that time due to the common use of compression by American radio stations to create a more dynamic sound (2014: 111). The influence of radio airplay (or not) in creating this early distinction between progressive rock's more mainstream status in the United States and its niche or 'underground' status in the UK can be illustrated through the aforementioned example of Pink Floyd's *Dark Side of the Moon* album. Following its release in March 1973, the song 'Money', the first track on the B-side of the original vinyl version of the album, was identified as a single for the American market. Issued in May 1973, the song became Pink Floyd's first hit in the United States, also charting in Canada, Germany, Austria and France. However, likely due to the lack of airplay being received by progressive rock bands on British radio at this time, the song was not released as a single in the UK. Indeed, following their early chart success in 1967, Pink Floyd had no further UK chart successes until 1979 when the band had its first and only British number 1 hit with 'Another Brick in the Wall, Part 2' taken from that year's double album release *The Wall*. Throughout the early to mid-1970s, Pink Floyd, together with other British progressive rock bands of the era, were essentially regarded as album-orientated rock (AOR) bands, a reputation shared with Led Zeppelin, who released singles in the United States but not for the British market (although ironically a cover of Led Zeppelin's 1969 track 'Whole Lotta Love' recorded by blues guitarist Alexis Korner's band Collective Consciousness Society (also known as CCS) was used as the theme tune for weekly UK television chart show *Top of the Pops* between 1970 and 1977). Progressive rock's lack of presence in the British singles charts and on radio and television served to create a quasi-avant-garde aura around the music and among those bands who created it. Indeed, as discussed later in this chapter, even as steps were taken to incorporate progressive rock and other elements of AOR music into British music television, the effect was to further deepen progressive rock's aura of avant-garde music rather than distil it.

Britain's AOR – Pop divide and national music television

While the term 'AOR' became transnationally recognized and applied as a means of denoting music of a more creatively involved and/or intellectual and abstract nature, in Britain AOR assumed a special, locally inscribed resonance as an essentially alternative form of musical taste and music listening. This was in part due to the aforementioned absence of AOR artists from the radio, given the often radio-unfriendly format of their music (at least in the eyes of music programmers of the time) underscored by an assumption that AOR music was too 'high-brow' for mainstream radio audiences. There was very little exception to this rule, two notable cases being celebrated BBC Radio 1 DJ John Peel, whose early 1970s weekly radio show *Top Gear* featured sessions recorded by a wide range of AOR artists, including Genesis, Fairport Convention, Soft Machine and the Incredible String Band (see Garner, 1993), and fellow Radio 1 DJ Alan 'Fluff' Freeman, whose *Saturday Rock Show* featured a weekly instalment of rock and progressive rock between 1974 and 1978, when the show was discontinued. A broadly similar situation prevailed in the case of British television where only limited opportunities to regularly view rock and pop music existed. The BBC's weekly music programme *Top of the Pops* (*TOTP*), Britain's longest running chart show (see Simpson, 2002), was the primary outlet for popular music in the early 1970s attracting an average of 15 million viewers each week. On ITV (Britain's independent regional independent television network), copycat shows such as *Lift off with Ayshea* and *Shang-a-Lang* (hosted by Scottish teeny-bopper pop band the Bay City Rollers, who were then at the height of their commercial popularity, see Frith, 1983) were also favoured by teen pop fans of the era. If limited opportunities for pop fans to see music on British television existed during the early 1970s, then this was even more so for rock fans at the time. Indeed, during the first part of 1970s, only one British popular music television show, *the Old Grey Whistle Test* (*OGWT*), regularly catered for British fans of rock and other AOR genres (see Fryer, 1997; Mills, 2010). Commencing in 1971, throughout the early to mid-1970s *OGWT* provided a critical outlet for AOR, introducing British audiences to a wide variety of artists, among them American rock avant-gardist Captain Beefheart, Irish blues-rock guitarist Rory Gallagher, English folk-rock band Fairport Convention, Scottish singer-songwriter John Martyn and English blues-rock outfit Vinegar Joe (a band characterized by the twin lead vocals of Elkie Brooks and Robert Palmer, who would each go on to have successful solo careers later in the 1970s and into the 1980s). Also featured on the show were a number of lesser-known progressive rock bands, such as Greenslade, Bebop Deluxe, Barclay James Harvest and Camel, who collectively represented a more localized chapter in British progressive rock history, their music failing to translate in the trans-Atlantic fashion of fellow progressive bands such as Jethro Tull, Yes, Genesis and ELP, who enjoyed a far greater level of popularity and commercial success at an international level.[4]

In comparison to most television chart music shows of the time, *OGWT* adopted a no-frills approach to the presentation of its guests. Among other things, this saw artists performing live or semi-live (with live vocals sung over pre-recorded backing tracks) in a sparsely furnished studio equipped with only basic lighting and no special effects. Such an approach helped to reinforce the fact that *OGWT* was a show primarily about the music and designed specifically for 'serious' music fans, essentially those who followed the album charts and read critical reviews of AOR artists in music press publications, such as *New Musical Express* and *Rolling Stone Magazine*. *OGWT*'s ascribed status as a *serious* music show was further emphasized through the in-depth interviews conducted both in-house and on location with many of the featured bands and artists. In the show's heyday of the early to mid-1970s, iconic *OGWT* presenter Bob Harris, then and now regarded as something of an authority on AOR music (Vickers, 2010), conducted interviews with guests that were designed to represent them as 'artists' rather than as show business celebrities as was typically the way that more mainstream pop artists were often positioned in the UK at this time. Harris's approach was underscored by the rock journalism of the day which, as noted in Chapter 1, functioned to separate rock and other designated 'serious music' from pop through the way it inscribed the former with a quasi-high art status (see Shuker, 2001; Kutulas, 2010; Toynbee, 1993). Again, in the case of Britain it could be argued that such an aesthetic divide was given extra depth, and perhaps made to feel more 'real', through the little exposure given to AOR artists in the mainstream British media. If bands such as Pink Floyd or Led Zeppelin did surface on British television from time to time, this was generally in the context of specialist arts and culture programmes such as BBC television's *Omnibus*. Similarly, concert and performance films by such artists frequently bypassed mainstream popular music television shows. For example, Pink Floyd's 1972 film release *Live at Pompeii* was premiered at that year's Edinburgh Film Festival while an extract from Led Zeppelin's 1976 concert film (accompanied by a live double album) *The Song Remains the Same* was previewed for British audiences on *OGWT*, the show's late-night slot excluding most early teen and pre-teen music fans. As later tributes to *OGWT*, notably the 2007 documentary *The Old Grey Whistle Test Story* (dir. Dionne Newton), serve to illustrate, the show is now regarded as an important promoter of AOR in Britain during the early 1970s. Indeed, the niche status of *OWGT* gave it significant license in the creation of an AOR canon in a British context. Work in the field of popular music heritage has suggested that a more recent process of cultural reclassification has transformed rock, once designated as a form of 'popular music' into a quasi-high art form with its own ascribed history and heritage (see, for example, Schmutz, 2005; Bennett, 2009). Although undoubtedly the case that rock music, or at least particular aspects of the genre now typically referred to as 'classic' or 'heritage' rock, began to achieve such a status in earnest during the mid-1990s, the forms of aesthetic distinction necessary for the future delineation and labelling of particular styles and/or artists as examples of classic and heritage rock were already well-entrenched by the beginning of the 1970s. Thus, it was at this point that rock music critics, together with rock filmmakers and other critical intermediaries, began the task of 'formulat[ing] an interpretation of the music which applie[d] the traditional parameters of art to the specificity of rock' (Regev, 1994: 87). Emerging at a time when the combined work of such intermediaries was crystallizing into a series of discourses regarding rock as art, *OWGT* was pivotal in articulating these discourses to a British audience, effectively becoming a localized platform for the rock taste-making process.

Although provision of a space for AOR artists was, and indeed has remained, a quintessential aspect of *OGWT*'s aura of attraction for artists and fans alike, it is also true to say that the actual distinction between AOR and singles artists was not always necessarily as clear-cut, even during the early 1970s, as it was often held to be. Indeed, reviewing those artists featured on *OGWT*, particularly during its earlier years, it is clear that the show sometimes actually played a key part in the 'conversion' of some of its featured artists from the AOR market to a more crossover market appeal. Thus, the very first *OGWT*, broadcast on 21 September 1971, featured the UK television debut of American rock artist Alice Cooper who was at that time little known to British audiences. The following year Cooper went on to dominate the singles' charts on both sides of the Atlantic (including appearances on *TOTP*) with the proto-punk single 'School's Out'. Similarly, *OGWT* often played a pivotal role in helping British artists who were beginning to achieve, or aspired to, chart success to establish a crossover appeal by introducing their music to AOR audiences in Britain. Salient examples of this include David Bowie, Roxy Music, Queen and Cockney Rebel who all benefitted significantly from early exposure on *OGWT* during 1972 and 1973.[5] Thus, in the sense that *OGWT* championed AOR music in Britain in the early 1970s, it can also be said to have created an important space for the emergence of artists, and particularly British artists, whose music crossed the divide between AOR and chart music in Britain at this time.

Stepping into the void between AOR and pop

If the notion of a progressive direction in British popular music during the early 1970s has been well mapped in the case of progressive rock, it is less well understood in just about every other sense. Similarly, while a number of academic authors have been quick to note the influence of the Beatles on the emergence of progressive rock, how this 'progressive' influence may have framed the aspirations of other British popular music artists has rarely, if ever, been considered. Earlier in this book it was noted how, in the wake of the success enjoyed by the Beatles during their later and more creatively experimental phase, record companies in Britain temporarily gave more control to many artists in determining the style and character of their musical output. It has similarly been noted how, during the early 1970s, music industry branding and the 'strategic' categorization of music was much less formulaic than it was to subsequently become, particularly in the video dominated 1980s (see Kaplan, 1987). Terms such as 'heavy metal' and 'alternative' were yet to appear and even genre labels such as glam and progressive rock, while they had an emerging currency in journalistic circles, were still relatively fluid terms that were often not properly understood, and thus not widely used, by the public or indeed in the retail marketing of music. Unshackled by the branding that would later come to dominate the popular music world, David Bowie, Roxy Music, Queen, 10cc, ELO and Cockney Rebel defined a new, if relatively short-lived, era in British popular music. Each of these artists, while to some extent aligned with then current musical trends, such as hard rock, progressive rock and glam, were at the same time distinct from these trends and indeed from each other, both musically and visually. What did connect each of them, however, was their proven capacity to operate artistically and commercially between AOR and the singles charts, producing music that was pop enough to appeal to an audience who based their purchasing choices on what was played on daytime radio and *Top of the Pops*, while at the same being progressive enough to attract the interest of more 'serious' music fans who tended to buy albums, listen to more niche radio programmes (such as those hosted by John Peel and Alan Freeman on BBC Radio 1), and tune in each week to sample the varied array of AOR music featured on the *Old Grey Whistle Test*.

Indeed, it is a by no means insignificant point that many of the artists described in this book as progressive pop were featured on both *Top of the Pops* and the *Old Grey Whistle Test* and seemed equally at home in both settings. Notable here are David Bowie and Roxy Music who in 1972 entreated *TOTP* audiences to their respective top 10 hits 'Starman' and 'Virginia Plain', appearing on the show merely weeks apart. Both of these tracks were strikingly novel in the context of the *TOTP* setting, the topic matter of their lyrics being strangely removed from what was usually featured on *TOTP*, the music featuring exotic and slightly eccentric melodies and chord changes. Put simply, compared to the other artists and songs featured on the show, the music of Bowie and Roxy Music appeared progressive – cut from a different cloth to the other mainstream pop offerings of the time. Yet at the same time each of these songs supplied a rhythm and beat that was as danceable as any other song generally featured on the show, something clearly in evidence from the enthusiastic response of *TOTP*'s in-house youth audience who danced away as Bowie and Roxy Music graced the stage during their respective appearances on the show (see also Chapter 4). In the same year, however, both of these artists also appeared on *OGWT*, where darker and far more AOR attuned aspects of their music were revealed. Bowie's appearance saw him performing the apocalyptically themed, and far less chart-friendly, 'Five Years' (see also Chapter 5), the opening track from his then current album *The Rise and Fall of Ziggy Stardust and the Spiders from Mars* (which also contained 'Starman').[6] In a similar vein, Roxy Music performed the musically abstract 'Ladytron' from their eponymously titled debut album, a track that quickly evolved from a minimalist vocal and electric piano opening to a cacophony of sound produced by instruments whose natural voices were radically altered through the sound-processing experiments of Brian Eno. Then referred to simply as Eno, his presence in Roxy Music gave the band an added air of distinction for pop and rock audiences alike. In subsequent years Eno would go on to have a highly successful solo career that included, among other things, experiments in the shaping of minimalist atmospheric soundscapes that would come to be known as ambient music (Tamm, 1995). Even in 1972, however, Eno's point of departure from conventional rock and pop music-making was obvious, he being one of the first popular music artists to appear on mainstream television using an electronic synthesizer (specifically a VC33) which, in addition to possessing a keyboard, featured a prominent, vertically positioned control panel containing a series of knobs and switches through which Eno was able to treat the sounds of the instruments being played by the other musicians in Roxy Music (see also Chapter 4). Famously labelling himself a non-musician, Eno pioneered the use of electronic technology, which gave Roxy Music art-rock credentials, while at the same time intriguing pop fans in an era when synthesizers and other aspects of electronic music-making technology were yet to become commonplace sights in popular music performance.

Queen's pop-AOR crossover also began to take form early in the band's career, although compared to Roxy Music, their emergence on the British music scene was a more slowburning and gradual process. Queen's first single, 'Keep Yourself Alive', written by guitarist Brian May and released in July 1973, failed to chart in Britain. It did, however, attract some attention when featured on *OGWT* and illustrates the show's importance in helping a number of artists with AOR credentials to also find their niche in the rock-pop crossover market. According to reports, OGWT's producer Michael Appleton received a 'white label'[7] of Queen's debut album *Queen*, on which 'Keep Yourself Alive' was the opening track (Hodkinson, 1995; see also Chapter 3). Both he and presenter Bob Harris were impressed by the sound of the album and having contacted EMI for more details about the artist elected to feature 'Keep Yourself Alive' on *OGWT*, accompanied by vintage animation footage originally used by Edgar J. Hoover during his presidential election campaign in the United States (see Gunn and Jenkins, 1992). This provided Queen with early exposure to AOR audiences in Britain (Frith, 1983) with the result that the *Queen* album peaked at number 24 in the UK album charts, paving the way for the band's following album *Queen II*, which contained what would become Queen's first UK top 10 single 'The Seven Seas of Rhye'. Further consideration is made of Queen's debut album to the emergence of a progressive pop aesthetic in Chapter 3. At this point, however, it is worthy of note that it provided the basis upon which Queen would build, between 1973 and 1976, each of their albums during this period containing a wealth of diverse material, including lengthier experimental pieces and segued tracks (reminiscent of the track segueing used on later Beatles' albums such as *Sgt. Pepper's Lonely Hearts Club Band* and *Abbey Road*), interspersed with more accessible material that the band ultimately drew on as single releases. In the very early stages of their career, Queen's singles output owed much to the hard rock style, and in particular to Led Zeppelin. However, while Led Zeppelin and other British hard rock outfits such as Deep Purple and Black Sabbath commanded only minimal mainstream music television presence in Britain at this time, Queen's more musically layered and chart-friendly brand of hard rock, together with their distinctive vocal harmonies, invested the band's music with a pop element missing in much other hard rock (this being several years before the melodic rock breakthrough of American and 'trans-Atlantic' melodic rock bands such as Journey, Styx and Foreigner). Moreover, as Queen's commercial foothold strengthened, their chart singles output began to show a range of influences that extended well beyond hard rock, as heard for example in the Freddie Mercury song 'Killer Queen', which reached number 2 in the UK charts in November 1974.

This chapter began by noting how an early impetus for the emergence of early 1970s progressive pop was the void left by the Beatles. While all of the progressive pop artists featured in this book would at some stage in their careers pay homage to the influence of the Beatles on their music, the two bands that most readily attracted comparisons with the Beatles were ELO and 10cc. In point of fact, however, as with each of the other progressive pop bands and artists considered here, ELO and 10cc were musically and stylistically distinct from each other. As such, the fact that both bands should be likened to the Beatles bespeaks an interesting facet of how multifarious the influence of the Beatles was judged to be – a fact that probably continues to reflect in how the band's legacy is felt today. In the case of ELO, the band's mission to carry on where the Beatles had effectively left off was evident not only in the sound of the band's music but in the early accounts offered by the band themselves, and particularly Roy Wood (see Spicer, 2018). Although Wood left ELO before that mission could be realized, under the creative leadership of Jeff Lynne (who on Wood's departure became the band's leader and principle songwriter), the sound of ELO evolved, retaining a clear Beatles influence but refining this so that it became more subtly infused within a style that was discernibly of the band rather than copy-cat style referencing of the Beatles (as had been the case with ELO's early work and typified in the band's debut single '10538 Overture'). Beyond this, ELO confirmed their progressive pop credentials by combining accessible pop singles with albums of more experimental, classically inspired and occasionally avant-garde material, culminating in what many consider to be ELO's most iconic and 'classic' album, *Out of the Blue* (1977) (see Chapter 6). Although sometimes referred to in music critic circles as a progressive rock band, during the early 1970s, ELO had far more mainstream pop visibility than the more commonly acknowledged British progressive rock acts of the era, scoring regular top 20 hits with songs such as the aforementioned '10538 Overture' (1972), 'Showdown' (1973) and 'Evil Woman' (1975). ELO's ongoing debt to the music of the Beatles was given a ringing endorsement when, speaking on US radio in 1974, John Lennon named 'Showdown' as one of his favourite songs and suggested that if the Beatles had remained together beyond 1970, their style may well have developed in a style akin to that of ELO (see Spicer, 2018: 109). More than anything else, Lennon's acknowledgement has possibly consolidated ELO's standing in the collective cultural memory of the 1970s as the British band that most vividly captured the spirit of the Beatles in their musical output.

The Beatles comparisons directed towards 10cc were of somewhat different order. Certainly, there were some obvious comparisons between the band's debut single 'Donna', released in 1972, and the Beatles' 'Oh Darling' from

Abbey Road (1969). But that comparison was relatively short-lived as future 10cc singles proved that the band's songwriting skills extended well beyond the scope of 'Donna' in increasingly diverse and eclectic ways. Rather, it was the concept behind 10cc that gave rise to the Beatles comparisons, particularly between 1972 and 1976, an era when 10cc were at their peak as progressive pop artists. The four-piece line-up at this time of Eric Stewart, Graham Gouldman, Kevin Godley and Lol Creme each contributed to the songwriting in 10cc and were multi-instrumentalists. Building on the creative partnership that had been forged between the Beatles and their producer George Martin, 10cc were perhaps the first British band of the 1970s to emerge with a fully formed competence of studio technology and the creative potential it offered. This was patently clear on 10cc's debut album (see also, Chapter 3), a record that announced 10cc to both British audiences and the music press as artists capable of crossing over between the singles and albums markets.

Beatles comparisons also resided in the fact that 10cc too hailed from the north-west of England, specifically from Manchester. Interestingly, though, while the Beatles 'northeness' quickly became something of a folk-memory as the band relocated to London following their initial success in 1963, 10cc's connection with the north-west continued well after their initial success and became something of a stance by the band against the London-centric nature of the UK music business at the time. In an interview conducted with the author in 2019, Grahman Gouldman offered the following reflections on 10cc's decisions to remain in the north-west:

> First of all [it was] because we were all from Manchester [but] the main thing was us having our own studio, this made all the difference ... [before that] you'd always record in London. Because up to the time of Strawberry [Studios] as far as I know there were never any really any decent studios in the north ... So to me the studio was vitally important. Because without the studio I don't think 10cc would have existed. (interview with author, January 2019)

During the interview Gouldman also referred to matters such as work ethic and shared sense of regional humour having contributed to the dynamic of 10cc as a band during the early 1970s. At the time, the band also suggested in various music press publications that their decision to compose material and record outside of London gave them a sense of autonomy from the music industry and a greater licence to make the music they wanted to make.

In essence then, where a Beatles spirit was located in the progressive pop of 10cc, this tended to spring from how the band took the conceptual blueprint of the Beatles' later years as a studio-outfit and re-inscribed this for their own creative ends. Indeed, one clear element that distinguished 10cc in a wholesale sense from their progressive pop peers was their visible shunning of show business trappings. Flagged at the time as a 'no-image' band, 10cc could in many respects be deemed an 'anti-image' act, a decision taken early in the band's career amidst discussions as to what they should wear for their first appearance on *Top of the Pops*, a show that was a focal point for artists to promote not only their music but also their overall 'product' of which image was held to be a critical component. In the event, 10cc elected to 'appear wearing their normal everyday denims' (Thompson, 2017: 49). While such a stance was becoming increasingly commonplace in AOR, during the early 1970s such a visual aesthetic was virtually unheard of in the world of pop. As such, this further galvanized 10cc's credentials as a band that transcended the pop world to draw on a richer legacy popular music, carrying forward with this the creative spirit of the Beatles for a new generation of music fans. The extent of 10cc's crossover appeal from the pop audiences of *TOTP* to AOR audiences is perhaps best illustrated by their regular appearances on the British rock festival circuit (see Tremlett, 1976) culminating in their appearance at the Knebworth festival in August 1976, the last ever performance by the original line-up of 10cc, sharing the bill with Lynyrd Skynyrd, Todd Rungren's Utopia, Hot Tuna, the Don Harrison band and headliners The Rolling Stones.

Conclusion

The distinctive composition of the singles and album chart lives that characterized progressive pop artists during the early 1970s marks an interesting and relatively unique period in the history of British popular music. Indeed, in many ways the first half of the 1970s marks a watershed moment, the last window of opportunity for artists, or at least those with a firm foothold in the albums market, to harness the creative license of the album as a marker of artistic credibility. The extent of the creative freedom afforded to artists in this respect is illustrated in the case of both Roxy Music and Cockney Rebel, whose early single releases were not taken from albums but were written and released as separate entities designed to appeal to chart audiences rather than as promotional devices for albums where sales had already proven healthy. Similarly, in the case of Queen, their first British top 20 hit 'Seven Seas of Rhye', although considered to be 'single material' by the band and their producer, Roy Thomas Baker, was only lifted from their second album, *Queen II* (1974), when a slot became available at short notice for Queen to appear on *TOTP* following a cancelled appearance by David Bowie (see Hodkinson, 1995). The progressive inroads made by these and other British artists into both the album and singles charts during the early 1970s has been largely eclipsed in the existing academic work due to the almost universally accepted discursive trope that progressive trends in British popular music during the early 1970s are wholly tied up with the evolution of progressive rock during this period. A critical issue with such a treatment of progressive rock, however, is the binary that it establishes, or at least strongly implies, between progressive rock and other aspects of popular music during the early 1970s. As noted earlier in this chapter, already during the late 1960s, some degree of experimentation away from the conventional pop ballads of the day was evident in more mainstream, chart-orientated music, not least of all because of the wide influence of the Beatles at this time. The Beatles' *Sgt. Peppers Lonely Hearts Club Band* is often cited as an influence on progressive rock music (Macan, 1997) and also commonly regarded as the first 'concept' album. It would, however, be erroneous to suggest that the influence of this album and other later work of the Beatles ended there. It is rather the case that the Beatles' influence permeated a broad range of popular music, encouraging many artists to develop their creativity and push the limits of pop, taking advantage of the new musical technologies at their disposal. It is also true to say that such an influence extended well into the 1970s. Indeed, during the period immediately following the break-up of the Beatles, a passing on of their creative mantle manifested as new bands emerged and began building on the Beatles' artistic legacy. In essence then what seems clear about British popular music of the early 1970s is that the notion of a progressive ethos assumed a far broader currency than that attributed to the limited number of bands that were clustered under the progressive rock banner. This point is taken up more forcefully in Chapter 3, where it is argued that, like progressive rock, what defined the British progressive pop artists of the early to mid-1970s was a willingness to innovate – to move beyond the comfort zone of 'conventional pop' in ways that stretched the abilities of the musicians and also challenged their listeners.

Notes

1. Auslander (2006) also includes Suzie Quatro in this book, claiming that Quatro can be considered the first, and only, female glam artist of the early 1970s.
2. For example, guitarist Steve Howe, who joined Yes in 1971, is also an accomplished jazz player and highly conversant with many other styles, including classical and ragtime.
3. While each of these three bands has become associated with the term 'heavy metal', during the early 1970s, this term was still not widely used. Both Led Zeppelin and Deep Purple have contested the heavy metal label being applied to their music.
4. The fact that such bands often fly under the radar of what is defined as progressive rock in academic accounts of the genre and elsewhere points the extent to which progressive rock's critical canon is linked with the genre's profile and representation in the United States. Anderton (2010) has gone as far as to suggest that progressive rock should be redefined as a meta-genre that encompasses a broad range of experimental music from the late 1960s and early 1970s, including the work of European artists such as German band Can and Italian artists Premiata Forneria Marconi (PFM).
5. Interestingly, while many of their progressive pop peers benefitted from the exposure they gained to the British AOR audience on *OGWT*, 10cc were excluded from the show. This was allegedly due to the show's producers deeming them not to be an album band. Following their departure from 10cc, however, Godley and Creme were interviewed on the show about their patented Gizmo invention, a device for bowing the strings of an electric guitar. This was followed by the preview of a track entitled 'The Flood' from the duo's debut album *Consequences* (1977). ELO were similarly absent from *OGWT* although in 1976 Jeff Lynne was interviewed by Bob Harris about the band's then current album *Face the Music* (1975) and forthcoming tour.
6. On this *OGWT* session Bowie also performed 'Changes' and 'Queen Bitch', two tracks from his previous album *Hunky Dory*. Released in 1971, *Hunky Dory* was Bowie's first recording for his new label RCA; although the album was well received, it was not until the release of *The Rise and Fall of Ziggy Stardust and the Spiders from Mars* that *Hunky Dory* began to attract more significant critical acclaim (see Trynka, 2011).
7. The term 'white label' refers to a vinyl record that is initially issued with a plain white label, that is, with no details of the artist or title, for promotional purposes and ahead of the record's general release.

3

Progressives in the world of pop

In the foregoing chapter of this book, reference has been made to how the emergence of progressive pop in Britain during the early 1970s may in part be considered as a response of the music industry, and the British record-buying public, to the break-up of the Beatles. Although this is not a novel claim, nor something that can be restricted to the early 1970s, or indeed to exclusively popular music in Britain, a specifically local sense of 'loss' does seem implicit in the trajectory of particular British popular music artists and their reception among local audiences at this time. With the break-up of the of the Beatles still very much in the national psyche, the British music industry, the music press and indeed the music-buying public seemed open to the prospect of new British pop and rock artists whose music drew on the Beatles' legacy. The release, on 2 April 1973, of two Beatles compilation albums, the 'Red Album' spanning the years 1962–1966 and the 'Blue Album' containing songs released between 1967 and 1970, was a clear indication of the continuing interest in the Beatles with the albums reaching number 3 and number 2, respectively, in the British album charts. Certainly the sentiment among emerging popular music artists at the beginning of the 1970s was often mixed in terms of how they discussed the influence of 1960s, including the Beatles, on their own musical approach. Thus, while artists such as ELO were unequivocal in their creative debt to the Beatles (see Spicer, 2018), others, ranging from Mark Bolan to Led Zeppelin, considered their music as being of a different genre and style. Furthermore, Bolan was also heard to comment that his audience was part of a new generation, ideologically and stylistically removed from the 1960s and in search of new pop icons to claim as their own.

But in other ways, evidence that the Beatles remained important as a creative template for those British artists who came after them, or whose careers only begun to take a more definitive shape in the early 1970s after the Beatles had broken up, is evident in a number of ways. David Bowie's collaboration with John Lennon while recording his celebrated *Young Americans* (1975) album is one example of this.

The album contains a cover version of the Lennon and McCartney song 'Across the Universe', and Lennon is credited as a co-writer of Bowie's trans-Atlantic 1975 hit 'Fame', which also features on *Young Americans*. Following Lennon's murder, in December 1980, Roxy Music paid tribute to the former Beatle with a cover of his post-Beatle's song 'Jealous Guy' (from the *Imagine* album released in 1971). Similarly, in 1976 Steve Harley and Cockney Rebel scored their last major British hit with a version of George Harrison's 1969 song 'Here Comes the Sun' from the Beatles' final studio album, *Abbey Road*. Cockney Rebel's version of the song was modelled on the original to a fair extent but featured state-of-the-art electronic synthesizer sounds that gave the arrangement a distinctively contemporary feel in an era when synthesized sounds were increasingly being heard in mainstream popular music. Evidence of the Beatles, influence on the new progressive pop trends in the British popular music of the early 1970s has been further accentuated in more recent years through various retrospectives offered by musicians who made key contributions during this era of musical innovation. Thus, for example, documentary interviews with Roger Taylor and Brian May of Queen as well as with the four original members of 10cc, Eric Stewart, Graham Gouldman, Kevin Godley and Lol Creme, have seen each of these musicians acknowledging a common debt to the Beatles and explaining how their varied musical styles and songwriting approaches were all initially inspired by the Beatles and particularly the band's later studio-focused albums.

Certainly, from an industry perspective it seems reasonable to suggest that the scope given to a number of new British artists in the early 1970s to engage in creative experiments and push the boundaries of rock and pop was at some level motivated by a desire on the part of the music industry to see if the creative and commercial achievements of the Beatles could be matched by a new British artist or perhaps by a cluster of artists. In any event, by mid-1972 it was evident that the new decade was generating some interesting and innovative turns in British popular music, with the year 1973 in particular being a pivotal one in terms of progressive musical departures both in the world of rock and, more importantly in the context of this book, in the world of pop.

A very progressive year

In the celebrated British television crime drama *Life on Mars*, when the show's unwitting protagonist police detective Sam Tyler travels back in time from 2007 to 1973 having been hit by a car and consequently, as the story line later reveals, sent into a coma, the link between Tyler's near-death experience and his shocked 'awakening' from unconsciousness in the past is the David Bowie song, 'Life on Mars' (1971) (Ticknell, 2010). An enduring track from the 1970s, 'Life on Mars' is also significant as a work of progressive pop in that its transition from album track to a top 10 single marks a period of eighteen months during which the progressive pop aesthetic took form as a palpable presence in the British popular music soundscape. Although the song had initially appeared in December 1971 on the *Hunky Dory* album, Bowie's fourth album and his first for his new label RCA, 'Life on Mars', was first released as a single in June 1973 when it climbed to number 3 on the UK singles charts. Earlier in the year Bowie had scored success with the album *Aladdin Sane* and the single 'Drive-in Saturday', a postmodern collage of fifties doo-wop influences and post-apocalyptically themed lyrics (see also Chapter 5), which had also been a number 3 hit for Bowie. The odd and in many ways provocative spectacle of Bowie's television appearances in 1972 and more prominently in 1973, portraying the androgynous alien figure Ziggy Stardust (the first of several fictitious aliases that Bowie was to assume in the ensuing years, see Bennett, 2017) was testament to a moment in British popular music when the creative boundaries of rock and pop were being continually tested. At that point in time, the notion of a progressive ethic assumed a particularly wide currency infusing the work of a broad and diverse range of artists. In this context, 1973 can in many ways be regarded as a watershed year for progressive trends in British popular music overall and a period of crystallization in terms of the musical and technological inspirations that a new generation of popular music artists in Britain drew from the Beatles and other musical innovators of the late 1960s.

Pink Floyd's *Dark Side of the Moon*, released on 1 March 1973 and generally considered to be the band's definite work, built on and refined the progressive elements of previous Pink Floyd albums, including *Atom Heart Mother* (1970) and *Meddle* (1971), channelling these musical traits into shorter tracks, conceptually linked through the disturbing theme of madness. Now considered to be Pink Floyd's most accomplished work, at the time of its release *Dark Side of the Moon* quickly proved to be their most commercially successful album (and has since gone on to be one of the best-selling albums of all time). A more surprising, but equally successful album release of 1973, and something that further demonstrates the depth of a progressive ethic in British popular music at this time, was Mike Oldfield's *Tubular Bells*. Building on the later Beatles' legacy of studio-based experimental rock, Oldfield's solo and understated approach to composition and recording was as novel as his reclusive stance, something that extended to not giving interviews to the British music press and shunning of live performance (things which almost every other rock artist at this point considered crucial to the promotion of their music) (see Palmer, 1977). Oldfield had previously been a member of ex-Soft Machine guitarist Kevin Ayers' band Kevin Ayers and the Whole World, playing bass and appearing with the band in an early television appearance on the *Old Grey Whistle Test* in 1972. With *Tubular Bells*, Oldfield took the concept of progressive music to a significantly new level, following the Beatles' ethos of using the recording studio as a musical instrument in its own right but evolving this approach to create highly elaborate soundscapes, whereby the use of tape loops and multiple overdubs allowed Oldfield to play most of the instruments on the album himself (see Jewell, 1983). While other rock artists had also begun to exploit studio technology to create music that extended beyond the limits of live performance, Oldfield was one of the very first artists to move away from the then strongly conventional band format in rock and recast the rock album as a solo project. While other artists, particularly in the world of electronic music, would subsequently follow Oldfield's example and work solo in the studio, in the spheres of rock and progressive rock, Oldfield's approach on *Tubular Bells* and his two subsequent albums, *Hergest Ridge* (1974) and *Ommadawn* (1975), remains a relatively unique and characteristically distinctive moment in British popular music (see Palmer, 1977).

Brian Eno, an artist more directly aligned, at least initially, with the progressive pop styles focused on in this book, was also beginning to explore the fuller creative possibilities of the recording studio in 1973. Moving beyond the song-based style of Roxy Music, whom he left in July 1973 to pursue a solo career, Eno was focusing on the creation of more sonically fragile, atmospheric and often quite ethereal soundscapes that would ultimately come to be referred to as ambient music (Tamm, 1995). Even during his tenure with Roxy Music, it was clear that Eno found the band format limiting and was searching for other ways to express himself musically. This ambition was to come steadily to fruition from the middle of 1973 onwards when, freed of his commitments to Roxy Music, Eno began a new musical career that, in addition to allowing for his creative maturation as an artist in his own right, also saw him collaborating with an increasing array of artists. This included contributions to David Bowie's three 'Berlin' albums, *Low* (1977), *'Heroes'* (1977) and *Lodger* (1979) and the co-writing of the song 'Heroes'. Eno's collaboration with Bowie also inspired an experimentation with ambient sounds, a feature heard most prominently on the album *Low*, whose B-side was largely instrumental ambient tracks. Enriched through the multiple layering of tracks, enhanced through the use of echo and other electronic effects as well the use of tape loops, Eno's initial foray into ambient music was on the album *No Pussyfooting*. Released in November 1973, this album marked the first of a series of collaborations with guitarist Robert Fripp, founder of King Crimson, one of the original exponents of progressive rock (see Chapter 2). Upon its initial release, *No Pussyfooting* failed to achieve anything like the commercial success enjoyed by *Dark Side of the Moon* and *Tubular Bells*, or indeed by much of Eno's subsequent work. However, the album's appearance in late 1973 further illustrated something of the diverse ways in which AOR in Britain was pulling away from more mainstream pop. The widening of the gap between AOR and pop was rife with possibilities for artists who took inspiration from both AOR and pop and wished to explore and combine the creative possibilities of each.[1]

Indeed, the year 1973 also saw the release of debut albums by 10cc and Queen, two new British bands who were ultimately set to play a particularly dominant role in the AOR-chart music crossover of the early to mid-1970s. These eponymously titled albums were released within two weeks of each other in July 1973. Although musically quite different, with Queen having more clearly discernible hard rock elements in their music than 10cc, the work of each band displayed a distinctly Beatles-influenced progressive pop quality. This was characterized by the diversity of the song material contained on each album, richly layered vocal harmonies, well-crafted arrangements and a high level of musicianship that manifested itself both in the individual performances of the band members and in the overall sound created. Perhaps more than any of the progressive pop artists documented in this book, the evolution of 10cc and Queen as consistent albums and singles artists during the 1970s (and in Queen's case well beyond that decade) drew parallels with the Beatles musical output, particularly from 1965 onwards. As noted earlier, in later years when reflecting on their songwriting and recording approaches, individual band members from both 10cc and Queen would acknowledge the key influence of the Beatles on their music and also in relation to the way that they took advantage of the technological and creative possibilities afforded by the recording studio. By the time each of these bands came to record their debut albums, recording studio technology had developed at such a pace that rather than being restricted to the eight track-recording machines used by the Beatles towards the end of their career, 10cc, and Queen, as well as each of the other artists discussed in this book, were presented with the opportunity to use sixteen track and later twenty-four track-recording facilities (see also Chapter 1). Among other things, the expanded number of tracks meant that the need to 'bounce' tracks (i.e. transfer several completed and mixed tracks onto an additional unused track to clear space for more tracks to be recorded) was somewhat reduced or could at least be delayed until later in the recording process. This gave artists and their producers an added level of flexibility when it came to recording songs and making decisions as to their construction and composition in the studio environment.

By the time of their debut album's release, 10cc had already begun to attract an audience based on the success of two singles drawn from the album, 'Donna' (1972) and 'Rubber Bullets', a number 1 for the band in the UK and Ireland in June 1973. The song parodied aspects of Elvis Presley's 1957 hit 'Jailhouse Rock' and also displayed echoes of early songs by the Beach Boys in the melody of the lead vocal and in the style of the rich vocal harmonies featured on the track. The parody on aspects of American popular culture heard in both 'Donna' and 'Rubber Bullets' also connects many of the other songs included on the *10cc* album. Indeed, if the then popular British glam scene was heavily invested in 1950s nostalgia, then the same is true of the songs on *10cc* but with a distinctly more satirical and pastiche-laden twist. For example, the track 'Sand in My Face' draws on the famous cartoon strip advertisement for famous body builder Charles Atlas's dynamic tension technique (see Reich, 2008), the latter being invented by Atlas as a low-cost and fast-track means for building muscles to create the archetypal body shape favoured among many male sports personalities and film celebrities in the 1950s and early 1960s. Featuring a lead vocal sung by Lol Creme, whose highly versatile voice, capable among other things of high falsetto, was often used to comic effect in 10cc's most well-loved songs. 'Sand in My Face' documents the story of Harry, a 'nine stone weakling' who uses the dynamic tension technique to build his muscles and win back his girlfriend from surfing hunk 'Big Alex'. Aside from the novel humour of a lyric that squarely overturns the celebratory and highly masculinist attitudes towards the muscle-toned male body often seen in 1950s and 1960s popular culture references to beach culture and surfing, 'Sand in My Face' (like the nine other tracks on *10cc*) also stood out because of the advanced studio production techniques applied in its making. As noted in Chapter 2, 10cc were able to take advantage of working in their own studio, Strawberry Studios in Stockport near Manchester. This allowed the band more time and scope to experiment with sounds and recording techniques, giving their music an added level of depth that contributed to the distinctive quality of their music in the British popular music soundscape of the early 1970s. A noticeable example of this is heard on the song 'Rubber Bullets', where the guitar solo is recorded using what is known as the 'double speed' technique. During the recording of the guitar solo, the tape used for the recording was slowed down to half speed and then brought back up to full speed again for the playback with the result that the pitch of the instrument was raised by a full octave. Although the double-speed technique had been used before, notably on Mike Oldfield's *Tubular Bells*, the inclusion of a double-speed guitar solo in 'Rubber Bullets' marked one of the very first times this technique had been heard in a chart-topping single and contributed towards the song's overall air of distinctiveness when heard on the radio and television during the middle of 1973. In addition to their proven ability to produce successful singles chart music, however, on their debut album, 10cc also demonstrated their capacity to write more musically complex tracks as well. This is heard, for example, on 'Speed Kills', the opening track on Side Two of the original vinyl album. The repeated guitar, bass and percussion riffs on 'Speed Kills' are all created using a series of tape loops, which form the main body of the piece. This is overlain with richly layered, harmonized vocals sung in real time but with minimal lyrics so that the voices function more as part of the song's overall soundscape (this technique would be used again but in a strikingly more innovative way two years later on 10cc's most popular song, 'I'm Not in Love', see Chapter 4). Again, the double-speed effect is used in 'Speed Kills' for the guitar solo, which on this occasion is faster and more harmonically complex than the solo featured in 'Rubber Bullets'. Indeed, when heard in the context of the full track, the double-speed effect gives the guitar a sonic quality that bears striking resemblance to a violin. The level of musical and technological ability evident in the composition and recording of 'Speed Kills' offered a clear indication that 10cc as a band were as comfortable working in more experimental fields of music composition and production as they were when working in the realm of more chart-focused pop music material. While three of the singles drawn from *10cc*, 'Donna' (1972), 'Rubber Bullets' (1973) and 'The Dean and I' (1973), were all top 10 hits, the album itself also received high critical acclaim from the British music press, who quickly latched on to the band's crossover appeal to both pop and rock audiences (Logan and Woffinden, 1977). In a review of *10cc* for British music magazine *Let It Rock* in September 1973, journalist John Pidgeon, in his closing remarks commented: 'What 10cc have done is combine all the elements of pop – infectious melodies, interesting lyrics and a distinctive vocal and instrumental sound – with (studio) sophistication' (Pidgeon, 1973).

The release of *Queen* similarly showcased the talents of a new British band, whose craft was to ultimately prove its strong adaptability to both the album and singles markets and to the respective audiences associated with these markets. Produced by Roy Thomas Baker, who would work with Queen on a further four albums during the 1970s, in 1994 *Queen* was named by *Guitarist Magazine* as the nineteenth most influential guitar album of all time[2]. At the time of the album's release, however, Queen was still a relatively unknown band both in the UK and elsewhere. Queen had initially experienced problems in finding a permanent bass player and had also struggled to perfect their desired sound in a live performance context (see Hodkinson, 1995). This resulted in the band playing only a relatively low number of gigs, mostly in and around London (Sinclair, 1983a), until late 1973, when they secured the support slot on a tour with Mott the Hoople, a band whose declining fortunes had reversed following their 1972 hit 'All the Young Dudes', a song specifically written for the band by David Bowie, who also produced it (see Sinclair, 1983b). Unlike 10cc, whose initial success in the UK singles chart with 'Donna' (1972) preceded the release of their debut album by around nine months, following the release of *Queen* its creators would have to wait for the best part of a year for their own chart breakthrough to materialize. A short instrumental version of 'Seven Seas of Rhye', the song that would eventually bring Queen to wider public attention in the UK (see Chapter 2), was included as the closing track on *Queen*, but in a form that was incomplete and essentially a taster of the fully formed version of the song that would appear on the band's follow-up album *Queen II*, released in early 1974 (Hodkinson, 1995). In that sense, while the *10cc* album represented a band whose song-craft and musical direction was already fully formed, the *Queen* album was more of an embryonic statement, containing a series of musical cues that Queen were to build on and refine over the next two years. Nevertheless, even at this early stage in the band's career, there was a distinctive edge to Queen's music that set them apart from other British rock bands of the time. The influence of hard rock artists including Cream, Jimi Hendrix, the Who and Led Zeppelin was clearly evident in many of the tracks on *Queen*, but at same time, the songs were honed and refined into a more contemporary feel that also reflected the influence of other artists whose music was located outside the hard rock field, such as David Bowie and Mott the Hoople. Other songs on *Queen*, such as 'Doing Alright', written by Brian May and his old bandmate Tim

Staffell during their tenure in Smile (see also Chapter 1) and 'The Night Comes Down' (another May song that reflects on his memories of growing up during the 1960s) have a distinctive Beatles influence, something that would also continue to be a trait of particular Queen songs on subsequent albums throughout the 1970s and into the early 1980s.

Another key point of innovation evident on *Queen* was guitarist Brian May's distinctive playing style, something accentuated by the design and tone of his highly unique guitar. Nicknamed 'the Red Special', due to the deep-red colour of the instrument's body, the guitar was built by May with the help of his father, an electrical engineer, while still at school (Tobler, 1978). In particular, the guitar's hand-wound pickups produced a thick, sweet tone that was not always instantly recognizable as a guitar (giving rise to May's insistence that early Queen albums include a 'no synthesizers' statement in the liner notes; see Zagorski-Thomas, 2014). This, combined with May's ability to overdub guitars in a way that created a quasi-orchestral effect, became as integral to the Queen sound as the unmistakable voice of lead singer Freddie Mercury. A further aspect of *Queen*'s production that gave the album a distinctive edge over many other hard rock albums of the time was the use of layered harmony vocals. Although this technique would be much refined and developed on Queen's subsequent four albums, notably on their 1975 breakthrough album *A Night at the Opera*, which contained the band's most remembered hit 'Bohemian Rhapsody' (see Chapter 4), in 1973 the presence of multi-layered vocals on their debut album already demonstrated a studio prowess on the part of Queen that helped to set them apart from other hard rock bands who, for the most part, either lacked the multi-vocal capacity possessed by Queen or were not prepared, or lacked the resources, to spend the time developing it in the studio.[3] In the making of *Queen*, the band enjoyed a similar situation to that of 10cc in that they were given free access to a recording studio, albeit making use of downtime, that is, time available when the studio had been vacated by other artists (Hodkinson, 1995). If Queen's debut album would not immediately lead to the kind of chart success enjoyed by contemporaries of the band, such as 10cc and Roxy Music, it did nevertheless earn them critical attention from the British AOR audience following a slot on *The Old Grey Whistle Test* (see also Chapter 2). The rapidity with which Queen's blend of AOR and chart music achieved success for the band is evident in the fact that *Queen II*, in April 1974 (only nine months after their debut album) reached the number 4 position in the UK album charts. Queen's third album, *Sheer Heart Attack*, released in November 1974, climbed to number 2 position, while 'Killer Queen' achieved the same position in the singles charts, consolidating Queen's status as a band capable of appealing to both rock and pop audiences in Britain.

The year 1973 also saw the return of ELO to the British singles chart, having scored a number 9 hit the previous year with '10538 Overture'. The band's follow-up single, a re-working of Chuck Berry's 1956 hit 'Roll Over Beethoven', marked a new chapter in the story of ELO, one that would see them flourish as an act whose unique blend of rock and stringed orchestral instruments was to become as suited to pop radio and television as it was to concert halls and, increasingly, the large arenas that the band would find themselves performing in. Although 'Roll Over Beethoven' had already been covered by the Beatles in 1963, ELO's version of the song constituted a significant reinterpretation, infusing the trademark 12-bar rock-and-roll riffs of the Chuck Berry original with classical overtones that seductively linked the song back to the historical German composer who had inspired it. This includes the iconic opening bars of Beethoven's 'Fifth Symphony', deftly played by ELO's three-person string section (Mike Edwards – cello, Wilf Gibson – violin and Colin Walker – cello[4]) at the beginning of the track before it segues into the more familiar guitar introduction heard on both Chuck Berry's original version of the song and on the Beatles' version. Although the success of '10538 Overture' had effectively launched ELO as a band with both ambitions as an experimental album band and significant potential for chart success, their version of 'Roll Over Beethoven' more strikingly showcased the rock-classical fusion that had been a core objective of ELO's establishment in 1970 (Spicer, 2018). Following Roy Wood's departure from ELO, Jeff Lynne took on the role as songwriter for the band, Lynne's songs successfully realizing the blend of classical and rock instruments and in the process assuring ELO a prominent place in the popular music soundscape of the 1970s. Pivotal in this respect was the success ELO enjoyed with their version of 'Roll Over Beethoven', this being in every respect the catalyst track for much of ELO's musical output throughout the rest of the 1970s. Certainly this was not the first time that attempts had been made to merge rock and classical music styles in British popular music, with various other bands from the Beatles and the Moody Blues to Deep Purple having experimented with this format in the years before ELO came to prominence. Nevertheless, ELO was the first example of a mainstream popular music act to focus their entire musical style around a rock-classical blend (something they were to maintain as a stylistic trademark until 1981 and the release of the album *Time*; see Chapter 6). While the amplification technology available at the beginning of 1970s often hampered ELO's early attempts to reproduce their music in a live performance setting, the high production standards applied in their studio recordings ensured that in the context of radio and television, ELO were able to generate a significant level of interest in their music, with many of the band's fans being old enough to remember tracks such as the Beatles' 'I Am the Walrus' and the Moody Blues' 'Nights in White Satin' and to realize songs such as these featured as influences in the musical approach of ELO. As live performance technology improved during the 1970s, ELO were able to more faithfully reproduce their studio-crafted material in a live context. This was highlighted by the band's 1978 concert appearances at London's Wembley Arena, with the first of these concerts being filmed and later released as a concert film, consolidating a vogue for high production concert films during the 1970s that also included Led Zeppelin's (1976) *The Song Remains the Same* (based on their 1973 performances at New York's Maddison Square Garden). By this time, 'Roll Over Beethoven' had become a staple of ELO's live set and was typically performed as a set closer (as seen in the Wembley concert film). In the hands of ELO the song could be said to have taken on a distinctly progressive pop feel, blending the rock-and-roll energy of Chuck Berry's original version of the song with the art music inflection of orchestral string sounds and fused together with smatterings of the progressive rock aesthetic that dominated AOR listening in Britain at this point. In terms of its production, two versions of the song existed – an edited 'single' version that compressed the dynamic energy of the song into four and a half minutes and a full-length album version of eight minutes, the latter also providing the basis for live performances of the song and designed to appeal to the more AOR elements of ELO's audience. Critical receptions to ELO at the time of the release of 'Roll Over Beethoven' and the album on which it featured, *ELO 2* (1973), were somewhat mixed. This perhaps betrayed a slight sense of confusion among journalists that during an era where a discourse of progressiveness was thoroughly permeating the world of rock and AOR, ELO seemed to be drawing too slavishly on an earlier set of musical references. Similarly, while the rock-pop crossover of ELO was clearly evident in their earlier work, the blend was not as seamlessly achieved as was the case with other progressive pop artists until later in the band's career. Nevertheless, in a 1973 review of *ELO 2*, *Let It Rock* journalist Phil Hardy described the album as 'progressive (musically and lyric-wise)' (Hardy, 1973).

Also in 1973, Roxy Music released their second album *For Your Pleasure*. As noted earlier, this was the last Roxy Music album to feature Brian Eno, whose departure from the band in May 1973 was to be followed by a string of increasingly successful solo albums that saw Eno moving always further away from the rock and pop territory of Roxy Music and their contemporaries. *For Your Pleasure* was a more musically ambitious record than Roxy Music's eponymously titled debut album, which had been released the previous year. Due to the success of its predecessor, Roxy Music had more studio time at their disposal to work on the songs and production of their new album. Making use of various studio effects, including phasing and tape loops, *For Your Pleasure* contained material that interrogated a social underbelly of psychosexual frictions as seen, for example, in the song 'In Every Dream Home a Heartache', about an inflatable sex toy, and 'The Bogus Man', an unsettling song that documents the obsessive mind of a sexual stalker (see also Chapter 5). Following on from a practice adopted by the Beatles early in their career (see Martin, 1979), the first two Roxy Music albums did not contain singles, these being released separately to coincide with the band's album releases. Like their progressive pop peers, however, what made Roxy Music distinctive in the early 1970s was their demonstrated ability to deftly tap both the singles and album markets, retaining a lofty presence in each. Upon its release, *For Your Pleasure* reached number 4 in the UK album charts, while the non-album single 'Pyjamarama', released ahead of *For Your Pleasure*, achieved a chart position of number 10. In terms of its critical reception, however, at the time of its release, *For Your Pleasure* received somewhat mixed reviews. The distinction here between how music buyers responded to the album compared with the response of journalists is interesting, suggesting that while Roxy Music resonated with AOR and pop audiences, the rapidly progressing and organic evolution of Roxy Music as a band that seemed to encompass so many different musical styles and influences made them difficult to assess, even at a time when the musical boundaries were being increasingly tested. That *For Your Pleasure* was perhaps too ahead of its time, even within an era of progressive pop, is supported by the fact that since 2000, the album has received increasing critical acclaim, including, among others, from British singer Morrissey, who has described *For Your Pleasure* as the only 'truly great British album' (Weisbard and Craig, 1995: 337). Further evidence that Roxy Music's early work was musically and conceptually progressive to the extent that it shaped rather than emulated trends in the fields of rock and pop is illustrated by the degree of influence that Roxy Music were to have on the future direction of British pop. This was particularly so during the 1980s and early 1990s when, in addition to Roxy Music, other artists from the early 1970s progressive pop era such as David Bowie, Cockney

Rebel and 10cc would also be frequently cited as highly influential by a new generation of British artists (see also Chapter 6).

Calling all teenyboppers – The crossover appeal of progressive pop

As illustrated above, progressive pop artists quickly established themselves with British AOR audiences during the early 1970s. However, evidence suggests – and the commercial success enjoyed by most of these artists essentially dictates – that the appeal of progressive pop ranged across a much wider audience, including a sizeable number of teenage and pre-teen fans. Scholarship dealing with the relationship between music and youth in Britain, particularly that published in or referring to the 1970s, has frequently identified a connection between class background and musical taste, often extending this to incorporate a discussion of gender. McRobbie and Garber's (1976) study of young female teenyboppers is an illustrative case in point. The study declares the object of female teenybopper fascination at this time to be artists such as David Cassidy (the only teenybopper star referred to in the study but suggestive of similar artists including the Bay City Rollers and the Osmonds, who also had a mass teenybopper following). The study progresses to define female 'worship' of teenybopper idols as a safe space for these girls to envisage heterosexual romance and fantasize about future courtship while also offering a pleasant diversion from the more mundane expectations placed upon them.

> The kind of fantasies which girls construct around these figures play the same role as ordinary daydreams. Narrative fantasies about bumping into David Cassidy in the supermarket, or being chosen out by him from the front row of a concert, both carry a strongly sexual element, and are also a means of being distracted from the demands of work or school or other aspects of experience which might be perceived as boring or unrewarding. (1976: 112)

McRobbie and Garber's analysis also looks at how female teenybopper fan practices of poster swapping and listening to their favourite chart hits on homemade cassette compilations consolidates this connection between gender, musical taste and socialization, such practices taking place in the 'safe space' of the teenage girl's bedroom, this in turn being nestled in the domestic space of the paternally regulated family home. While the more sociological observations of

McRobbie and Garber regarding the restrictions placed on the liberty of female working-class teenagers in Britain during the early 1970s may have credence, the interpretation of teenybopper culture as an exclusively working-class, or indeed female, practice seems less credible. Also, given the nature of British top 20 chart music in Britain, and in particular the practice on radio and television chart shows of interweaving teenybopper hits with songs by more progressive pop artists such as Queen, 10cc and Roxy Music, it seems likely that many of these tracks also found their way onto the compilation cassettes, and thus into the ambient bedroom soundscape, of many teen and pre-teen popular music fans in Britain. In itself, such a feature of popular music consumption disturbs any neat analysis of female teenage music fans as exclusively fixated on those artists strategically marketed by the popular music industry to serve as teenybop icons.

The fact that the actual music listened to by British youth in the 1970s is so underdiscussed, this being vastly overshadowed by the discussion of youth style (see, for example, Hall and Jefferson, 1976), counts in retrospect as something of a lost opportunity. This extends both to an understanding of the extent that so-called youth 'subcultures' of the early 1970s were in fact representative of British youth overall and also in having a better knowledge of what music youth in early 1970s Britain were actively consuming on a day-to-day basis. Even where an occasional attempt is made in the scholarship to focus on and name musical styles, genres and artists that appealed to youth in the early to mid-1970s, a strong focus on class and its significance for musical taste remains. This is illustrated in a study by Murdoch and McCron published in the same year as McRobbie and Garber's (1976) previously referenced work. Thus, in discussing their findings, Murdoch and McCron note how

> [t]he basic technological and stylistic division between 'progressive' rock and mainstream pop largely corresponded to a social division within the youth audience, between those who had left school at the minimum age and those who stayed on to take up a place in the rapidly expanding higher education sector, a division which in turn largely reflected the class differentials in educational opportunity. (1976: 23)

In attempting to locate musical taste as contingent on social stratification, Murdoch and McCron's somewhat rudimentary categorization of the popular music listened by early 1970s youth into two 'distinct' camps, 'progressive rock' and 'mainstream pop', appears somewhat blunt and insensitive to the overall variety of popular music in Britain during this time and the interplay that frequently existed between progressive and more standard musical elements that characterized British pop.

A similarly problematic binary between musical taste and social class is proffered by Willis in *Profane Culture*, an ethnographic study of the contrasting musical tastes displayed by working-class bikers and middle-class hippies. According to Willis, the bikers in his study demonstrated a marked preference for musically straightforward 1950s rock-and-roll songs by artists such as Chuck Berry and Gene Vincent, while the hippies' musical preference was for the more musically complex, album-orientated progressive rock groups of the early 1970s. According to Willis, this stark differentiation in the musical tastes of the bikers and hippies directly related to their respective class backgrounds. For the bikers, the simplicity of rock and roll 'clearly resonates and develops the particular interests and qualities of [their] life-style [possessing] an integrity of form and atmosphere as well as an immediate, informal confidence' (1978: 71). By contrast, the more educated middle-class hippies, according to Willis, demanded music that challenged the listener and offered a more diverse listening experience. In combination with the use of psychedelic drugs, the complex rhythms and exotic soundscapes characteristic of progressive rock music became a way of achieving altered states of perception and awareness, subverting conventional notions of time: 'Electronic techniques ... such as echo, feedback, stereo [and] loudness itself ... [gave] the impression of space and lateral extension', a sensation that was significantly enhanced when the music was listened to under the influence of drugs (1978: 167). Willis then proceeds to explain the professed musical preferences of the bikers and hippies in terms of a homological fit between class background and taste, homology representing 'the continuous play between the group and a particular item which produces specific styles, meanings, contents and forms of consciousness' (1978: 191).

Despite its status as one of the few existing ethnographic snapshots of youth musical taste in Britain during the early 1970s, Willis's study arguably also presents as something of an oddity. To begin with, the 'motorbike boys' discussed in the book exhibit musical tastes that would seemingly place them towards the middle of the 1960s rather than the early 1970s. Indeed, by the early 1970s the musical tastes of youth-centred British bike culture were as much focused around hard rock and heavy metal as they were around rock and roll. Similarly, although the remains of a hippy culture existed in Britain, by the early 1970s more 'intelligent' hard rock bands such as Led Zeppelin and Deep Purple were as much a feature of this listenership's musical taste. One wonders then how typical the bikers and hippies selected by Willis actually were of these youth cultural groups – and their musical tastes – in a broader sense.

Subsequent research has argued that the use of class in such a reductive fashion to explain away musical taste as essentially predetermined is unworkable given the propensity for individuals to acquire personal tastes, including tastes in music, that do not uniformly map onto class and education (see, for example, Lewis, 1992; Peterson and Kern, 1996; Bennett, 1999). Thus, as Lewis observes:

> the relationship between [musical preferences and social class] is not the clean and neat one that some, perhaps naively, have assumed it to be – especially in our modern, mass-mediated technological society. In such a society ... the link between social and cultural structures becomes a question not a given. Rather than assume it to be simply correlative, it is perhaps better to view it as contingent, problematic and variable, and – to a higher degree than we might imagine – subjectively determined. (1992: 141)

These debates are perhaps by now well-worn in the context of academic writing. What has been less well investigated, however, is the extent to which other institutions, that is to say those beyond the academy, may also have played a role in both suggesting and, indeed, actively promoting class-based distinctions and consequent divisions among British popular music audiences during the early 1970s. Indeed, there is reason to suggest that the British music press and music radio may also have been complicit in the way that music was deemed to be received by audiences from different class backgrounds. An interesting example of such possible media bias is seen in the memoir of Mike Rutherford (2014). Thus, in reflecting on the early reception of his band Genesis in Britain and the United States, Rutherford notes how in the UK much was made by the music press of the band's middle-class, public school background. Indeed, this much is evident from an interview with Genesis keyboardist Tony Banks conducted by music journalist Keith Altham and published in the *New Musical Express* in February 1973. Thus observes Altham: 'Speaking to Tony last week at Charisma Records I found him to be a polite but curiously laid-back product of a public school education and classically trained musical mind' (Altham, 1973).[5] Later in the article Altham notes how five of the original members of Genesis had met while studying at Charterhouse School in Godalming, Surrey. American music journalists, by contrast, seemed far less interested in such aspects of the band's history and more interested in their music and live performances. This is typified in an article written by John Swenson for *Crawdaddy!* and published in March 1974 that describes Genesis as 'combining a penchant for surrealistic songwriting with an interesting instrumental approach and a well-conceptualized visual presentation' (Swenson, 1974). Likewise, whereas in the US progressive rock's classical influences were a novelty and played into its grandiose stature as a stadium-based music, in the UK this aspect of progressive rock was often judged to smack of highbrow pretentiousness. A similar fate befell Queen, whose music, together with the band's higher education background, was often presented in the British music press as indications of Queen's aloofness (see Thomas, 1999). Laing (1994) has argued that the British music press of the 1970s frequently applied romanticized discourses of class relations as reflected in and through popular music. This assumed a critical pitch with the emergence of punk, which was often depicted as the soundtrack of working-class housing estates. In reality, however, punk musicians and audiences alike originated from both working-class and middle-class backgrounds with a number of punk musicians, notably Paul Simonon and Mick Jones of the Clash, Budgie of Siouxsie and the Banshees and Pete Shelley of the Buzzcocks having attended art school or studied art and design prior to embarking on a musical career (see Fryer, 1986; Frith and Horne, 1987; Frith, 1997).

Given the observed critical bias in both academic and popular representations of British popular music and its significance for youth audiences during the early 1970s, there is little wonder that the potential audience crossover appeal of many artists and genres has often been overlooked or simply airbrushed out of existence. Nevertheless, a small amount of evidence that such a crossover could and indeed did occur opens an important window on how the relationships between rock, pop, class and musical taste were not as set in stone as they were often made out to be during the early 1970s. Taylor and Wall's (1976) study of David Bowie was written at the time when Bowie was beginning to enjoy commercial success in Britain as Ziggy Stardust, with two well-received albums and a string of top 10 chart releases between 1972 and 1973. In the study, Taylor and Wall consider Bowie's art rock credentials, the erudite nature of his song lyrics and how his shrewd understanding of artifice made him one of the first examples of a popular music artist come pop entrepreneur. At the same, however, Taylor and Wall also note how the music and style of Bowie was able to find appeal among young working-class listeners and particularly working-class males youth, for whom Bowie was seen to challenge dominant working-class notions of masculinity (see also Chapter 5). As one of the few pieces of academic work published during the 1970s to consider what was actually happening in mainstream British popular music of the time, not only in terms of the music itself but also with regard to audience reception, Taylor and Wall's study is significant in terms of the light it casts on who was listening to this music and how musical taste then (and now) may not be exclusively shaped by class and education. More specifically, what this work suggests is a less tightly regulated fit between class, gender and taste among British youth in the early 1970s than is frequently represented in academic scholarship. Bowie's songs, and particularly his lyrics, were something of a departure from much of the other more conventional song-craft in the British charts at this time. The same can be said of Roxy Music and Cockney Rebel, and to a lesser extent Queen, 10cc and ELO.

The album success of a number of these artists has already been documented, but these were also artists who not only frequently found their way into the UK singles charts but regularly occupied positions in the top 10. Indeed, a cursory look at the British singles charts for 1973 illustrates that David Bowie had no less than four top 10 hits in that year[6] as well as two in the following year.[7] A broadly similar level of chart success can be seen in relation to other progressive pop artists during 1973, with top 10 placing being achieved by singles from ELO (1), Roxy Music (2), Brian Ferry (3) and 10cc (2). A similar pattern is evident in 1974 when newcomers Cockney Rebel scored two top 10 hits, while Queen's 'Seven Seas of Rhye' reached number 10 in April followed by their November release 'Killer Queen', which, as noted earlier, reached the number 2 position in the UK charts. Other progressive pop artists to make the top 10 in 1974 included Brian Ferry (1), Roxy Music (1) and 10cc (1). It seems improbable that it was in every case the same fans that bought the singles of these artists as bought their albums. Nor does it seem likely that teen fans of these artists were all from the same class background or of the same gender. Rather, it seems plausible to assume that a broad youth audience was also attracted to these artists through their television appearances on programmes such as *Top of the Pops* and *Lift off with Ayshea* as well as their regular featuring on chart radio shows (see also Chapter 4). Further evidence of the fact that the chart presence of progressive pop artists meant they were able to connect with and appeal to a younger teen and pre-teen audience is provided by their frequent inclusion in weekly teen magazines of the day such as *Jackie* and *Look In*. With a large teen and pre-teen readership bolstered by regular promotion on commercial television, these publications were dedicated exclusively to catering for youth tastes in popular culture. In the case of *Jackie* (published between 1964 and 1993), its content was largely focused on music with the highest selling edition being the double issue dedicated to teenypop icon David Cassidy issued to coincide with Cassidy's tour of the UK in 1972. This statistic would appear to locate *Jackie*'s readership firmly within the teenybopper bracket. However, the magazine's content, including features on David Bowie and Bryan Ferry in 1973 and a Queen poster series featured in 1976, indicates that the musical tastes of the *Jackie* readers extended beyond what was then typically categorized as teenybopper artists. *Look In* (published between 1971 and 1994) was more focused on children's television programs but also ran features on popular music artists who appealed to a teen and pre-teen audience. Artists featured in *Look In* during the early to mid-1970s included some predictable choices such as The Sweet and David Essex but also extended to the realms of AOR-chart crossover artists including Queen and Bryan Ferry, both of whom were featured twice in the magazine and on its cover between 1974 and 1976. Again, this is suggestive of fact that the audience for such artists, rather than being restricted to older listeners, extended to early teen and pre-teen music fans in Britain.

In this same time period, all of these artists also made significant inroads into the UK album charts. David Bowie's *Aladdin Sane* stayed at the number 1 slot for five weeks between May and June 1973, while in December, Roxy Music's third album *Stranded* stayed at number 1 for a week. While 10cc's debut album reached number 36 in the UK album charts, Roxy Music's earlier album release that year, *For Your Pleasure*, attained a position of number 4. In 1974, David Bowie's *Diamond Dogs*, an album that marked a change in musical direction for Bowie away from the style of his previous two albums and contained the proto-punk song 'Rebel Rebel', also held the number 1 slot for a period of four weeks between June and July. *Sheet Music*, the second album by 10cc, went to number 9, while Roxy Music's *Country Life* attained a position of number 3. In the same year, Cockney Rebel's second album, *The Psychomodo*, featuring the top 10 hit 'Mr. Soft', went to number 8 in the UK charts and stayed in the top 50 for twenty weeks. Finally, Queen's two album releases of 1974, *Queen II* and *Sheer Heart Attack*, achieved chart positions of number 5 and number 2, respectively. The success enjoyed by progressive pop artists across both the singles and album markets strongly indicates how, at a time when singles and album bands in Britain were still often regarded as separate entities, progressive pop was successfully straddling the singles and album markets, finding a significant crossover audience in the process.

Conclusion

The purpose of this chapter has been to consider how, during the early to mid-1970s, a new generation of British popular music artists wrote songs that bridged the albums and singles markets, contributing along the way to an era of what this book describes as 'progressive pop'. By dint of music journalism and the perceptions of those responsible for the programming decisions of music radio and music television in Britain, the albums and singles markets had frequently been considered distinct, attracting audience clusters that were separated by features of class, age and taste. A quasi-elitist sensibility inherent in much journalistic writing about AOR at the time suggested that this was a musical world beyond the grasp of a *mainstream* audience, whose tastes were shaped by the fads and fashions of the popular charts. And yet, while David Bowie, Roxy Music, Queen, 10cc, ELO and Cockney Rebel were each lauded as significant new album artists on the British popular music scene, their music was also being eagerly consumed by a chart-focused audience of teens and pre-teens. Thus, for a brief period of time, these artists embodied a 'progressive' aesthetic that drew creative nourishment from the broader ambit of progressively attuned popular music prevalent among British artists at this time but framing their music in such a way as to transgress the confines of AOR to become a progressive voice of British pop. Indeed, such musical border crossing also gave these artists and their music a ubiquity during the early 1970s that was not accessible for artists in the progressive rock field and thus enshrined with the mantle of AOR. Thus, in addition to their aforementioned presence on chart radio and television programmes in the early 1970s, the music of progressive pop also worked seamlessly in a range of everyday, mundane spaces and situations where vernacular culture held sway. For example, through their regular chart exposure, the songs of David Bowie, Roxy Music, 10cc, ELO, Queen and Cockney Rebel made their way into the hands of DJs running the then popular mobile discotheques up and down Britain. In this way, tracks such as 'Rubber Bullets', 'Killer Queen', 'Virginia Plain', 'The Jean Genie' and 'Make Me Smile (Come Up and See Me)' became regular favourites at events such as wedding receptions, twenty-first birthday parties, village galas and at holiday camp discos. As such, these and similar songs by progressive pop artists found their way into the cultural memories of audiences, becoming part of a signature soundtrack of early 1970s Britain, informing the way the era was experienced and is now remembered by those who lived through it. The following chapter considers in more depth how and why British progressive pop has become inextricably connected with the early 1970s and why specific songs in particular appear to be uniquely significant as tracks that sum up the seventies era. Key here, it will be shown, is the way that these songs form part of a generational soundtrack, thus becoming a means through which a generation marks itself off as distinctively tied to a specific moment of musical innovation with the sound of progressive pop as one of its centrally defining characteristics.

Notes

1 Although with the fullness of time *No Pussyfooting* came to be regarded as a highly important album and has been influential for a number of artists.
2 'The Top 50 Most Influential Guitar Albums of All Time Ever!' December 1994. Archived at rocklistmusic.co.uk.
3 Another British band whose multi-vocal prowess was often evident on their recorded output was glam rock outfit The Sweet. However, given the lack of their albums' success (see Chapter 2), recording budgets allocated to The Sweet were far lower than those enjoyed by Queen, who were thus able to devote more time in the studio, creating the lush vocal overdubs that became a trademark of their sound, both as a singles chart band and as an album band.
4 ELO has undergone various line-ups during its career, but the most well-remembered version of the band, considered by many to be its classic line-up, consisted of Jeff Lynne (guitar, vocals), Kelly Groucutt (bass, vocals), Bev Bevan (drums), Richard Tandy (keyboards), Mik Kaminski (violin), Hugh McDowell (cello), Melvyn Gale (cello). This line-up existed from 1974 until 1980 and recorded ELOs' most well-remembered albums, including *Face the Music* (1975), *A New World Record* (1976) and *Out of the Blue* (1977).
5 Charisma Records, founded in 1969 by Tony Stratton Smith, signed Genesis in 1971 and released each of the band's subsequent albums up to and including *Invisible Touch* (1986). The label was acquired by Virgin Records in 1983, who then absorbed it following Virgin's purchase by EMI in 1986.
6 http://www.severing.nu/music/1973UK.html (accessed 2 December 2017).
7 http://www.severing.nu/music/1974UK.html (accessed 2 December 2017).

4

Big songs and generational soundtracks

In Chapter 3 it was noted that a quintessential aspect of progressive pop was its ubiquity in the British popular music soundscape of the early 1970s. By dint of the quickly established crossover market of progressive pop bands, in addition to their established AOR identity, they also had an enduring presence in the British singles chart during the early 1970s. This was punctuated by the release of several tracks that quickly came to be considered as 'classics' and, in the case of Queen, a song that also led to a pioneering entree into the world of popular music video in late 1975. The fact that so many of the artists defined as progressive pop in this book maintained such a sustained commercial consistency during the 1970s, and in some cases beyond that decade, has also played an important part in ensuring that these artists and their work have remained entrenched in the minds of British popular music fans as a pivotal aspect of the musical soundtrack that defines the early to mid-1970s. A critical aspect of such appeal was the apparent ongoing musical evolution of these progressive pop artists who, like the Beatles before them, seemed to make new musical strides with each new album and, in some cases, each new single release. In a time and context where the musical boundaries of both rock and pop were shifting, due in large part to the aforementioned improvements in studio technology and the greater control this allowed over the recording process, progressive pop became signature to the musical sensibility of a new generation of British music fans seeking to assert ownership of a pop-rock soundtrack that they could call their own.

Another salient aspect of British progressive pop music during the 1970s, and also a part of its enduring resonance during the following decades, is what could be referred to as 'nostalgic innovation'. In the same way that British glam in the 1970s has been defined as a music that looked to a post-sixties future by invoking the music and culture of the past, specifically the 1950s (see, for example, Stratton, 1986), so progressive pop also frequently worked at the level of pop-pastiche, combining musical elements and cultural references from previous eras but in ways that gave them a freshness to the ears of a new generation in search of new music. Several years later, aspects of progressive pop, along with progressive rock, were derided by punk for their apparent self-indulgence and concomitant lack of concern with the gritty politics and austere sociopolitical landscape of 1970s Britain (see Chapter 6). As will be considered in Chapter 5, it is erroneous to suggest that progressive pop artists were entirely devoid of a critical voice in their work although this was certainly of a different nature to the more overtly voiced political messages issued by many rock and folk artists in the late 1960s and by punk artists in the later years of the 1970s. But in an era following the demise of the counterculture and before the emergence of punk, progressive pop also tapped into and serviced a desire among music fans for music that promoted a 'good-time' feeling and sensibility, a quality propelled by the radio-friendly nature of the music and the chart prominence of the artists concerned.

Popular music as an everyday soundtrack

> We absorb songs into our own lives and rhythms into our own bodies; they have a looseness of reference that makes them immediately accessible. Pop songs are open to appropriation for personal use in a way that other popular cultural forms (television soap operas, for example) are not – the latter are tied into meanings we may reject. (Frith, 1987: 139)

The notion of popular music as forming part of the everyday soundtrack to which individuals live their lives has surfaced many times and at various levels of discourse, both scholarly and non-scholarly. This ranges from Kassabian's (2013) critical rendering of pop as part of what she refers to as 'ubiquitous' music to the late Glen Frey's assessment of the impact of his band, the Eagles, on audiences, and their memories of specific Eagles' songs, when he noted how people 'did things' – such as leave college and start a career, fall in love, raise children – to the music of the Eagles (see, *History of the Eagles Part 2*, 2013). As Frey's observations suggest, rather than music's everydayness being a passive process, it depends to a large degree on the agency of music listeners who actively 'own' music and inscribe it with meanings of their own. Frith (1987) has argued that among the various forms of material culture and cultural consumption engaged in by individuals in late modernity, music seems to evoke feelings of ownership more frequently than most other forms of popular culture (with the exception of sport). Although this observed quality in music could ostensibly be applied to many different musical genres and across different eras and generations, popular music from the 1950s onwards has received particularly focused attention in academic work when it comes to issues of appropriation and ownership (see, for example, DeNora, 2000; Bennett and Rogers, 2016). There are several key reasons for this. First, it was during the early 1950s that the industrial production and mass mediation of popular music assumed a specific shape and character as new playback technologies, such as the plastic 45' rpm record (or 'single'), arrived along with the portable record player and the transistor radio (Frith, 1988). Second, in terms of its cultural significance, during the 1950s popular music was increasingly designated as a 'youth music', a shift heralded by the arrival of rock and roll and the emergence of new, young artists such as Elvis Presley and the Beatles (Chambers, 1985; Shumway, 1992). Commenting on the cultural fit between such youthful artists and their equally youthful audience, Plasketes and Plasketes observe: 'There existed a strong bond between performer and audience, because there was the sense that the stars were not being imposed from above but had sprung up from similar ranks as the audience' (1987: 30). Following rock and roll, a rapid succession of youth musical genres and associated styles emerged, including beat music in the early 1960s, psychedelia in the mid-1960s, through to glam and punk in the early and mid-1970s, respectively. As noted in Chapter 3, it was also the case that the progressive pop artists of the early 1970s were young enough to appeal to a youth audience, as demonstrated by their frequent and often quite colourful appearances both on chart shows such as *Top of the Pops* and in teen magazines of the time.

Taking stock of this rapid shift in the cultural meaning of music towards a youth aesthetic during the post–Second World War era, scholarship focusing on the connections between music and memory has often looked at how music acts as a medium for the framing of generational notions of shared identity and belonging (see, for example, Kotarba, 2002; Bennett, 2013). The notion here is of (popular) music as a soundtrack of shared generational experience, whereby the value and significance of a specific song (or collection of songs) is rooted in its capacity to evoke a clear and vivid sense of meaning associated with a specific time and place. Indeed, more recently, such qualities of music have also been recast as a means through which music intersects with memory to produce a sense of generational place and belonging not only in the present but also over time and in a way that connects the present with the past. Thus, as

Green observes: 'One way in which people discuss music is by talking about particular experiences with it that stand out in memory. For example, some music experiences are described as especially affecting, important, influential or even pivotal for the individuals involved' (2016: 334). Music, then, serves as an important vessel of 'cultural information', providing an instantly accessible means through which people can situate themselves, spatially, temporally and emotionally.

The connections observed between music, memory and belonging are worthy of scrutiny as this connection underlines one of the ways that canonical concentrations of the popular past, including the role of music therein, are established. In its conventional form, the musical canon is often deemed to principally emerge from the work of particular taste-making institutions, notably the music press, whose privileging of certain artists, songs and albums over others to elevate some aspects and eras of popular music history to iconic status while concealing others from view except in the case of the most die-hard and specialist music fans (Jones, 2008). Indeed, in this respect there has been some discussion over whether, in presenting specific eras of popular music, for example the late 1960s, as seminal moments in music and cultural history, the music press and associated media are serving to emphasize the historical and cultural importance of particular memories of music and culture over others and producing what is, in effect, a 'golden age' of youth, generation and popular music (see, for example, Lipsitz, 1994; Grossberg, 1994). Evidence of such a golden-age effect and its plausible impact on collective musical memory is presented in Schmutz's study of *Rolling Stone Magazine*'s contribution to the retrospective cultural consecration of selected rock and pop artists through the publication of its '500 Greatest Albums' list. Thus observes Schmutz:

> *Rolling Stone* ("500 Greatest Albums," 2003) clearly sees itself as a preserver and celebrator of the best its art world has to offer and often refers to the historical significance of the albums it consecrates. Although there are no restrictions on the age of the albums selected, there is clearly a preference for older albums. The median age of the 500 albums on *Rolling Stone*'s list is 28 years. (Schmutz, 2005: 1515)

Other work, however, has pointed to the distinction that often occurs between such official renderings of popular music as an aspect of cultural memory and the more localized and 'unofficial' renderings that also take place in an everyday context. Indeed, according to Bennett and Rogers:

rather than responding to mediated texts in ways that align with more generally represented and 'official' understandings of their cultural significance, late modern individuals may find within the realms of textual mediation multiple frames of reference through which to organise and rehearse their own, more locally informed memories of the past. (2016: 49–50)

It is in such a context that we may begin to consider how a far broader range of popular music, much of which is often elided in official, prestige conferring accounts of popular music history such as the *Rolling Stone* example considered above, also resonates as a marker of generational affect and belonging. Indeed, given its prominence in the mediated popular music soundscape and its essential status as 'ubiquitous music' (Kassabian, 2013), it stands to reason that popular music in its broadest sense, that is say in its manifold forms extending even to the most unabashedly commercial and/or novelty-focused songs, also possesses a significant capacity to register in relation to aspects of memory, affect and belonging. One critically important thing that needs to be considered here is the sheer extent to which music of a more consciously 'mainstream' nature has figured, and continues to figure, in the everyday soundscapes of people's lives. To this extent, what are often categorized as 'meaningful' songs in a more critical context, be this in *quality* journalism or indeed in academic work, can be laid open to scrutiny. Certainly, some of those songs that have acquired canonical status in this regard – for example John Lennon's 'Imagine', Bob Dylan's 'All along the Watchtower' and Joni Mitchell's 'Big Yellow Taxi' – fall into the category of more mainstream ubiquity simply because they are played on the radio, television and as 'piped music' in public spaces such as shopping malls and sports stadiums and so on, so often. However, it is far more often the case that the music that has piqued the public interest, and thus becomes readily assigned to memory, are those songs that achieve significant amounts of radio and television airplay, rather than those that necessarily assume a canonical status and/or more niche audience, a situation that actually applies to many of those genres, such as punk and (heavy)metal, that have been a core focus in popular music scholarship. Frith (1996) has argued that the role of the popular music academic is not simply to take record sales and airplay as indicators of musical value but rather to use musical texts themselves as a starting point for uncovering the combined artistic and cultural value of particular songs over others. For Frith: 'There are … political as well as sociological and aesthetic reasons for challenging populism … The utopian impulse that Adorno recognized in high art, must be part of low art too' (1996: 20). This kind of argument has steered the academic study of popular music for many years and has certainly helped to invest the loose discipline of popular music studies with the same kind of criticality observed in the 'parent' disciplines, from which popular music studies most readily draws its intellectual nourishment, notably media and cultural studies, (ethno)musicology and (cultural) sociology. At the same time, however, the fact cannot be avoided that in assuming this approach, vast tracts of the popular music landscape in each decade since the 1950s have often been systematically overlooked in the field of popular music studies as scholars rely on established canonical interpretations of 'meaningful' popular music as a benchmark of which artists, genres, albums and songs to focus on in their work.

As already alluded to in Chapter 1, early 1970s British popular music serves as a salient example in respect to the above observation, being an era that still remains very thinly mapped in terms of both how newly emerging music was received at the time of its release and, similarly, how it has continued to function as a collective soundtrack for those who claimed it as the music of their generation. Sandwiched between the politically edged rock of the late 1960s and the often more politically, or at least sonically, abrasive approach of punk from the mid-late 1970s, the popular music of early 1970s Britain, and more pointedly the mainstream music of this era, registers as a conspicuous gap in popular music studies' critical canon. The fact remains, however, that irrespective of the lack of critical attention paid to it, this music formed a dominant part of the musical soundscape of the era and continues to inform popular perceptions of Britain in the early 1970s as demonstrated in the various forms of pop nostalgia media, including documentaries on artists such as David Bowie, 10cc, ELO and Queen, that are now increasingly being produced (see also Chapter 1). As the audience appeal of such media products helps to illustrate, much of the music being discussed in this book forms the basis of a generational soundtrack, a means through which people who lived through the era related to it and indeed continue to relate to it when reflecting back on their memories of the seventies decade.

Progressive pop, then, was sonically interwoven into the pop soundtrack of early 1970s Britain. Moreover, the chart impact of many songs by progressive pop artists was, for a specific period of time, also somewhat localized – a British phenomenon that found its key following among a British audience. While progressive pop found a relatively fast appeal with a national audience, it would take time for this success to translate to an international market – and particularly the all-important US market. For example, while Roxy Music's debut single 'Virginia Plain' peaked at number 4 in the British singles charts at the time of its release in August 1972, it would be three years before the band achieved mainstream international success with the track 'Love Is the Drug' (1975). The same was true for David Bowie, who, despite having been a recording artist since the 1960s, would not begin to achieve consistent international success until 1975 when the song 'Fame', co-written with Carlos Alomar and John Lennon, would earn him his first US number 1 (Trynka, 2011). In the UK, however, Bowie's 1969 song 'Space Oddity' had peaked at number 5 and in 1972 'Starman', the song that introduced Bowie's Ziggy Stardust character to a mainstream British audience via a rousing appearance on *Top of the Pops*, went to number 10 in the singles charts. A broadly similarly scenario applies in the case of Queen. Thus, while 'The Seven Seas of Rhye' (1974) reached the top 10 in Britain, it failed to chart anywhere else and it was not until the end of 1975 that Queen would score a major international hit with 'Bohemian Rhapsody'. ELO were also something of a local sensation in Britain during the very early 1970s, where they scored top 10 hits with '10538 Overture' (1972) and 'Roll over Beethoven' (1973). However, like Queen, ELO had to wait until late 1975 to achieve their first major international hit with the song 'Evil Woman', taken from the band's fifth album, *Face the Music* (1975). The same is broadly true of other artists in the progressive pop vein, notably 10cc and Cockney Rebel, whose major international success also came later than their chart success in Britain and was also more short-lived than David Bowie, Roxy Music, Queen and ELO.

On my radio

> People become aware of their emotional and affective memories by means of technologies, and surprisingly often, the enabling apparatus becomes part of the recollecting experience. Songs or albums often get interpreted as a 'sign of their time' in part also because they emerge from a sociotechnological context. (van Dijck, 2006: 358)

Given the ubiquitous nature of digital music capture and playback that now permeates the way that music is accessed and consumed across the developed world, it is easy to overlook the fact that the relationship such technologies have forged between music and audiences is a relatively recent development (see,

Nowak, 2015). During the early 1970s, well before the widespread introduction of the internet and associated technological developments that impacted music consumption, such as the MP3 (digital sound file), YouTube and music streaming services, such as Spotify, Pandora and Tidal, the discovery of 'new' music was primarily through the medium of radio. Indeed, while radio remains a significant tastemaker in the realm of popular music (see Baker, 2012; Nowak and Bennett, 2014), in the pre-digital era, a song's commercial fate rested primarily on the levels of radio airplay it received, which shows it was featured on and what times of the day it was played. Writing at the beginning of the 1990s, and thus during a period just prior to the emergence of the earliest examples of digital music technology, Rothenbuhler and McCourt offer the following insightful account of the unrivalled power of radio to make or break a pop song at that point in time. Thus, they state:

> Most radio programmers base their decision about what artists and songs to play on industry indicators of popularity. In fact, radio airplay is determined in part by radio airplay. Radio stations frequently add a song to their playlist simply because it is being played by a competitor or an influential station in another market ... Songs that receive sufficient initial attention will eventually gain maximum popularity through accelerated exposure, while songs receiving less initial attention recede quickly from public exposure and awareness. (1992: 102)

As Rothenbuhler and McCourt's observation aptly demonstrates, in the pre-digital era, radio's part in the creation of popular music taste was even more dominant than it is in the post-digital world purely because of its monopoly position as a public disseminator of recorded music. In the pre-digital era, people essentially relied on the radio to a significant extent to hear both new music and their favourite hits and, in essence, assumed a basic expectation that music radio programmes would perform that service for them. Indeed, as Simmons (2009) explains, music fans frequently formed a highly interactive relationship with radio, often writing in with requests to hear their favourite song. It was this trend among radio audiences that ultimately led to the appearance of dedicated radio request shows. In early 1970s Britain, a popular teen and pre-teen radio request show was BBC Radio 1's *Junior Choice*, broadcast on a Saturday morning and hosted by Ed 'Stewpot' Stewart (see, Witts, 2012). Featured songs on *Junior Choice* were many and varied, but the majority reflected songs in the British pop charts at the time when young listeners sent in their requests. Another Radio 1 show that played a key role in shaping the nation's musical taste during the early 1970s was *Pick of the Pops*, a show hosted by Alan Freeman that moved to Radio 1 from the BBC Light Programme in late 1967 (see Devlin, 2018). In 1972 *Pick of the Pops* was replaced by *Solid Gold Sixty*, hosted by new presenter Tom Browne. Featured in the same popular early evening weekend slot as its predecessor had been (Sunday between 6.00 and 7.00 pm), *Solid Gold Sixty* was instrumental in building the reputation of many seminal 1970s popular music artists and, together with the BBC television music show *Top of the Pops* (see Chapter 2 and below), was majorly responsible for producing some of the biggest hits of the decade, among them 10cc's 'I'm Not in Love' and Queen's 'Bohemian Rhapsody', songs that will be returned to later in this chapter.

Progressive pop artists were a mainstay of British music radio during the early to mid-1970s and thus a dominant part of the nation's everyday musical backdrop throughout this period. Barely a day went by in daytime radio when songs from these artists were not featured with the result that their chart releases frequently made it into the top 10, often remaining there for several weeks at a time. In this way, progressive pop artists found a level of mainstream appeal that their progressive rock counterparts, even if the latter frequently enjoyed significantly higher album sales, found difficult to procure due to their absence from the singles market. Indeed, from the point of view of the record-buying public in the UK, it could be argued that it was often bands and artists such as 10cc, ELO, Queen, Roxy Music and David Bowie who signified the more *progressive* element in British popular music at the time purely because their crossover into the singles market gave them exposure to a large audience of mainstream pop fans. This included a significant teen and pre-teen audience, for whom AOR was often an unknown quantity – something they may have heard about from their older siblings or fellow students in more senior years at their schools but usually not sampled for themselves. Certainly, this is not to claim that there was no avenue for progressive and hard rock bands to be heard on British radio. However, where these bands tended to receive radio airplay was through programmes such as Alan 'Fluff' Freeman's *Saturday Rock Show*, which was broadcast in weekly instalments on a Saturday afternoon and attracted a niche audience whose tastes were more orientated towards AOR (see also Chapter 2). As such, it tended to be progressive pop artists who assumed the mantle of more 'serious music' creators when it came to weekly daytime radio where their songs were heard throughout the day and also in prime-time slots, rather than being restricted to particular days, or evenings, of the week.

What progressive pop and progressive rock did have in common, however, was an often superior sound quality evident in the recording and production of their music. It has already been noted (see Chapter 3), for example, how 10cc benefitted from being able to work at Strawberry Studios, the latter being partly owned by several members of the band. Other artists, while not having the same kind of luxury, did enjoy the advantage of significant backing from major recoding labels of the day. With the benefit of higher recording budgets and often more experienced producers than many of their more mainstream pop peers, progressive pop artists were also able to take strategic advantage of high-quality studio facilities. This granted them the capacity to make state-of-the-art recordings that gave their music a critical edge over much of the more low-budget pop present in the radio soundscape at this time. Also, because progressive pop singles were often drawn from albums, rather than quickly recorded as stand-alone products to capitalize on the taste trends of a fickle and capricious pop market, they often sounded more rounded and honed when compared to artists whose output was more stridently directed towards the singles charts. Such a mark of distinction is evident, for example, in David Bowie's early 1970s hits, such as 'Starman' and 'The Jean Genie', and in 10cc's 'Rubber Bullets'. In the case of 'Rubber Bullets', the song was released at a time when the troubles in Northern Ireland were at their height. Consequently, the BBC restricted airplay of the song as it was assumed that the title was, or could be construed as, a reference to the British Army's controversial use of rubber bullets in the conflict (Tremlett, 1976). Nevertheless, airplay was sufficient to ensure the success of the song in reaching the top of the British charts in June 1973. Another song from the same era that became something of a surprise hit was Queen's, 'Seven Seas of Rhye', hastily drawn from the band's second album *Queen II* when a chance opportunity arose for the band to appear on *Top of the Pops* (see Chapter 2). A standout track when featured on the radio, the song's hard rock pedigree, overlain with multitracked vocals and layered lead guitar work, provided an early indication of Queen's rock-pop crossover appeal, later summarized by music journalists Logan and Woffinden, who described the band as 'exotic enough to appeal to crossover bopper fans [while] equally well-geared to hold the attentions of new-generation hard rock enthusiasts' (1977: 407). A little under two years later, in late 1975, Queen would dominate the UK radio airwaves with a song that produced a perfect blend of progressive rock aesthetic and pop sensibilities in the shape of 'Bohemian Rhapsody', a track that continues to serve as a quintessential example of the elements that defined British progressive pop during the early 1970s.

'This week on *Top of the Pops*'

In the annals of British popular music television *Top of the Pops* holds a special and indeed iconic place for successive generations of music fans, particularly in relation to their youth, as the music show that most reliably introduced them to new music and new artists (see Fryer, 1997). It is undoubtedly the case that a broad mapping of connections between popular music and cultural memory in Britain would quickly reveal the pivotal importance of *TOTP* as both a place where music fans forged a connection with particular popular artists and where 'peak experiences' (Green, 2016) of these artists and their hit songs were often formed. As with the observations made earlier in this chapter about radio's importance as a musical medium in the pre-digital age, for those young Britons living in a time before access to digital media technology, *TOTP* was in many cases their tangible 'introduction' to new music artists. While they may in some cases have initially heard new artists on the radio, *TOTP* was more typically the place where young fans actually 'saw' these artists in the 'televisual' flesh for the first time and thus formed a closer bond with them. First broadcast on 1 January 1964 *TOTP* had a weekly spot until 30 July 2006, when the show was cancelled. For the majority of this time, *TOTP* was shown on BBC1, only moving to BBC2 in 2005 when its popularity began to decline. In its forty-two years on air, *TOTP* became a significant aspect of British popular culture and was responsible for helping establish the careers of a great many artists. The show was also a place where each of the progressive pop artists discussed in this book were first seen by a mass public and thus where they began to generate a more mainstream audience in Britain. *TOTP* was known for presenting an eclectic roster of artists, ranging from rock and pop performers and singer-songwriters to novelty songs, such as comedian Benny Hill's 1971 hit 'Ernie – The Fastest Milkman in the West' (Caterson, 2006). In an era before the arrival of the pop video (see Kaplan, 1987), the custom was for bands appearing on *TOTP* to perform live in the studio. In truth, the actual extent to which artists actually performed live on the show is a moot point as most simply mimed to their latest hit (Gittens, 007), a practice adopted from earlier British popular music television shows such as *Oh Boy!* (see Frith, 2002). In the case of many artists, however, this combination of mimed 'live' appearance worked to their strategic advantage, particularly in cases where the featured song had relied on a significant element of studio production in its making. As Frith (2002) observes, miming had jarred with notions of rock 'authenticity' during the 1960s, but by the early 1970s, many artists were coming to value the importance of spending time in the studio creating versions of their songs that went beyond the confines of live performance. Such was clearly the case with progressive pop artists. Although each of these artists were touring acts and ultimately became highly adept at playing their music in a live context, the fact that they were also able to introduce new songs to the record-buying public as highly polished studio versions in the *TOTP* setting was clearly advantageous. Appearing on *TOTP* also meant that progressive pop artists quickly gained exposure to a much wider audience than would necessarily go and see them live, particularly given the fact that a sizeable amount of *TOTP*'s audience was pre-and early teen. Given the constraints of time and also the limits of the sound technology available to the *TOTP* production team during the early 1970s, it is unlikely that the tracks that introduced these artists to a mass audience in Britain would have had the same impact had they been performed live and thus at the mercy of an inferior sound mix or other technological impediments that may have compromised the overall quality of the performance.

Among the many artists for whom *TOTP* provided a galvanizing moment of public exposure was David Bowie. Although Bowie had previously appeared on *TOTP* performing his 1969 hit *Space Oddity*, it was his appearance on 6th July 1972 in the guise of his new persona, Ziggy Stardust, that piqued mass interest in Bowie and truly established him as a pop icon for a new generation of music fans in Britain. Even with glam rock by then an established and staple genre on *TOTP*, and one that had already served to produce a weird and wonderful succession of artists, Bowie's bright-red, backcombed hair and rainbow-patterned jumpsuit gave the singer a standout appeal as he sang his new release 'Starman'. The song depicted an alien visitor to Earth, a topic consolidated by Bowie's own quite alien visual appearance. Although the embodiment of a new and original sound that perfectly blended pop and rock aesthetics, for older viewers 'Starman' had an element of nostalgic appeal about it too, its chorus melody bearing traces of Judy Garland's pre-war hit 'Somewhere over the Rainbow' from the 1939 film *The Wizard of Oz* (see Nathanson, 1991). A further galvanizing effect of Bowie's performance was the license that it gave to other artists working outside the parameters of the more conventional popular music formats employed by glam, teenybop and other staples of *TOTP* at that point to pursue more performative and theatrical dimensions of live performance. It has frequently been observed how, in the context of the early 1970s, rock performance had become synonymous with an image of long hair and blue jeans (an image exemplified by British boogie-rock band Status Quo, who would transform it into their trademark look during the 1970s, as exemplified by the cover of their 1976 album *Blue for You*, which features the band wearing clothing supplied by the Levi company, with whom they had recently signed a sponsorship deal). In the space of one brief performance on *TOTP*, Bowie and his backing band, the Spiders from Mars (see Trynka, 2011), transformed the perception that being a 'serious' rock artist meant a sidelining of image considerations. As the early 1970s progressed, it became clear that Bowie's message of visual extravagance was registering far and wide as an increasing number of artists, among them Elton John, Queen and Cockney Rebel, although highly noted for their music, also generated a level of audience appeal through the flamboyant images they created for themselves – and presented to a mainstream British audience on *TOTP*. The fact that so many of these artists are also featured on the popular *TOTP* reruns on BBC television is indicative of how well they are remembered in the context of the British popular culture of 1970s.

Another British band combining exotic influences, both musically and visually, whose impact on the national music scene of the early 1970s was significantly enhanced by an early performance on *TOTP*, was Roxy Music. Like David Bowie, Roxy Music stood out on the show as artists whose image and music seemed to bear little relation to anything else that was currently going on in the British hit parade. Appearing on *TOTP* in August 1972, several weeks after Bowie's enigmatic performance of 'Starman', Roxy Music's debut single 'Virginia Plain' deviated from the pop norm on several notable accounts. To begin with, the song featured a slightly unusual assortment of instruments, including a clarinet and a VCS3 electronic synthesizer (synthesizers at this time being a revolutionary and quite novel form of technology in the worlds of rock and pop). Furthermore, the song was devoid of a chorus – a sing-along chorus being at that point considered an absolute necessity for a radio-friendly and teen-accessible hit single. If Bowie's slightly earlier *TOTP* performance had been suggestive of new territories opening up in British popular music, Roxy Music's appearance seemed to confirm this in unequivocal terms. Many years later in an interview commissioned for a box-set containing highlights from the classic television programme *Old Grey Whistle Test*, a show that continues to be best remembered for its featuring of AOR music during the early 1970s (see Chapters 2 and 3), Scottish singer-songwriter Roddy Frame (formerly with pop and new wave band Aztec Camera) described how upon seeing Roxy Music for the first time they appeared to him to be a band without definable rock or pop influences. This sense of the band's 'left-fieldness' was undoubtedly also felt by many of those who experienced the spectacle of Roxy Music's debut performance on *TOTP*. Like Bowie, the fashions worn by Roxy Music had an 'other-worldly' appearance to them. This exotic quality also extended to the lyrics being sung by lead vocalist Bryan Ferry, which Fuller describes as '[a] camp, kitsch, Pop-Art collage of movie, advertising and Americana' (1983: 1805) and to the sounds produced by the band. Even the more familiar musical instruments featured on 'Virginia Plain', such as keyboards, guitar and bass, were processed through electronic effects to the point of a musical transgression unheard of by British fans of more mainstream pop at this point.

Although the practice of *TOTP* was to encourage featured artists to make a physical appearance on the show, the frequent unavailability of artists meant that other measures had to be taken to promote their latest single. Pan's People, *TOTP*'s all-female dance troupe, were a weekly feature on the show throughout the early to mid-1970s, dancing their way through many hits of this period (see Fryer, 1997). In November 1975, however, *TOTP* made a fundamental contribution to popular music history when it featured what was to become regarded as the world's first official popular music video, a clip produced by Queen to accompany their new single 'Bohemian Rhapsody'. By this point, Queen were recognized faces on *TOTP*. In the case of their previous appearances, however, they had performed in the *TOTP* studio, taking their turn in lip-syncing to their current new release. 'Bohemian Rhapsody', however, provided a challenge for Queen due to its complex and highly overdubbed construction, with any attempt to mime the song likely to have looked odd and out of place, particularly during the track's mini-opera section, a novel and quite dramatic departure from anything attempted by a popular music artist up until this time (a point returned to later in this chapter). Moreover, with their popularity in Britain growing rapidly at that point, Queen were in fact scheduled to play a show in Dundee, Scotland, on the same night that 'Bohemian Rhapsody' was due to be featured for the first time on *TOTP*. As such, Queen took a decision that was to have a pivotal impact on the popular music industry, choosing to make a special promotional video for their new single release. This was not the first time that a 'pop promo', as they were referred to at this point, had been made. For example, in February 1967 pop promos for the Beatles' double A side single 'Strawberry Fields Forever' and 'Penny Lane' had been shown on *TOTP*, and two months later, the release of Pink Floyd's single 'Arnold Lane' was also accompanied by a promotional film. In the early 1970s this trend continued with pop promos for various tracks, including Marc Bolan and T-Rex's 'Hot Love' (released in 1971) and David Bowie's 'Life on Mars' (1973), these also being featured on *TOTP*. 'Bohemian Rhapsody', however, marked the beginning of a radically different chapter in the history of the popular music video, ushering in a new aesthetic understanding of video as something capable of making an artistic statement in and of itself rather than merely serving as a promotional device for a song. During the 1980s, pop videos would see artists utilizing a range of formats, from straightforward 'performance' videos featuring a 'live', on-stage look to videos that took artists beyond the performance context to act out quasi film-like roles designed to accentuate particular aspects of the song and its lyrical meanings (see Kaplan, 1987). The 'Bohemian Rhapsody' video cleverly cuts across these two different types of pop video text. Its striking opening sequence depicts the illuminated faces of the four members of Queen in a sea of darkness achieved through backlighting to create a similar effect to that seen in the photograph of the band taken by Mick Rock for the cover of the *Queen II* album (Hodkinson, 1995). The band are depicted singing the a cappella opening of 'Bohemian Rhapsody' before the scene changes to lead singer Freddie Mercury playing the piano opening to the ballad section of the song, with bass player John Deacon standing in the background, supplying the accompanying bass line. The action then settles into a performance video mode until the beginning of the opera section, when the image of the four backlit faces is re-introduced and special camera effects used to visually accentuate the cascading effect used on Mercury's voice in the studio at critical points in the dramatic light and shade of the operatic vocals. As the opera section ends and a new 'rock' section of the song begins, the video returns to performance mode. Directed by Bruce Gowers, who had also directed *Queen Live at the Rainbow* (later released on DVD as *Queen Live at the Rainbow '74*), the 'Bohemian Rhapsody' video was apparently recorded in four hours and at a cost of £4,500. For the *TOTP* audience, however, the video had a very clear novelty value, enhancing 'Bohemian Rhapsody's' already unusual quality to a new level. In 1986, Michael Appleton, producer and director, known among other things for his work on British late-night rock television the *Old Grey Whistle Test* (see also Chapter 3), commented on the Queen documentary *Magic Years: Volume 1* that the 'Bohemian Rhapsody' video marked a major turning point in how popular music would be marketed from that point onwards. The video became a major talking point among television audiences, undergoing a slight edit after being aired on *TOTP* for several weeks and almost certainly contributing majorly to the song's incredible success. As Appleton remarked, while the music of 'Bohemian Rhapsody' was itself a major draw for audiences, its visual interpretation in the video was unlike anything seen up to this point in popular music history.

Big sounds, big songs

Ultimately, 'Bohemian Rhapsody' would hold the number 1 position in Britain for a period of nine weeks, being the Christmas number 1 of 1975. Following the death of Freddie Mercury in November 1991, 'Bohemian Rhapsody' would again reach the number 1 slot, making it the only song to have been a Christmas number 1 twice by the same artist. Returning to 1975, however, this was something of a watershed year for progressive pop in Britain, seeing the release of not only one but rather two songs that between them significantly pushed the boundaries of the then accepted format of the pop single. Five months before the release of 'Bohemian Rhapsody', 10cc had topped the British charts for two weeks with 'I'm Not in Love', the song for which the band are still most well remembered as pop innovators of the 1970s. Music journalist and radio presenter Paul Gambaccini has described 'I'm Not Love' and 'Bohemian Rhapsody' as 'the great multi-track hits of ... all time'.[1] Between them, the two songs have scooped a number of awards and accolades. These include three Ivor Novello awards for 'I'm Not in Love' and two Grammy Award nominations for 'Bohemian Rhapsody', with the 2002 *Guinness Book of Records* naming 'Bohemian Rhapsody' as the all-time top British single. Notably enhanced by the use of studio technology, each of these songs remains relatively unique in the popular music soundscape, significantly expanding and refining principles of studio innovation established by the Beach Boys and the Beatles during the mid- to late-1960s (Martin, 1979; Wilson, 2016) and taking these to a new level of complexity and sophistication.

'I'm Not in Love' was written by Eric Stewart and Graham Gouldman. However, the song also benefitted from significant creative input from Kevin Godley and Lol Creme during its transformation from an almost abandoned project to a studio masterpiece. 'I'm Not in Love' is the second track on 10cc's third album *The Original Soundtrack*, released in March 1975. This was the band's first album for the Mercury label, with whom they signed with in February 1975, having become dissatisfied with UK Records, who had released their first two albums, *10cc* (1973) and *Sheet Music* (1974) (see Tremlett, 1976).

The release of *The Original Soundtrack* saw 10cc building on the success of their previous two albums, its songs again being distinctive and diverse, ranging from 'Une Nuit a Paris', a multi-section mini-operetta mooted to have been a key source of influence for Queen's Freddie Mercury in his writing of 'Bohemian Rhapsody' (see below), and 'The Film of My Love', a mock-mariachi-style ballad sung by Graham Gouldman that closes the album. 'I'm Not in Love', however, is a standout track on the album as indeed it was in the broader context of the British charts, due to its unique sound, which is primarily created through the richly layered, multitracked voices heard throughout the song. According to Eric Stewart and Graham Gouldman in the 2015 BBC documentary *I'm Not in Love – The Story of 10cc*, 'I'm Not in Love' began life as a bossa-nova-style song based around the guitar. The four members of 10cc recorded a working version of the song in its original style but were dissatisfied with the result. Work on the song was dropped and the original recording erased (although elements of the original melody were later incorporated into the reworked version of 'I'm Not in Love'). Having noticed that staff at Strawberry Studios continued humming its main melody, 10cc decided to revisit 'I'm Not in Love' to see if a more satisfactory version of it could be produced. Godley's suggestion was to rework the structure of the song using voices rather than instruments to create the backing track. Stewart's original understanding of this was that Godley felt the song would work best in an a cappella style, but Godley remarked that what he had actually meant was a 'wash' of wordless voices. This suggestion, combined with the fact that having access to their own studio gave 10cc the luxury of time to experiment with their music, resulted in one of the most ambitious pieces of studio production as yet undertaken by the band. In order to create the lush vocal effect suggested by Godley, Stewart spent three weeks recording the voices of Godley, Creme and Gouldman, who sang separate single notes in a chromatic scale spanning top C to bottom C onto a sixteen-track tape machine. In order to create a quality of infinite sustain, the tapes used to record the voices were looped (a trick suggested by Lol Creme), using microphone stands and capstan rollers so that the loops could be extended in length to around twelve feet. As batches of looped tracks were completed, they were bounced down to two tracks to make room for additional loops to be added with the result that when the three-week recording process was completed, a total of 624 voices had been committed to tape. The vocal tracks were then played back through the mixing console, with each member of the band manipulating multiple faders in a similar fashion to pressing keys on a keyboard instrument with the effect that chords could be created by using the multitracked voices. A backing track, making use of a Fender Rhodes electric piano played by Stewart, a rhythm guitar played by Gouldman and a simple bass drum pattern reminiscent of a heartbeat played by Godley using a Moog synthesizer, had also been created primarily as a guide to the creation of the vocal backdrop. However, when it was heard together with the newly added vocal wash, the decision was taken to leave the backing track in the mix as part of the song. Similarly, according to Stewart, the lead vocal used on the final version of the track was actually his original guide vocal. Additional backing vocals by Godley and Creme (specifically the hypnotic phrase 'it's because'), acoustic piano and effects including the chimes of a musical box were then added to the track. A final, yet in the event, iconic touch was added when the secretary of Strawberry Studios, Kathy Redfern, was asked to contribute a whispered motif, 'be quiet, big boys don't cry' in the middle eight, which also includes a short bass guitar solo, itself a novelty both in the music of 10cc[2] and in the soundscape of early 1970s popular music overall. In an interview with the author, Graham Gouldman reflected on the recording and production of 'I'm Not in Love' and how it typified the close and collaborative working relationship of 10cc during the early 1970s:

> One thing I should say about that record, which shows how unified we were and how reliant we were on one another [is that] the contributions of everybody [in the band] made that record. It wasn't just a great song, it was a great record as well. And all credit to all of us for creating it. Even though two people wrote it the record that we know would not have existed without the other two members [of the band]. (interview with author, January 2019)

Like 'I'm Not in Love', Queen's 'Bohemian Rhapsody' also presented as something of a novel surprise in the pop world of 1975, not only in Britain but also further afield. Indeed, the song, a mini-suite comprising several different sections, would prove to be Queen's international breakthrough hit. In addition to its chart-topping success in Britain, 'Bohemian Rhapsody' also reached number 1 in eight other countries, including Australia, where the previous year Queen had met with a somewhat negative reaction to their performance at the Sunbury Festival (see Hawkings, 2014). In addition, 'Bohemian Rhapsody' provided Queen with their first top 10 hit in the United States. In similar fashion to 'I'm Not in Love', 'Bohemian Rhapsody' was an ostensibly unusual choice for a single. At just under six minutes in length,

Queen's record label EMI had expressed concerns about whether the song would be adopted by radio DJs for airplay (an incident comically portrayed in the 2018 Queen bio-pic *Bohemian Rhapsody*, where actor Mike Myers plays the EMI executive charged with the task of disabusing Queen of their unrelenting belief in 'Bohemian Rhapsody's' potential as a single). However, Queen and their record producer at the time, Roy Thomas Baker, gave a reel-to-reel tape copy of 'Bohemian Rhapsody' to Capital Radio DJ and friend of the band Kenny Everett on the 'condition' that the tape was for his personal use only. Everett then proceeded to play segments of 'Bohemian Rhapsody' on his daily radio show and, as listener interest increased, played the song in its entirety a total of fourteen times over a period of two days. As demand for 'Bohemian Rhapsody' grew among Queen fans, who were perplexed that they couldn't actually buy a copy of the record, EMI relaxed its previous opinion about the unsuitability of 'Bohemian Rhapsody' as a single and, in late October 1975, released a full, uncut version of the song.

'Bohemian Rhapsody' was written and conceptualized by Freddie Mercury, lead vocalist and frontman of Queen. Although several of the distinctive elements that gave rise to the song had been heard in a more embryonic form on previous Mercury compositions, notably 'My Fairy King' (from *Queen*, 1973) and 'The March of the Black Queen' (from *Queen II*, 1974), the scale and production of 'Bohemian Rhapsody' was unlike anything that Queen, or indeed any other popular music artist, had attempted up to that point. As noted above, it has been suggested that a source of inspiration for Mercury in writing 'Bohemian Rhapsody' was the 10cc track 'Une Nuit a Paris', a lesser-known but equally ambitious track written by Kevin Godley and Lol Creme and featured as the opening song on *The Original Soundtrack*. Indeed, Graham Gouldman has reported to the author that 10cc had initially wanted to release 'Une Nuit a Paris' as a single but had met resistance to this suggestion from their record company. Like 'Bohemian Rhapsody', 'Une Nuit a Paris' consists of several sections and is also characterized by richly layered, multitracked vocals. Both songs embody an obvious progressive rock influence in terms of their compositional structure. In November 1975 during an interview with American music journalist John Ingham, Kevin Godley revealed how initially 'Une Nuit a Paris' had been envisaged as taking up one complete side of *The Original Soundtrack* but was then pared back to eight minutes and forty seconds (see Ingham, 1975), a track length still more comparable with a progressive rock aesthetic than with pop.

However, while 'Une Nuit a Paris' was destined to remain an album track, the decision to release 'Bohemian Rhapsody' as a single delivered a taste of progressive rock's 'high-brow' technicality to a more mainstream pop audience, this meeting with an obviously wide approval given the significant success of the song.

The compositional structure of 'Bohemian Rhapsody' is such that the song is presented in five discrete sections. A five-part harmony, a cappella section introduces the song (augmented by piano at fifteen seconds into the track). While the promotional video that accompanied 'Bohemian Rhapsody' depicts all four members of Queen 'singing' (i.e. lip-syncing) this opening segment, in reality, the entire section was sung by Mercury using studio multitracking to layer up harmonized vocals. In the ballad section that follows, the song begins to build dynamically, beginning with piano and bass accompaniment, with drums coming in at the beginning of the second verse, with the entry of the guitar slightly later accentuating the dramatic tone of Mercury's lyrics concerning the despair of a young man who, having committed an act of murder, now contemplates the punishment he will receive. While the moribund nature of the lyric befits the ballad format (and had by this time become a well-trodden format in pop), what follows in the musical evolution of 'Bohemian Rhapsody' was entirely unprecedented, the slow rolling momentum of the ballad giving way to the staccato tempo of a mini-opera. When Mercury first suggested his idea for an opera section to Queen producer Roy Thomas Baker, this was apparently conceived as a relatively small interlude, comprising, according to Baker's description in the Queen documentary *Magic Years* (1986), of 'a few little Galileos' (see also Thomas, 1999). As work continued on this section of the song, however, further material was added with the result that in the finished version of 'Bohemian Rhapsody' the opera extends to just over one minute in length with 180 overdubbed vocal tracks, sung by Mercury, guitarist Brian May and drummer Roger Taylor, providing a dramatic opera-esque soundscape. This was made even more exotic in a pop context through a lyric comprised of largely unfamiliar references to things such as 'Scaramouche' (a clown character of the Italian commedia dell'arte) and 'Bismillah' (a word that appears in the Qu'ran and has the literal meaning 'In the name of Allah'). The rock section that follows the mini-opera marks yet another shift in tempo and features one of the most recognizable and distinctive guitar riffs of the 1970s. This riff was in fact composed by Mercury on the piano and shifts between sequences of notes in A sharp major and E flat major, both keys being uncommon in rock guitar at this time. The last section of 'Bohemian Rhapsody' marks a return to the style and tempo that begins the track with the grand finale again being a novel motif in the pop landscape of the time, as Roger Taylor strikes a tam tam (a gong-like instrument of Chinese origin).

Conclusion

As this chapter has illustrated, both musically and visually, progressive pop played a major role in shaping British popular music in the early to mid-1970s. Similarly, key songs from progressive pop artists have become pivotal to how these years, and perhaps the 1970s decade overall, are remembered and represented in the cultural memory of those music fans who lived through the decade. In an era before access to digital media, radio and television were the main mediums for music consumption outside of the live music experience. With a critical AOR/chart music crossover, progressive pop artists commanded a wide audience and their songs became highly revered both among AOR listeners and within the mediascape of British chart pop. With the release of Queen's 'Bohemian Rhapsody', popular music edged closer to the video age, while this song, together with 'I'm Not in Love', demonstrated how the creative legacy of the Beatles retained an enduring presence in the British popular music of the early to mid-1970s. When asked about the meaning of 'Bohemian Rhapsody', its composer Freddie Mercury declined to offer any specific insights into his inspiration for writing the song. Eric Stewart, on the other hand, declared that the sentiment behind the unconventionally titled 'I'm Not in Love' was motivated by his feeling that daily expressions of love for his wife had become routine and hollow – the song's 'hidden' meaning being that it is, after all, a love song. For many, though, there was an uneasy feeling that these and other examples of 1970s popular music had become effectively 'too clever' for their own good – that self-indulgence and vacuity had become new 'standards' in British popular music at the expense of any obvious engagement with social and political issues. Such an apparent lack of sociopolitical concern, it was felt, was made all the more pressing given the deepening crisis in Britain following the end of political consensus and the onset of a socio-economic downturn. The following chapter offers an evaluation of such criticisms of British popular music during the early to mid-1970s, suggesting in the process that while lacking the more overt reactionary voice of late 1960s 'political rock' or the subsequent anger of punk, early to mid-1970s popular music in Britain was not entirely devoid of sociopolitical commentary with songs in the progressive pop category in particular often providing important insights concerning the pathologies of seventies society.

Notes

1 *I'm Not in Love – The Story of 10cc* (BBC4 Documentary, 2015).
2 On 10cc's live album *Live and Let Live* (1977) (see also Chapter 6), Graham Gouldman contributes a bass solo to an extended version of the four-piece suite 'Feel the Benefit' from the band's fifth studio album *Deceptive Bends* released earlier that year.

5
Small 'p' politics

In January 1974, rock band Hudson-Ford scored a top 20 hit in the UK singles charts with the song 'Burn Baby Burn'. Formerly members of British folk-rock group the Strawbs, for whom they had written 'Part of the Union', a number 2 hit in 1973, John Ford and Richard Hudson left the group later that year to form their own band. In the context of early 1970s British popular music, 'Burn Baby Burn' presented as a slightly unusual song in that, through its candid commentary on high taxation and rising unemployment, the track seemed to chime with the state of the British nation, exercising a political voice that appeared to be absent almost everywhere else in British chart music of the time. The song's lyrics also extended to critical reflections about human threats to the natural environment, specifically the dumping of toxic waste into rivers. With the formation of the nongovernment organization Greenpeace in the Canadian city of Vancouver in 1971 (Ostopowich, 2003) during the early 1970s, environmental politics begun to assume greater visibility as concerns about an emerging environmental crisis took hold across the developed world. Had 'Burn Baby Burn' been released five or six years earlier, it would have seemed less out of place, the late 1960s having been something of a watershed period for songs with a more overtly articulated political message (Bennett, 2001; Eyerman and Jamison, 1998). In the context of the early 1970s, however, 'Burn Baby Burn' seemed oddly out of place – a song with an anthemic sixties flavour commenting in a direct way on topical themes of the 1970s that seemed to be of little concern elsewhere in British rock and pop. Performing the song on *Top of the Pops*, Hudson-Ford also appeared as relics from the late 1960s, their image as much as out of place in the *TOTP* studio as the themes they sung about in 'Burn Baby Burn'.

As previously noted in Chapter 1, the seeming absence of a political agenda among rock and pop artists of the early 1970s may be one reason why this era of popular music has been largely overlooked, particularly in the UK. And yet, despite a commonly rehearsed rhetoric that the post-Beatles and pre-punk years of British popular music represented a markedly sallow period in terms of political aspirations, to date little sustained analysis has been attempted to either support or properly refute this claim. To say that British popular music in this era lacks the staunchly anti-hegemonic themes of its late-sixties counterpart is one thing. To claim, as such, that popular music in Britain at this time was lacking a critical voice in any kind of respect is quite another. If British popular music, and particularly those artists clustered under the banner of progressive pop, absorbed influences from the late 1960s, then it was at the same time cut from a different cloth, one that responded to a new generation of fans and a new sociocultural milieu where old social conventions were beginning to break down and cracks in the weathered veneer of a post-war sociocultural reality beginning to show. In this sense, progressive pop could be seen to have embraced a new sensibility of the times, playing its own part in the negotiation of Britain's social and economic stagnation and cynically poking fun at the British establishment and its crumbling system of values.

Back to the future

By the beginning of the 1970s the post-war consensus that had seen Britain enter an age of technological advancement and economic prosperity (Leys, 1983) during the 1950s and 1960s was beginning to falter in a dramatic fashion. Harold Wilson's Labour government, which had been a mainstay of Britain's optimism and prosperity during the 1960s, suffered a surprise defeat by the Conservative Party, led by Edward Heath, in 1970 (Ramsden, 1996). This paved the way for increasing friction as Britain entered a period of recession accentuated by the oil crisis in 1973 and further exacerbated by the three-day week. The latter was an extreme measure imposed by the Heath government in January 1974 to conserve supplies of coal following the announcement of a second national miner's strike (Richards, 1997). Electricity power cuts became a frequent occurrence across the nation, particularly at night when millions of homes would suddenly be plunged into darkness. In the same period, Britain was experiencing monetary inflation that reached a height of over 20 per cent (Nelson and Nikolov, 2003). Amidst such bleakness, a national state of emergency was declared by the UK government.

If British popular music in the 1960s had been frequently infused with a political voice, as heard for example in adopted countercultural anthems such as the Beatles' 'Revolution' and the Rolling Stones' 'Street Fighting Man' (Platoff, 2005; see also Chapter 1), during the early 1970s popular music in Britain appeared to have become decidedly apolitical even as the country slumped into a deepening crisis that was far worse than anything experienced since before the Second World War. Indeed, much of the popular music that filled the British airwaves during the early 1970s seemed to revert back to the melodic motifs and lyrical topics of the late 1950s and early 1960s. The Bay City Rollers, a group whose mid-1970s global popularity gave rise to the term 'Rollermania' (designed as a means of comparing the impact of the Bay City Rollers with the excitement of 'Beatlemania' in the early 1960s, see Spence, 2016), are an illustrative case in point, the band achieving huge commercial success, in Britain and elsewhere, during 1974 and 1975 with a string of bubblegum hits, including 'Shang-a-lang' and 'Bye Bye Baby'. With the teen appeal of the Bay City Rollers well established, other British pop bands such as Mud, the Rubettes and Showaddywaddy also proved successful in cornering the local teen market with a brand of music that drew heavily on influences from the 1950s, such influence also extending to the visual style of these artists. In the same period, the New Seekers (founded by Keith Potger after the disbanding of his former group the Seekers, who had enjoyed significant commercial success during the 1960s) were marketed to a more mature audience. The band's international breakthrough hit 'I'd Like to Teach the World to Sing' was a slight re-working of a song that had already become popular through its use in a 1971 Coca-Cola commercial. Smokie, a soft-rock band from the northern English city of Bradford in West Yorkshire, also found success in the early to mid-1970s with music that appealed to a slightly older audience. Similarly, some of the more established British popular artists who had first come to prominence during the late 1950s and early 1960s consolidated their success by reaching out and adjusting to the more 'middle of the road' tastes of their maturing audience. Such was the case with Cliff Richard, whose number 4 hit 'Power to All Our Friends' in 1973 was also the British entry to the Eurovision song contest that year where it was placed third. In one clear sense then, the response of British popular music to the crisis of the early 1970s seemed to be through engaging in a game of 'hauntology' (Reynolds, 2011), effecting an escape to a popular past – in this case the 1950s and early 1960s – a period re-presented as a golden age of popular music and youth culture. In itself, such a trend could be seen as something of a deflection from the pressing issues of the 1970s, a cluster of bands whose songs were both musically and lyrically inoffensive, designed to be 'good time' music during a period of mounting crisis and insecurity. Certainly this was the image often portrayed of these artists on *Top of the Pops*, where the emphasis was largely upon the creation of a party atmosphere. The show's invited youth audience were encouraged to dress as if going out to a club or 'disco' to dance – the music providing the backdrop for this spectacle. Shumway (1992) has discussed how since the 1950s youth audiences have frequently been a prominent feature of televised popular music performances, their filmed responses to the artists and the music performed providing a strong basis upon which other young people viewing the show will respond to and understand the music. This may certainly have added to the impression among some critical observers of the time that British popular music in the early 1970s was becoming increasingly effete – with shows such as *TOTP* appearing as significant tastemakers among youth and their perception of music.

Even as mainstream British pop seemed to engage in this game of retreatism from the harsh socio-economic realities of Britain, however, from the point of view of many British music critics, the genre that most stridently appeared to have deserted the political spirit of the 1960s was progressive rock. Although musically speaking, progressive rock owed much to the more experimental bands of the late 1960s, with the exception of Pink Floyd (whose political voice only became more strident on the band's 1977 album *Animals*), in terms of its lyrical content progressive rock seemed as far removed from any form of political voice as it was possible to get. In the eyes of the British music press, progressive rock's seeming disinterest in political matters was compounded by its musical self-indulgence. Amidst a scenario of increasing austerity in Britain, the response of progressive rock was an increasingly lavish approach to the production and performance of their music, with individual tracks becoming longer and more complex while the venues for progressive rock performances became larger and featured increasingly more elaborate light shows and stage props. The antagonism generated by progressive rock came to a head with the release of conceptual double albums by two of the leading English progressive rock bands of the early 1970s, Yes and Genesis (see Macan, 1997), whose respective offerings, *Tales from Topographic Oceans* (1973) and *The Lamb Lies Down on Broadway* (1974), both met with a decidedly mixed critical reception. As will be further discussed in Chapter 6, progressive rock is largely held to have inspired the musical backlash of punk during the mid-1970s. In truth, some elements of progressive rock were arguably more in tune with the period of crisis experienced by Britain during the early 1970s than has been acknowledged. A salient case in point is the Genesis album *Selling England by the Pound* (1973), where both the title of the album and its and opening track, 'Dancing with the Moonlit Knight', resonated with Britain's worsening socio-economic situation at the time of the album's release. However, steeped in the imagery of often-abstract lyrics and set to music trading on technical intricacy and complex time signatures, the political message of progressive rock, such as it existed, remained largely inaccessible to the majority of British music listeners at the time, something not helped by the fact that it received little airplay on national television and radio.

On the face of things, progressive pop did not appear to provoke much in the way of a response to Britain's deepening crisis either. Certainly, given their AOR-mainstream pop crossover quality, such bands were musically more accessible than their progressive rock counterparts to a mainstream music audience. But the music and lyrics of progressive pop seemed as removed from the gritty reality of Britain's economic problems at this time as progressive rock. In subsequent years, the anger of punk at some, if not all, progressive pop artists would squarely question their apparent lack of engagement with the sociopolitical status quo and seemingly unquestioning service to a music industry, whose profit motivation they supported with increasingly healthy albums and singles sales (see Chapter 6). A decade later, in the significantly alerted sociopolitical context of the 1980s, the notion of the pop-rock entrepreneur had not only become an established maxim but was also positively celebrated in many areas of the arts and culture world (see, for example, Hill, 1986). During the early 1970s, however, overt entrepreneurial intentions on the part of artists often created a sense of confusion or in some cases outright disdain, particularly among music journalists and critics. Writing about Queen in the late 1990s, British music journalist David Thomas observed:

> For a young band to have Queen's rampant ambition might come across as cool, sod-you cockiness in Blairite '90s Britain. In the strike-ridden, right-on early '70s it was infinitely more offensive. So music press disapproval dogged Queen right from the start. (1999: 76)

This was, however, by no means a level-playing field situation either. Thus, while such music press disdain was directed at Queen, an artist such as David Bowie was able to speak openly about the self-conscious creation of his glam-aligned Ziggy Stardust character and purposely playing on the ephemerality of pop culture (Trynka, 2011). In essence, Bowie was in every way as entrepreneurial as Queen, but as an artist, he was positioned differently by the music press and received critical acclaim rather than disdain. The same was true of Roxy Music, a band whose image and music were also strategically conceived to align with and exploit the fashionable era of glam, during which they emerged onto the British music scene.

Such an uneven response on the part of the music press was, however, in many ways telling of a period of transition in popular music, and particularly in rock, that was occurring in Britain and elsewhere in the early 1970s. During the 1960s the splitting of rock, albeit cosmetically, from 'pop' in music journalism was made to seem like a naturalistic division through the application of strongly formulated tropes of rock 'authenticity' and pop 'plasticity' (Shuker, 2001; see also Chapter 1). In truth, however, the discourse of 'rockism' quickly created its own problems and contradictions in the ways that rock artists were presented (and indeed presented themselves). Thus, while music critics continued to invest notions of authenticity and subversive intent in those artists whom they had collectively christened 'rock stars', the reality was frequently quite different. The overt contradiction in the claims of rock musicians, and their pundits, to be countercultural leaders while at the same time pursuing highly lucrative careers in the music industry was brought into sharp relief by legendary rock concert promoter of the late 1960s and early 1970s, Bill Graham, when he lamented:

> An artist would get on stage and say: 'Let's get together ... and fight and share and communicate.' Then he'd get into his jet and fly off to his island and play with his sixteen-track machine. It was hypocrisy. The misuse of power was devastating. (Palmer, 1977: 247)

A broadly similar point is made by Frith and Horne, who argue that, despite their often brazenly articulated countercultural, anti-capitalist rhetoric, as far as most rock musicians were concerned: '"Commercialism" was only opposed when it interfered with the musicians' plans. When commerce helped them to be realized there were no complaints' (1987: 90). Even at the 1969 Woodstock festival, an event that has been frequently described as a highpoint of the counterculture's ideological struggle against more 'mainstream' cultural values (see Bennett, 2004), festival organizer Michael Lang has noted how he encountered problems with several high-profile acts who enjoyed countercultural 'kudos' demanding payment before they would agree to perform their set at the event (see Young and Lang, 1979).

The message of rock as community (Frith, 1981) with world-changing potential was thus naïve in its articulation, and therefore a fundamentally flawed concept, from the very beginning. As such, by the early 1970s, rock was beginning to reposition itself, maintaining a status inherited from the late

1960s as a more 'high-brow' and 'intellectual' style of music but distancing itself from the political agendas of old. Rock musicians by and large no longer saw themselves as figureheads of the counterculture; nor did they regard their music as a vehicle for bringing about large-scale socio-economic and political change in the world at large. Rather, those who considered themselves 'serious' artists became more squarely invested in musical innovation (an obvious example here being Mike Oldfield) – see also Chapter 3 – utilizing the new technologies that were increasingly at hand to make ever more ambitious music. Progressive pop, as an aspect of British popular music that embraced elements of art rock and progressive rock, also reflected this transition. In the few short years since the break-up of the Beatles, studio technology had developed at a fast pace (see also Chapters 1 and 3), rapidly expanding the creative palate of those musicians with a desire to explore what the recording studio had to offer. Progressive pop artists, although musically diverse, were united in their common embracing of the new creative possibilities offered by the recording studio. The critical reaction to this trend was mixed, with some artists such as David Bowie and Roxy Music being praised as musical innovators, while others, such as Queen, were often rebuked for their apparently self-absorbed nature, producing music of a highly clinical, perfectionist nature that thus lacked warmth and sincerity.

And yet, when viewed as a broad field of musical output, it is difficult to discount the presence in progressive pop of subversive, counter-hegemonic and critical elements in an overall sense. Certainly, this was not the hard-edged subversive voice of 'Street Fighting Man' or 'God Save the Queen'. But the popular cultural heritage on which progressive pop drew, combined with the fact that many of those who found their way into progressive pop bands in the early 1970s had served important creative apprentices as art school students (Frith and Horne, 1987) provided a ready basis for the critical edge, often satirically or cynically intoned, that was evident in many progressive pop songs of the early 1970s. In essence then, in progressive pop the large 'P' politics of the late 1960s metamorphosed into a small 'p' politics that frequently focused on the social pathologies of the 1970s.

Social disease

In June 1974, 10cc had their fourth top 10 hit with 'The Wall Street Shuffle'. Taken from the band's second album *Sheet Music*, released in May 1974, this song was the first 10cc single to feature a lead local from Eric Stewart. As its title suggests, 'The Wall Street Shuffle' deals with the infamous American stock market crash of 1929, from which began the Great Depression, which would severely impact the world economy for the next twelve years (Romer, 1990). Although focusing on an economic disaster that gravely affected the lives of a great many people in many different nations, the lyrical thrust of the song is its satirical portrayal of the self-concerned greed at the root of much that went wrong in 1929 when share prices on the New York stock exchange collapsed. Although a direct comparison is difficult to make, it is interesting that this song appeared precisely at a point when the British economy was entering a steep decline, the references to the crumbling value of the pound sterling having a poignant resonance with events overtaking Britain in the early 1970s. At just over three minutes in length (with a slightly longer, unedited album version) the song's minor key, aggressively distinctive fuzz-tone guitar riff and harrowing mellotron string-voices in the song's bridge were at odds with much of the other more happy-sounding music in the UK top 20 at that point, songs that included the Wombles' 'Banana Rock' and 'Hey Rock and Roll', the debut single by rock-and-roll band Showaddywaddy.

Having displayed a penchant for songs whose lyrics explored social pathology on their debut album (see Chapter 3), the following three albums from 10cc would continue in this vein. In addition to 'The Wall Street Shuffle', *Sheet Music* contained tracks such as 'Silly Love', a song about the hang-ups and inhibitions that frequently interfere with contemporary rituals of romance, and 'The Sacro-Iliac', a comic ballad that issues a message of resistance to social pressures to present as 'cool' and 'fashionable' even when such conventions feel uncomfortable or alien to the individual concerned. The song 'Brand New Day', from 10cc's following album, *The Original Soundtrack* (1975), is a soliloquy of the nine-to-five existence of the average individual. The lyrics are written in second person, addressing an unspecified character working in an unspecified job, the sentiment being that it could be about anybody listening to the song. Kevin Godley and Lol Creme, the song's writers, would later reprise and refine the topic matter of 'Brand New Day' in their first post-10cc single 'Five O'clock in the Morning' from *Consequences* (1977), a triple album whose songs also focused closely on aspects of contemporary everyday paranoia and its myriad social contexts.

The focus in 10cc's music on social pathology and paranoia was consolidated in 1976 with the release of the band's fourth album *How Dare You!* (the last 10cc album to feature songwriting and musical contributions from Kevin Godley and

Lol Crème; see also Chapter 6).[1] Commenting upon the imminent release of *How Dare You!*, band member Graham Gouldman explained in an interview for British music newspaper *Melody Maker* that the album contained songs about divorce, obsession with money, a psychopath and someone who wants to rule the world. Although 10cc never claimed to have released concept albums, many of the songs included on their albums, particularly those released between 1973 and 1976, were conceptually linked. This is probably most keenly observed in the case of *How Dare You!*, where six out of the nine tracks included on the album focus on an individual problem or dilemma and are sung in first person – an approach that acutely accentuates the personally inflected nature of the material. If the music of 10cc is often said to exemplify the more adventurous elements of popular music in the 1970s, then similarly the band's lyrics often speak directly to the social and individual dysfunctionalities of the decade. While the 1960s have been described as an era during which social norms were challenged, and in some cases subverted, the 1970s are frequently seen to be a darker era, characterized by social-psychological insecurities and the dawning of what is now more readily referred to as 'therapy culture' (Furedi, 2004). If the 1960s were symbolic of a challenge to the technocratic, progress-obsessed mode of Western society from without (Roszak, 1969), then the 1970s witnessed the start of that same society's unravelling from within. In songs such as 'I Wanna Rule the World', 'Iceberg' and 'Art for Art's Sake', *How Dare You!* points in a very direct fashion to the social disease that was beginning to eat away at the fabric of everyday existence, these songs respectively discussing issues of material greed, neurosis and psychopathy. 'Art for Art's Sake', a number 5 hit in the UK for 10cc in late 1975, plays on the 19th century French slogan which declares that art should be considered a form of expression free from any utilitarian value. Against this notion, however, the song pitches a refrain declaring 'money for god's sake', suggesting that for many the accumulation of personal wealth has become an essentially quasi-religious practice. This sentiment is then driven home by messages in the song's lyrics regarding the significance of money as a form of power, in love, work and political aspirations. In essence, 'Art for Art's Sake' can be read as a track that explores the emerging neo-liberal obsession with wealth and status as this was beginning to assert itself during the mid-1970s at the time of the album's release.

The issue of personal power, and its potential for abuse, is also a topic of 'I Wanna Rule the World'. The song's lyrics are based upon the perspective of a young school boy bullied and excluded by his classmates who stereotype him as a 'weakling'. This progresses to the point where the school boy develops sociopathic tendencies centred around a lust for power that trades in delusional episodes reminiscent of those displayed by James Thuber's (1939) Walter Mitty character in his short story *The Secret Life of Walter Mitty*. Similarly, the song 'Iceberg' delves into the mind of a psychopath stalking their prey on the streets of New York, a city that during the 1970s had become synonymous in the public imagination with crime of every description. At a deeper level, the song indirectly draws on the media moral panics (Cohen, 1987) of the time that depicted New York as a haven for sinister characters such as the one described in the song who, along with others such as muggers, sex offenders and drug dealers, functioned to make the city's streets inherently unsafe to walk through at night. As with most of the material written by 10cc at this point in the band's career, the songs approach their topic matter in a comically satirical fashion. Nevertheless, the themes addressed in these songs and the lyrical approaches employed do provide a clear illustration of how progressive pop, if less obviously political in the sentiment of its song material, nevertheless maintained a focus on social issues and social ills.

The themes of Roxy Music's songs during the early 1970s also frequently explored a range of dark and often socially taboo topics. This aspect of the band's music was significantly accentuated by singer Bryan Ferry, whose vocal style, at this time relatively unique in the world of rock and pop, was highly suited to conveying the complex web of individual angst and emotional insecurity that played into the lyrics of many of the band's songs. In his essay 'The Grain of the Voice', Barthes (1990) suggests that the voice acts as a form of bodily communication that subverts and circumvents linguistic processes to convey meaning in a more universal and intuitive sense. In the latter years of Roxy Music, Ferry was noted for the smooth, crooner style of his voice. During the initial years of the band, however, Ferry's voice possessed an edgy and often tense quality that has since drawn comparisons, among others, with David Byrne, lead singer of the US new wave band Talking Heads. This quality in Ferry's early singing with Roxy Music lent a bizarre and sometimes macabre feel to songs such as 'In Every Home a Heartache' and 'The Bogus Man', both from Roxy Music's second album *For Your Pleasure* released in March 1973. The first of these tracks focuses on a blow-up doll (fast becoming a popular sex toy during the early 1970s) and the underlying sexual frustrations of a user who otherwise lives in a state of middle-class affluence with all of the associated and highly prized home comforts. This song is followed on the album by 'The Bogus Man' an altogether more sinister song but one that also focuses on the dysfunctional nature of a society increasingly riddled with social and psychological problems of a deep seated nature. 'The Bogus Man' plays on the potent myth of the bogey man (Warner, 2011), a mythical figure across many different cultures and typically used by parents to warn children off acts of bad behaviour. In the song, the fear generated by the bogey man is focused on adults through its depiction of a character in the contemporary urban landscape who acquires enjoyment though following people and instilling fear in them. The actual goal of the 'bogus man' character is never fully explained in the song, but the lyrics hint at themes of intimidation, sexual assault, abduction and murder. The 'bogus man' thus becomes a composite of the various folk devils, real and imagined, that prey on the ordinary citizen (both in reality and in the mind) and convert the apparently safe and mundane spaces of suburbia into zones of fear and paranoia.

The pathology of self-absorbing wealth obsession is also a topic of the Queen song 'Good Company' from the band's breakthrough album *A Night at the Opera* (1975). Although Queen's lyrics are generally held to be socially and politically vacuous, several tracks during the band's career did address more socially and politically themed issues, with two songs in particular from the album *The Works* (1984), 'Hammer to Fall' and 'Is This the World We Created?' speaking to topical themes of the time, notably the escalation of the Cold War and the famine in Ethiopia. While 'Good Company' lacks this more consciousness-raising intent, its anecdotal narrative of a life spent building a career and an obsession with business concerns at the expense of meaningful personal relationships was a theme that harked back at some level to the late 1960s counterculture's discontent with mainstream social values and focuses on the fall-out from this kind of existence. Themes of loneliness and frustration resulting from self-obsession and misplaced values are also evident in several songs from Cockney Rebel. The track 'All Men Are Hungry' from the 1976 album *Timeless Flight* depicts a male character who is growing to appreciate the finite nature of human existence. This is accompanied by a realization that a childlike sense of time as boundless can have only a limited sense of satisfaction and, in many instances, results in a nostalgic yearning for youth. A yearning for a return to the innocence of childhood is also present in the song 'Everything Changes' (1976), where such innocence is pitched against the protagonist's memories of having served in the army, lamenting the fate of many young soldiers who are in many cases barely old enough to carry a rifle. In the song 'Psychomodo' (1974) from the album of the same name, Harley takes the topic of alienation and disillusionment further, pre-empting punk and grunge commentaries on teen and post-teen life with lyrics that reference addiction, schizophrenia and suicide. As the song suggests, even in the pre-punk years of the early 1970s, economic decline and social fragmentation were beginning to instil feelings of anomie and powerlessness in British youth.

Aliens and the (post)apocalypse

During the late 1950s and early 1960s, there had been growing concern about the increasing threat to world peace and possibility of nuclear annihilation due to the escalation of the Cold War between the United States and the Soviet Union. At its most extreme, the resulting widespread public and official concern had seen a proliferation of home-made fallout shelters and the practicing of the notorious 'duck and cover' action in schools around the United States in preparation for the possible event of a nuclear attack. The 1960s saw various protest songs against the mounting aggression between the world's superpowers, with more famous examples including Bob Dylan's (1963) 'Masters of War' and Barry McGuire's (1965) 'Eve of Destruction'. During the 1970s such direct concern with the threat of a nuclear war was less evident in popular music until the end of the decade, with songs such as the Clash's (1979) 'London Calling'. When such 'end of the world' images did arise in early seventies popular music, they were more cryptically discussed with reference to various themes ranging from escape, as in the Kinks' (1972) 'Supersonic Rocket Ship', to transformations that might alter the path of humanity and what might become of the human race as it sought to rebuild a new world from the ashes of the old. These latter themes were nowhere more evident than in the work of David Bowie, whose three consecutive albums *Hunky Dory* (1971), *The Rise and Fall of Ziggy Stardust and the Spiders from Mars* (1972) and *Aladdin Sane* (1973) each contained tracks that dealt directly with these topics. 'Oh You Pretty Things' (1971), a song that was initially recorded and released by Peter Noone (singer with sixties pop group Herman's Hermits), discussed the possible decline of the latter-day human race to be replaced by a more superior race of beings. Hinted at in the lyrics is that the so-called 'homo superior' might result from a convergence between alien visitors to earth and the youth culture of the time. Stories of the 'troubled times' of the early 1970s continued with Bowie's transformation into Ziggy Stardust, the persona that was to ultimately bring the artist international fame (Bennett, 2017). In the early days of Ziggy Stardust and his backing band, the Spiders from Mars, however, it was British teen audiences who first came to witness and experience the strange spectacle of Ziggy Stardust's androgynous alien figure, gracing music television shows such as *Top of the Pops* and touring medium-sized venues right across the country, including in provincial cities and towns most badly hit by the national recession. In these social and economically grim environments, Ziggy introduced songs such as 'Five Years' and 'Starman' to a disenfranchised youth audience who were trying to make sense of the rapidly changing world around them. 'Five Years', the opening track of *The Rise and Fall of Ziggy Stardust and the Spiders from Mars* (1972), is an anthem to the apocalypse that many feared would overtake the earth through either natural or manmade causes (or a combination of both). At its heart, the song depicted the demise of the earth over a five-year period, though equally it could have been read at the time as the prophecy of a cataclysmic event that would occur after a period five years – an event such as a nuclear war or the impact of an asteroid. The despairing tone of the music and the increasing hysteria in the tone of Bowie's voice offer the listener little relief as the song depicts the fear and anxiety of the human race being forced to face the fact that Earth's days are numbered. The track 'Starman', also from the *Ziggy Stardust* album, again speaks of imminent change occurring on earth, but this time due to the arrival of an alien from another world, whose introduction to the human race, although initially an unsettling prospect, will ultimately bring about positive change away from the destructive path that humanity has found itself on. In an age where belief in aliens and other worlds continued to grow, buoyed up by other popular culture offerings, such as Stanley Kubrick's *2001: A Space Odyssey* (an early inspiration for Bowie, see Trynka, 2011) and popular US television shows such as *Lost in Space* and *Star Trek* (which also had significant audiences in Britain), 'Starman's more optimistic tone and lyrics suggested the coming of a new age, where humanity could benefit positively from alien contact. Bowie's follow-up album *Aladdin Sane* (1973) also contained a track that dealt with the future of humanity, this time struggling to rediscover its humanness in a post-apocalyptic world. 'Drive in Saturday' was apparently inspired by an unusual luminosity witnessed by Bowie on a night train travelling through a deserted landscape in 1972 during a tour of the United States. With reference to intense heat, radioactive fallout and 'strange ones' living in a dome, the track, which draws musically on 1950s doo-wop, focuses on how the youth inhabitants of this future world look back at images of popular culture icons, notably Mick Jagger and British model Twiggy, using these icons as role models of how to be and behave in a time devoid of such icons. The conjuring up of such images in

'Drive in Saturday' suggests that despite the despairing times of the early 1970s, future generations may actually look back to the era as a 'golden age' and thus draw inspiration from it to rebuild their own lives and cultural identities in a desolate, post-apocalyptic world.

New awakenings

Thus far it has been established that if the British popular music of the early 1970s was ostensibly less invested in the more hard-edged political messages that had characterized the political rock and other music during the late 1960s, it would at the same time be erroneous to suggest that all of the music emerging during this period was without a sociopolitical conscience. Rather, the oppositional stance of the popular music of early 1970s Britain, it has been argued, was fashioned according to a different range of issues, these often assuming a more micropolitical aspect. Indeed, if politics continued as an element of music at this time, then it was often centred upon a more everyday form of cultural politics, including the politics of individual identity. Most striking in this respect were the beginnings of a challenge towards then dominant notions of male identity and masculinity. In truth, the early manifestations of this in popular music had been seen much earlier with American artists such as Little Richard (White, 1994) and, towards the end of the 1960s, the Velvet Underground (Cagle, 1995). In Britain, however, if the music had been revolutionary in some ways during the 1960s, then this did not extend in any overt sense to gender politics. During the early 1970s, however, the emergence of glam rock offered an alternative rendering of gender identities and ways of performing them. Interestingly it was those artists positioned at the 'high glam' end of the spectrum (see Trynka, 2011), those identified in this book as a part of the 1970s progressive pop movement, who made the most strident contributions to glam rock's gender-bending stance. Among these artists, David Bowie was an early trendsetter, subverting the then dominant hyper-masculine ethos of the rock singer (Frith and McRobbie, 1990) with a radically new look that saw him and his band wearing sequined cat suits, lipstick, eyeliner and other elements of facial make-up. As Bowie's new persona, topped off with the fictional alias of Ziggy Stardust, developed, his cat suit was traded for a leotard, an image that made his look increasingly androgynous (Hebdige, 1979). It was during this period, in 1972, that Bowie was caught on camera by photographer Mick Rock performing what resembled fellatio on the guitar of bandmate Mick Ronson during a performance in Birmingham, England. Featured as a full-page spread in British music newspaper *Melody Maker*, the image of Bowie kneeling in front of Ronson and clutching the guitarist's buttocks caused mild controversy (Trynka, 2011). It was, however, an image that resonated well with a sea change that was being ushered in by glam and one that went beyond the middle-class art-school audiences that, up until that time, had been regarded as rock's only 'natural' audience in Britain. Indeed, as Taylor and Wall (1976) note, Bowie's experimentation with this radical new look also piqued the interest and imagination of working-class youth, the new comprehensive schools around Britain at this time being notable for the many teenage Bowie lookalikes to be seen in playgrounds and classrooms (see also Chapter 3).

Others in the British pop world of the time reinforced Bowie's message to youth that a shakedown of the nation's traditionally gendered society was in the air. Notable here was Roxy Music, a band who crafted an image that was equally challenging to the dominant and accepted image of the male rock star at that point in time. With band members Bryan Ferry, Andy McKay and Brian Eno all having studied at art school, Roxy Music was among the first British rock bands to carefully craft an image alongside their music as means of ensuring a distinctive appearance and 'brand'. Although referred to as a glam rock band in their early days, like Bowie it is clear in retrospect that while Roxy Music may have drawn on aspects of the glam aesthetic, this was done in a highly self-reflexive way – and one that regarded the glam image as a vehicle through which to bring their music to a wider, rock-pop crossover audience. Nevertheless, as with Bowie, Roxy Music's early publicity, including their appearances on *Top of the Pops* (*TOTP*), cut a striking pose and one that hinted at a sexuality which deviated from the more clearly defined and hegemonic male look of many of their rock and pop peers. This was nowhere more pronounced than with Brian Eno (then referred to simply as Eno), whose varnished finger nails, eye liner and lipstick, pale complexion, rail-thin physique and slender hands rendered him an interesting and highly distinctive figure in the iconography of early 1970s British rock and pop. Equally remarkable was his 'musical' role in Roxy Music. At that point, young *TOTP* viewers were well used to seeing male rock and pop stars brandishing electric guitars or striking imposing postures from behind a microphone. Eno did neither of these things. As one of the first synthesizer players to appear on *TOTP*, Eno's musical role in Roxy Music appeared to amount to pushing buttons and twirling knobs, a role that was well removed from what many young viewers understood to be what a rock musician did. In effect, like Bowie, Eno appeared as a kind of androgynous alien, taking this stance further through mysteriously tinkering with technology in a way that, to the untutored ear at least, seemed to have little to do with the music that the rest of the band were producing. Just as Roxy Music's collective image subverted the dominant modes of male posturing associated with rock and pop bands at the time, Eno's then unconventional musical contributions to the band's sound offered its own form of subversion through its suggestion of Eno as a 'non-musician', a term he would subsequently come to embrace and further explore in his subsequent solo work (Tamm, 1995).

Another British band whose image served to challenge the dominant male sexuality associated with rock during the early 1970s was Queen. Certainly, when Queen first appeared on *TOTP* in April 1974, their featured song on that occasion, 'Seven Seas of Rhye', while demonstrating an exceptionally high degree of musical competence, offered few clues as to the music the band would subsequently produce over the coming years. At that point, Queen appeared as a high-quality hard rock band with the classic hard rock line-up of lead singer, guitarist, bass player and drummer. And yet, like Bowie and Roxy Music, Queen deviated from the staple rock image of the day. With all four members of the band possessing higher education qualifications (a fact that was in itself unusual at this time in the world of rock and pop), the manner of Queen was more erudite and articulate than many other artists associated with British rock and pop at this time. The band's visual image also suggested an air of difference, a flamboyance and attention to detail in terms of fashion not routinely associated with hard rock bands at the time. Prior to their debut appearance in *TOTP*, in January 1974 Queen had travelled to Australia to play at the Sunbury Festival in Victoria. Reports as to how the group was received vary, but it is clear that Queen's image confused a predominately white, male audience who heckled the band and issued homophobic remarks during their set (see Hawkings, 2014; Hodkinson, 1995). The reception of Queen in the UK was certainly more positive, but mild controversy pertaining to the band and their 'sexuality' was also apparent. Within this, it was the band's lead singer Freddie Mercury who attracted most attention. Although Mercury would later declare himself to be bisexual, at the point when Queen emerged onto the British popular music scene, no such statement had been made and the speculation about the singer's sexuality was largely based on his image. A few years after Queen's significant commercial success and rapid rise to stardom, Simon Frith and Angela McRobbie (1990) published an essay in which they outlined what they saw as the defining characteristics of the typical male rock vocalist's hegemonic masculinity. While Mercury is inevitably not mentioned in the essay due to his by then overtly articulated bisexuality, in his early years as Queen front-man, many of the qualities outlined by Frith and McRobbie could just as easily have been assigned to Mercury. And yet, through a subtle deviation in his portrayal of the male rock singer, even during Queen's formative years, there was a quality in Mercury's rock-pop persona that aligned him far more readily with the more ambiguous male sexuality of artists such as David Bowie and Roxy Music than with other male rock vocalists (including those referenced by Frith and McRobbie) such as Led Zeppelin's Robert Plant and Deep Purple's David Coverdale (who replaced former vocalist Ian Gillan in 1973). Such features included the eye liner, back nail varnish and fur coat worn by Mercury for Queen's *TOTP* appearance in November 1974 to promote their new single 'Killer Queen'.

Partying in the ruins

In discussing the appeal of David Bowie as an emerging artist in early 1970s Britain, Trynka suggests:

> [Bowie's] blend of space-age futurism and glamour lodged in the consciousness of a generation in sore need of escapism ... References to the 1920s Weimer Republic, or 1930s Hollywood and Art Deco, and even the threadbare glamour of Edwardian music hall – all images of partying amid the ruins – pervaded David's music, as it did that of emerging rivals like Roxy Music's Bryan Ferry; this was their time. (2011: 163)

In the context of Britain's escalating economic decline during the early 1970s, this is a highly telling statement. Against an increasingly bleak backdrop of rampant socio-economic decline, the fact that much of the music listened to by young Britons appeared to evade head-on discussion of such a grim reality might in itself have proved a subversive medium for fans of artists such as Bowie, Roxy Music and indeed the other progressive pop artists discussed here. As noted at various points in this book, rock music in the 1970s retained an aura of 'high seriousness' while at the same jettisoning the claims of its late 1960s predecessor to world-changing potential. Rock in the early 1970s proved to be a very different animal, as did its audience. The endgame by and large became not one of trying to change the world but rather trying to create and sustain a meaningful existence within an everyday reality, which seemed increasingly to close down options for a generation of youth striving to find its voice. Certainly, factions of British youth remained political during the early 1970s, as seen for example through student involvement in groups such as the Socialist Review Group (which later became the Socialist Workers Party) and the Campaign for Nuclear Disarmament (CND). However, such political sensibilities among youth appeared to roam free from any direct anticipation of music, and specifically rock music, as a unifying call to arms at this point. Punk would realign the connection between music and social change to a significant degree, but at this point, punk was still some years away and British youth in the early 1970s were thus wary and, to a fair extent, weary of the hippie rhetoric of old.

Through its appropriation of the new rock sensibilities of the early 1970s, progressive pop resonated with youth's desire to distance itself from the more radicalized stance assumed by much of the rock music associated with the late 1960s. This stance had dramatically unravelled during the ugly scenes at Altamont, where a festival-goer was stabbed to death amidst mounting unrest in the audience (Schowalter, 2000), and the glaring contradictions of the counterculture's professed rejection of the technocracy (Roszak, 1969) whilst readily buying into those forms of commodification that serviced countercultural ends – specifically, music, fashion and drugs (that latter having also become a major 'industry' for hippie youth by the later 1960s). Tarnished by such contradictory features of rock's countercultural associations, progressive pop and its audience appeared to embrace the significance of music as something of a Tabula rasa during the early 1970s, looking towards its renewed energy as something that could continue to ignite a sense of youth cultural 'togetherness' while at the same time sidestepping the overblown claims of rock musicians and their music during the late 1960s. In the event, however, British youth found themselves in a far more precarious socio-economic state as the 1970s wore on than had been the case for the previous youth generation. Faced with these gritty circumstances, music became a form of escapism. Progressive pop with its range of sometimes spectacular and carnivalesque figures and its song craft – sometimes comic, often satirical and occasionally lifting the lid on dark and taboo aspects of everyday life – brought a lightness and bearability to a period when so much in the lives of young people seemed to be subject to repression from outside forces. Still coming to terms with itself as a post-colonial nation and teetering on the brink of a new political era that would see its industrial base rapidly dismantled, Britain in the early 1970s was a place of transition. For British youth, the colourful world of progressive pop provided a necessary subversion, the often lavish production of records from Queen and David Bowie through to 10cc and ELO offering moments of transcendence. During the long nights as houses around the UK were plunged into darkness due to power cuts, battery-powered radios and portable cassette players became vital accessories for youth whose bedroom culture (McRobbie and Garber, 1976) ensured an ongoing connection between youth and its music during this bleak period in Britain's post-war history.

As noted previously, progressive pop was also very much a live music too. And in the Britain of the early 1970s, a time before the UK acquired the arena-sized venues common at that time across the United States, touring frequently meant appearing at smaller venues dotted around the country. For example, on their 1973 tour, Queen played a string of concerts at places such as St Georges (Blackburn), Victoria Hall (Hanley), Civic Hall (Wolverhampton), Kursall (Southend) and County Hall (Taunton). Similarly, in the same year 10cc's British tour took them to venues including the Palace Lido (Douglas, Isle of Man), Woods Leisure Centre (Colchester), Flamingo Ballroom (Hereford), Top of the World (Stafford) and the Baths Hall (Scunthorpe). Such performance settings, many of them in provincial towns, provided a degree of intimacy between performer and audience and would often give rise to a party atmosphere. In an era before pop video and the internet, a live concert performance by a nationally profiled band in a local venue continued to be primary form of leisure for youth fans of popular music – a chance to meet friends and socialize while at the same time seeing their favourite band or artist. As progressive pop artists became bigger, they would outgrow such small provincial venues, gravitating to the new bigger venues that started to appear in the UK's regions at the end of the 1970s and into the 1980s. For a brief period of time, however, and in one of the bleakest periods of Britain's economic crisis, progressive pop and its audience connected as the bands strove to find their musical feet in front of young fans who were happy for moments of communal distraction from thoughts of the uncertain future that presented itself in their daily lives and punctuated by gloomy reports in the British media.

Conclusion

This chapter has explored the connections between progressive pop and political themes emerging in Britain during the early 1970s. At the outset, it was noted how the staunchly political voice of many popular music artists during the late 1960s was absent in the British popular music of the early 1970s, this also extending to progressive pop artists. This, it was explained, reflected to a fair extent a wariness and weariness on the part of artists and their audiences with many of the overblown claims that had been made during the late 1960s concerning the capacity of popular music to engage with politics and bring positive change in the world. By the early 1970s, if rock music continued as a discourse pertaining to the high-art qualities of many particular popular music artists and their music, this did not extend to a political agenda as such. That said, however, there was at the same time a critical quality in progressive pop, with many artists using their music, and in many cases their image too, to question social values and conventions as these began to unravel during the early 1970s. Bands such as 10cc and Roxy Music, it has been noted, considered in their songs some of the deep-seated social pathologies that were manifesting in the early 1970s, ranging from obsessions with material wealth to sexual frustration and psychopathology. Roxy Music, David Bowie and Queen became leading figures in a new sexual revolution that challenged then dominant male stereotypes and forms of hegemonic masculinity based around a softer and more androgynous look. Particular songs of David Bowie during this period picked up on increasing public fears of nuclear war and the apocalypse during the early 1970s as the Cold War escalated and also mused over how the decade might one day come to be regarded as a golden age by a post-apocalyptic youth of the future. Finally, it was considered how in an era where it was still common for relatively high-profile bands and artists to play smaller venues in the UK due to the absence at that point of a regional area-circuit, progressive pop bands were able to reach out to their audience in the relatively intimate setting of small, provincial venues. Such settings allowed an artist and their audience to connect in a way that, according to punk, was lost once artists began playing in larger, arena-style venues (see Laing, 1985). As such, progressive pop became an important, if temporal, antidote for British youth audiences who were frustrated as the nation slipped into economic decline.

Note

1 Godley and Creme also contributed vocals (including a lead vocal from Godley on the song 'The Stars Didn't Show') to 10cc's 1992 album *Meanwhile*. Although promoted as a reunion of the original 10cc line-up by Polydor, who released the album, *Meanwhile* comprised songs written by Eric Stewart and Graham Gouldman backed by a number of session musicians, including bassist Freddie Washington and guitarist Michael Landau. Drummer Jeff Porcaro and Paul McCartney also made guest appearances on the album.

6

The end of an era

Introduction

The year 1977 is often perceived as a watershed moment in the history of British popular music. More specifically, 1977 is generally considered to be the year during which punk took hold of the popular music industry in Britain and begun to radically reshape it (see, for example, Chambers, 1985). There can be little doubt regarding the impact of punk in Britain and in particular its impact on British youth for whom punk's extreme visual style and outspoken DIY (do-it-yourself) quality made it a highly accessible cultural medium through which young people could vent their collective frustration as the nation went into a critical and sustained period of economic decline (Hebdige, 1979). Punk music was also praised by the British music press for its back-to-basics approach, whereby a lack of musical expertise on the part of punk artists was transformed from a hindrance into a positive virtue (Toynbee, 1993). In this way, punk set out to distance itself from much of the popular music that had characterized the first half of the 1970s. Assuming a staunchly anti-rock stance, punk decried the perceived musical excesses and artistic pretention of artists such as Led Zeppelin, Pink Floyd, Emerson, Lake and Palmer, Yes and Genesis. In taking popular music into the realms of large-scale production, both in the studio and in a live context, these artists, it was claimed by punk, had deserted the spirit of the rock-and-roll aesthetic that had created so much excitement in popular music during the 1950s and early 1960s (Laing, 1985). Unsurprisingly, given the nature of its critical onslaught, progressive pop artists such as Queen, 10cc and ELO also became something of a target for punk's criticisms concerning the increasing aloofness of British popular music during the pre-punk 1970s.

Such was the anti-rock rhetoric of punk and those who supported it in British popular music press publications, such as the *New Musical Express* (see Laing,

1994). Certainly, however, and despite the undeniable element of hype in the posturing of punk, it was clear that a new game was afoot and was one that would ultimately usurp rock's dominant position in British popular music, with many rock artists who had emerged during the late 1960s and early 1970s failing to survive into the 1980s without any discernible disruption in their careers. To say, however, that punk represented a sudden and wholesale transformation in British popular music would be inaccurate. The transformations that punk did instigate were more gradual than is often represented in retrospective accounts of punk's reach and influence and many artists, including those identified in this book as progressive pop, continued to enjoy significant levels of commercial success even at the height of punk. Indeed, the years 1977 and 1978 were highly diverse ones in the sphere of British pop, issuing some surprises including a clutch of radio-friendly singles by some of the more staunchly AOR-positioned progressive rock bands as well as the emergence of some fresh talents who would propel a new era of progressive elements in British popular music into the 1980s and beyond. In the long run, however, survival in this new musical climate would not be possible without a degree of evolution, and while some progressive pop artists were capable of making this transition intact, others were not.

Are they talking about us?

The air of tension in the British popular music world that was created by the first stirrings of punk in late 1976 and early 1977 was difficult to ignore. Whether or not they expressed this openly at the time or not, many established British popular music artists perceived punk as a threat. Indeed, one of the more notorious punk moments, and something that would also instantly cast punks as folk devils and create a moral panic (Cohen, 1987) around the punk scene in Britain, began with a seemingly harmless decision made in the EMI offices in late 1976. Queen, who by then had become one of the most successful signings to EMI during the 1970s, were due to appear on *Today*, a current affairs programme screened on prime-time television. When Queen were forced to cancel their appearance at short notice, EMI suggested that the Sex Pistols, a new (and as it was to turn out relatively short-lived) signing to the label, take their place on the *Today* programme. What is generally remembered about the Sex Pistols' appearance on *Today*, which took place on 1 December 1976, is the programme's presenter Bill Grundy goading the band into swearing on live television in front of a family audience. Indeed, as Laing observes, in the space of a one-minute, forty-second interview, Grundy 'managed to sketch in the popular stereotype of punk' (1985: 36). What is less reliably remembered, however, are the moments leading up the tirade of expletives that shocked the nation's parents and excited much of its youth, when Grundy compared the Sex Pistols to Mozart and Beethoven with the express purpose of suggesting that the band's music was inferior, inherently uncultured and perhaps unworthy of any claim to actually being classed as 'music' at all. Sex Pistols' bassist of the time Glen Matlock had made a quirky retort that these *great* composers were 'all dead', which succinctly asserted a deeper sensibility of punk, pronouncing its 'of-the-moment' vitality over the top-heavy assertions of worth frequently ascribed to existing forms of music, including the more recent and, in punk's view, creatively dead contributions of artists in the rock and progressive rock vein.

Punk's antipathy towards the establishment and what it regarded to be 'establishment music' (both more recent and historically) was thus forcibly communicated. At the same time, however, and despite the media hype, both pro- and anti-punk, the relationship between punk and the existing forms of rock and pop music was by no means one of complete sonic and stylistic separation. Indeed, the tenacity of this alleged rock-punk bifurcation encapsulates one of the most enduring myths of punk as somehow throwing down the gauntlet for rock during 1977 in what is often romantically depicted as a musical year zero. Most obviously, punk, by and large, still relied on the familiar guitar-bass-drums musical format established through rock, while many punk bands, from the most celebrated likes of the Sex Pistols and American counterparts the Ramones through to other more locally profiled British acts such as Sham 69 and 999, preserved the classic four-piece line-up of lead vocals, lead guitarist, bass guitarist and drummer that was also a staple in rock music at the time. Similarly, while Punk's back-to-basics approach clearly set it apart from the more technical arrangements of bands such as 10cc, Queen, ELO and their progressive rock counterparts, at the same time punk was not the musical free-for-all that it was often professed to be (including in the British music press). Many punk musicians had had earlier careers in bands that formed part of London's early 1970s pub rock scene (see Laing, 1985). For example the Clash's Joe Strummer had previously been in pub rock band The 101ers (Friedlander, 1996). Similarly, other bands, such as the Jam and the Stranglers, although initially aligning themselves with the punk scene to gain exposure (in much the same way as Bowie and Roxy Music had aligned themselves with glam to the same ends during the 1970s; see Chapter 2) subsequently developed musical directions that took them away from punk. This is evident, for example, in the Strangler's 1982 hit 'Golden Brown', which features a harpsichord and combines 3/4 and 4/4 timing to create a highly distinctive arrangement that connotes a radical departure from their previous guitar and electronic keyboard-driven singles. Similarly, as their career progressed, the Jam embraced an increasingly eclectic range of influences as heard, for example, in their 1980 hit 'Start' (featuring a guitar and bass riff reminiscent of the Beatles' song 'Taxman') and the white soul sound adopted towards the end of the band's career, notably in the single 'A Town Called Malice', released in January 1982 and achieving the number 1 position in the British charts. Finally, the Sex Pistols' first and, as it was to turn out, only original album, *Never Mind the Bollocks* (1977), was produced by Chris Thomas, who had previously worked with the likes of the Beatles, Pink Floyd, Procul Harem, Queen and Roxy Music; and Bill Price, who had previously worked with Mott the Hoople. Contrary to punk's allegedly anti-musician stance, the Sex Pistols' new bass player, Sid Vicious (who replaced Glen Matlock in early 1977), was not considered competent enough by Thomas and Price to play on the sessions for *Never Mind the Bollocks*, with the result that the majority of the bass tracks were later added by Steve Jones, the band's guitarist.[1] While it was certainly a rawer sounding record than many other albums around at the time, *Never Mind the Bollocks* also exhibits a number of established rock traits such as layered rhythm guitars, overdubbed guitar solos and other embellishments. There are also several indications of rock influences on musical techniques employed on the album, notably the crisp and perfectly timed bass and snare syncopation played by drummer Paul Cook that provides the segue from the first to second verse of the track 'God Save the Queen' (a moment that is reminiscent of Beatles' drummer Ringo Starr's similar work on 'The End', the penultimate track on the 1969 album *Abbey Road*).

Despite such continuities between rock and punk, however, the emergence of punk undoubtedly sent shock waves through the music industry, and its antagonistic affront towards the rock establishment did not go unnoticed. Led Zeppelin vocalist Robert Plant was apparently seen at several early punk gigs in London (Fyfe, 2003), and much of the British rock music that appeared in the wake of punk's emergence exhibited an obvious punk influence, notably a new generation of heavy metal artists that attracted the label New Wave of British Heavy Metal (NWOBHM). NWOBHM was distinctive for its fusion of punk and metal styles (Waksman, 2009), a notable example being the band Motörhead. Lemmy, the singer-bassist-frontman of Motörhead, was a former member of British post-psychedelic space-rock band Hawkwind, among whose followers were several notable British punks, including Sex Pistols lead vocalist Johnny Rotten (see Clerk, 2006). Other established British bands displayed a discernible shift in musical orientation in the wake of punk. For example, Pink Floyd's 1977 studio album *Animals*, loosely based on George Orwell's (1945) allegorical novella *Animal Farm*, is musically and lyrically darker and more aggressive sounding than the band's previous two albums *Dark Side of the Moon* (1973) and *Wish You Were Here* (1975). This quality remained apparent with the follow-up to *Animals*, 1979's *The Wall*, which produced Pink Floyd's first hit single in twelve years, 'Another Brick in the Wall (Part 2)' (see also Chapter 2). This song quickly gained notoriety as an anti-school anthem whose lyrics may well have been a nod to punk's anti-hegemonic stance in their focus on the everyday anxieties experienced by many British schoolchildren, both then and since, during the course of their primary and secondary education.

The arrival of punk also registered in the British progressive pop world, but the effects of its arrival there were uneven, with some artists finding themselves more negatively impacted by punk than others. In the case of David Bowie, for example, it is clear that his music, both during the artist's tenure as Ziggy Stardust and during his post-Ziggy era, pre-empted punk to a fair degree with his 1977 hit 'Heroes' in particular appearing to slot seamlessly into the punk soundscape. On the whole, however, for those artists who had contributed to the progressive pop era in the early 1970s, the advent of punk and its successor new wave were the catalyst for a noticeable and unwelcome change in the way that their music was increasingly responded to by significant sections of the British record-buying public and the British music press. A palpable indication of this change came in 1978 when Bob Harris, long-time presenter of the British AOR-focused television programme the *Old Grey Whistle Test* (*OGWT*) (see also Chapter 2), left the show to be replaced by Annie Nightingale. Harris had first come under fire among a younger generation of music fans when he referred to US proto-punk band the New York Dolls as 'mock rock' following their appearance on *OGWT* in November 1973. In 1977 it is reported that Harris was assaulted by punk icon Sid Vicious amidst mounting criticisms of *OGWT*'s elitism, judged among other things by its failure to invite punk artists onto the programme. With Nightingale at the helm, *OGWT* quickly reversed this trend and began to feature an increasing number of punk and new-wave acts. As a consequence, the programme was able to distance itself from its former reputation as a show exclusively committed to the promotion of AOR artists and their music.

Even in 1977, as the presence of punk in the UK was fully asserted, however, there were also some surprises in the world of British popular music. For example, in October of that year ELO released what would turn out to be their most successful album (and one with some established traits of a 'concept' album at that). More surprising still, despite the fact that they were very much a central focus for punk's repulsion at the state of British popular music, a number of progressive rock artists had major chart success in 1977 (and in the following year), suggesting that as these artists began to feel hemmed in by punk, progressive pop's demonstrated ability to bring more ambitious music into the British charts served as a source of inspiration for high-profile progressive rock bands such as Yes, Genesis and Emerson Lake and Palmer together with several less well-known artists from the progressive rock genre such as Renaissance and Gordon Giltrap. Finally, the year 1977 saw the re-emergence of Peter Gabriel, former Genesis vocalist who had left the band in 1975, with a new solo album, while in 1978 newcomer Kate Bush (whose influences included Pink Floyd and Peter Gabriel-era Genesis) scored a number 1 hit with her debut single 'Wuthering Heights' based on the Emily Brontë (1847) novel of the same name. During the late 1970s and into the early 1980s, artists such as these would successfully negotiate the rapidly shifting territory of British popular music, reshaping some elements of progressive pop for a new era and a new audience in the age of pop video.

Mixed fortunes

For many progressive pop artists, survival beyond the mid-1970s demanded a significant degree of musical change, including in most cases an element of stylistic adaptation as well. One of the most obvious examples of this was seen in the case of Queen. As noted in previous chapters of this book, between their emergence in 1973 and the consolidation of their commercial success in 1976, Queen had been a prime example of a band who were able to seamlessly combine AOR and chart music success, appealing as credible rock artists while also producing a string of high-performing pop singles that peaked with 'Bohemian Rhapsody' in late 1975. The enthusiasm of Queen's crossover audience was not, however, shared by the British music press (see Thomas, 1999), and when, in late 1976, Queen found themselves signed to the same record label as the Sex Pistols, several stories appeared, including one that documented a meeting between Sid Vicious and Freddie Mercury where Vicious had allegedly quipped that Queen had succeeded in bringing ballet to the masses, while Mercury apparently responded by referring to Vicious as 'Mr Ferocious'. Irrespective of the accuracy of such stories, they ultimately served to strengthen a music press narrative of bands such as Queen as old fashioned and out of touch with current musical trends and the audiences who followed these new trends. Queen's next album *News of the World*, released in October 1977, following a summer in which the newspapers had been dominated by the apparent outrage caused by the Sex Pistol's single 'God Save the Queen' during Queen Elizabeth II's silver jubilee (see Savage 1992), seemed to respond directly to the criticism the band had received from the British music press and to the undoubted resonance of punk with a significant section of British youth at the time. Unlike previous Queen albums, and particularly the band's two most recent albums at that point, *A Night at the Opera* (1975) and *A Day at the Races* (1976), *News of the World* saw the band adopting a more stripped-back approach to production, featuring far less of the vocal and instrumental layering that had characterized their earlier albums. Consequently, *News of the World* had an instantly more accessible feel to it. Indeed, the first two tracks on Side A of the original vinyl version of the album, Brian May's 'We Will Rock You' and 'We Are the Champions', written by Freddie Mercury, had each been written and recorded with a specific view to eliciting audience participation in a concert setting. It is no great coincidence that in the subsequent years each of these tracks also became significant sporting anthems (see, for example, McLeod, 2016). The rawness exhibited by many of the tracks on *News of the World* continued with the Roger Taylor song 'Sheer Heart Attack'. Originally written for but not completed in time to be included on Queen's third album *Sheer Heart Attack* (1974), the heavy, driving rhythm and somewhat trashy style of the track's arrangement (including a guitar solo comprising of pure feedback) was very much in keeping with punk's musical zeitgeist and also pre-empted the punk-metal style that would become increasingly prominent in the late 1970s and early 1980s. Other tracks on the album, while less punk inspired, also demonstrated a new straight-ahead approach in Queen's music; for example Brian May's blues influenced 'Sleeping on the Sidewalk', for which the rhythm track was apparently recorded in a single take (Doherty, 2011).

Since the release of *News of the World*, Brian May has suggested that rather than constituting a direct response to punk, the idea of a more stripped-back and accessible album had been on Queen's agenda for some time prior to the album's release due to the mixed feedback the band had received following the release of *A Day at the Races* (see Doherty, 2011). Whether *News of the World* was consciously inspired by punk or not, however, the release of the album proved timely and marked a definite change in direction for Queen that would also serve as a blueprint for subsequent albums including *Jazz* (1978) and *The Game* (1980). In the case of the latter album, the featured songs and emerging hits saw Queen attempting to broaden their musical range and, with it, their audience. 'Crazy Little Thing Called Love' incorporated influences from the early rock and roll recordings by Elvis Presley, while 'Another One Bites the Dust', one of three Queen hits written by bass player John Deacon over the course of the band's career, saw Queen further diversifying into funk and disco territory. This would be more fully realized on Queen's 1982 album *Hot Space*, which also included a one-off collaboration with David Bowie on the song 'Under Pressure', Queen's first number 1 hit in the UK since 'Bohemian Rhapsody' in 1975. During the 1980s Queen would go on to be one the most successful bands in the world, becoming the first rock band to tour in South America, in 1981. By that point, however, the richly layered and often complex arrangements of their earlier albums had been replaced by a more pop-dominated style as heard, for example, on mid-1980s hits such as 'Radio Gaga' and 'It's a Kind of Magic'. Only at the end of the 1980s did Queen return to some of the musical reference points evident during the early years of their career with songs such as 'I Want It All' and 'The Miracle', both of which feature-marked tempo changes (something that continues to remain a rarity in the context of pop chart material). Similarly, the song 'Innuendo', released in January 1991, returned more squarely to the territory of 'Bohemian Rhapsody', being six minutes and thirty seconds in length and featuring different sections, including an opera section, and the richly layered vocals characteristic of much of Queen's early work. The track also features sections in 5/4 and 6/4 time, which are again unusual elements in chart-orientated popular music. Like 'Bohemian Rhapsody', 'Innuendo' climbed rapidly to number 1 in the British charts. At this point, however, Queen had become to all intents and purposes a studio band, having given up touring due to the failing health of Freddie Mercury, who had been diagnosed with AIDS in 1987 (Gunn and Jenkins, 1992). Although the details of Mercury's illness were not released to the public until the day before his death, in subsequent years his former band mates Brian May and Roger Taylor revealed the extent of Mercury's resolve to continue making music for as long as his failing health permitted (Doherty, 2011). As such, and with the need to consider how new material would translate into a live performance context no longer an issue, a refocusing of the band on the creative possibilities of the studio was perhaps inevitable, as was the return to some of the more ambitious song formats and arrangements that had established Queen's progressive pop credentials during the early 1970s. *Innuendo* (1991), the last Queen album to appear during Mercury's lifetime (a further album featuring Mercury, *Made in Heaven*, being released several years after his death), is critically considered to be Queen's best album since 1975's *A Night at the Opera* (Thomas, 1999) and is equally diverse in terms of the eclectic range of musical styles featured on the album.

An equally surprising development in 1977, and one that critically demonstrated the British music audience's ongoing appetite for progressive pop sounds even as punk music was increasingly heard on television and radio, was the release of ELO's double album *Out of the Blue*. Released in the same month as *News of the World*, if the former displayed a marked change in the musical direction of Queen, *Out of the Blue* was something of a consolidation in musical direction for ELO, firmly showcasing the sound and style through which the band had earned its reputation during the first half of the 1970s. Indeed, as an album, *Out of the Blue* is interesting for several reasons, not least of all because it appropriates the established progressive rock trope of the double album, complete with a semi-conceptual thread, at the very point in contemporary British popular music history when such components of progressive rock were attracting the harshest criticism, from punk and its supporters. *Concerto for a Rainy Day*, which, in classic progressive rock style, takes up an entire side of the album, culminates with the song 'Mr Blue Sky', which became a top 10 hit for ELO in January 1978. As one of ELO's more obviously Beatles-influenced songs, 'Mr Blue Sky' served as a point of connection for 1970s progressive pop artists to the late 1960s era of experimental pop while at the same time reinforcing progressive pop's established blending of album-orientated rock and mainstream chart music. Becoming one of ELO's most commercially successful albums, eventually achieving worldwide sales of around 10 million copies, *Out of the Blue* represents a consolidation of Jeff Lynne's attempts to blend classical, rock and pop sounds. Most strikingly, at a point where the emphasis in punk was on a more minimalist approach to music-making, on *Out of the Blue*, Lynne expanded the already richly layered musical contours of ELO through taking the decision to hire a full orchestra, in place of ELO's three regular string players, Mik Kaminski (violin), Melvyn Gale (cello) and Hugh McDowell (cello), to play on the album (Shearman, 1983).

In many ways, the unprecedented success of *Out of Blue* marked a pinnacle, if not a swansong moment in progressive pop's seventies legacy as music capable of straddling the progressive rock and chart-orientated pop landscapes. Harking back to the Beatles' *Sgt. Pepper's Lonely Hearts Club Band* (1967) but also likely inspired by the subsequent commercial successes of Yes's (1973) *Tales from Topographic Oceans* and the Genesis's (1974) *The Lamb Lies Down on Broadway*, *Out of the Blue* signified a point when the expressive logic of the concept album, which up until that point was predominantly the preserve of AOR, successfully crossed over into the pop world. Indeed, it is true to say that *Out of the Blue* remains the only example of a British 1970s progressive pop concept album (if only in part) and, artistically speaking, ranks as something of a counter-hegemonic statement given the derision being directed at that time by punk towards the concept album as an illustration of progressive rock's pretentiousness.

Despite the success of *Out of the Blue*, musically speaking, things began to change significantly for ELO beyond that time. While ELO's subsequent album *Discovery* was also a commercial success, reaching number 1 in the UK album charts, it demonstrated the band's move into more contemporary musical territory. Released in May 1979, when disco was at its height (see Dyer, 1990), *Discovery* demonstrates a clear disco influence, particularly on the first single to be drawn from the album, 'Shine a Little Love'. Certainly, ELO were not alone in this respect with other artists, notably Roxy Music, who had begun their careers in the early 1970s as AOR-singles crossover artists, also releasing highly successful disco-influenced songs in the final year of the decade (see below). In the case of ELO, however, the change in style that had begun with *Discovery* was to continue with their next album *Time*. Appearing in July 1981, this album abandoned the rock-orchestral fusion that had been a trademark of ELO's music throughout the 1970s and embraced instead the electro pop styles being made popular by a new generation of British artists such as Gary Numan and the Human League. *Time* was a concept album, based on the story of a man who travels through time from 1981 to the year 2095. As such, the album can be seen as embodying a progressive pop aesthetic and attempting to re-apply this in a post-punk pop environment, harnessing the technologies to hand. Ultimately, however, ELO audiences found the rapid transition of the band to this new style difficult to accept, and the band itself struggled with line-up problems to the point that in 1986, with Jeff Lynne, Bev Bevan and Richard Tandy as the only original members of the band, ELO disbanded. The band reformed in 2000, eventually becoming Jeff Lynne's ELO in 2014, with Lynne singing and playing all instruments on recordings and using a touring band to reproduce the music in a live context. Although remaining a sought-after live act, ELO have essentially become a heritage rock group (Bennett, 2009) primarily performing music from their classic 1970s era. Indeed, ELO are by no means the only band from the 1970s to have found success under the heritage rock banner with a variety of rock and pop bands from the decade, sometimes with only one original member, finding huge appeal among audiences comprising both original fans and younger listeners.

Another progressive pop band whose transition to the 1980s proved to be problematic and ultimately short-lived was 10cc. Indeed, the survival of 10cc beyond the end of 1976 had surprised many observers given events that beset the band at this point in their career. Specifically, this focused around the departure of Kevin Godley and Lol Creme, who had been key contributors to the band's songwriting and also supplied some of the more experimental and avant-garde elements in 10cc's musical output, including songs such as 'The Hospital Song' (1973), 'Somewhere in Hollywood' (1974), 'Une Nuit a Paris' (1975) and 'I Wanna Rule the World' (1976). While both Queen and ELO demonstrated an ability, not to say desire, for musical change in the latter half of the 1970s towards a more chart-orientated footing (each of these bands releasing an increasing number of hit singles from 1977 onwards), in the case of 10cc, such a transition was not consistent with the creative preferences of all members of the band and resulted in one of the most unanticipated artistic 'falling outs' in 1970s British popular music (see Thompson, 2017). During the recording of 10cc's fourth studio album *How Dare You!*, released in January 1976, Godley and Creme had also been working on a separate music project that would eventually surface as the triple album set *Consequences* (1977). Following the completion of *How Dare You!* and the promotional tour of the UK and Europe that followed the album's release, Godley and Creme continued working on their new project, while Eric Stewart and Graham Gouldman set about writing new material for the next planned 10cc album. While Stewart had not contributed to the writing of the three hits drawn from 10cc's eponymously titled debut album (see Chapter 3), from the second album, *Sheet Music* (1974), onwards he had collaborated on the writing of each of 10cc's hit singles, including their major 1975 hit 'I'm Not in Love'. In the 2015 documentary *I'm Not in Love: The Story of 10cc*, Kevin Godley claims to have felt uncomfortable with 10cc's approach to songwriting as early as the planning for *How Dare You!* at which point he felt that a changed, more formulaic approach was beginning to take hold as the band discussed what kind of tracks were needed for the new album. As Godley further explains in the documentary, in late 1976 when Stewart played a new song entitled 'The Things We Do for Love' for the other members of the band, both Godley and Creme disapproved of it, this event bringing their musical frustrations to a head and signalling their ultimate departure from 10cc. As an interim measure, Stewart and Gouldman took the decision to continue 10cc as duo and recorded their next album *Deceptive Bends* (1977) with the help of drummer Paul Burgess, who had performed live with the band as a supporting musician (supplying additional drums, percussion and keyboards) ever since 10cc had become a touring concern in 1973. *Deceptive Bends* was commercially successful as an album, reaching number 3 in the UK album charts, while the first two singles taken from the album, 'The Things We Do for Love' (released in November 1976) and 'Good Morning Judge' (released in April 1977), had comparable success to previous 10cc singles, both becoming top 10 hits for the band in the UK. Similarly, *Deceptive Bends* was well received, climbing to number 3 in the British charts. Nevertheless, some critics suggested that the album lacked the depth and diversity of 10cc's first four studio albums (with Gouldman admitting in an interview for the *I'm Not in Love* documentary that when writing some of the tracks on *Deceptive Bends*, he and Stewart had tried to mimic Godley and Creme's approach to songwriting in order to preserve their spirit in the mix of songs presented in the album).

Following the release of *Deceptive Bends*, 10cc undertook a tour of the UK, Australia and Japan with a new expanded line-up that resulted in the band's first live album, *Live and Let Live*. Released in late 1977, the album met a mixed response from the British music press, which, among other things, questioned the need for a 10cc live album given the high and enduring quality of their studio albums up to that point (Doherty, 1977). The band's new line-up was largely retained for the recording of 10cc's next studio album *Bloody Tourists* (1978), which yielded 10cc's third and last number 1 hit in the UK, the reggae-inspired composition 'Dreadlock Holiday'. The following year, Eric Stewart was involved in a serious car accident, which left him with ear and eye injuries, meaning he was unable to play music for approximately six months. Stewart reflected on this some years later in a BBC radio interview, where he remarked on how the British popular music scene changed significantly during his period of convalescence to point that by the time he was ready to return to recording and performing with 10cc the band's music was beginning to feel increasingly out of step with the punk and new wave hits that featured in the British popular music charts at the time. Similarly, without the creative moderation of 10cc, Godley and Creme's music became increasingly avant-garde. *Consequences* and follow-up albums such as *L* (1978) and *Freeze Frame* (1979) were poorly received, although in 1981, the duo had two top 10 hits in the UK with 'Under Your Thumb' and 'Wedding Bells'. By this time, however, Godley and Creme had also broken into the rapidly emerging world of pop video, achieving their biggest success during the 1980s as directors of over fifty videos for artists, including Culture Club, Duran Duran, the Police, Toyah and George Harrison (for whom they directed the video to Harrison's 1987 song 'When We Was Fab', a nostalgic reflection on his days with the Beatles and Beatlemania). In the ensuing years, all four members of the original 10cc line-up have acknowledged that in hindsight Godley and Creme's departure from the band in late 1976 was unfortunate and leaves a question mark over how the band, then at its creative peak, might have progressed beyond 1976. In an interview with British music writer Dave Thompson, Graham Gouldman observed:

> When Kevin and Lol left it was a blow, an artistic blow and although we carried on and we had hits, and some tracks show all the humour and imagination and style of the early 10cc, we lost Kevin and Lol's abstract, bizarre attitude and there was nothing we could do about it. (Thompson, 2017: 73)

Two exponents of progressive pop who experienced better fortunes during the late 1970s were Roxy Music and David Bowie. With the departure of Brian Eno in 1973, Bryan Ferry had increasingly assumed control over the creative reins of Roxy Music, who achieved a series of eight top 10 singles between November 1973 and April 1982, including 'Love Is the Drug', which remains one of the band's most well-known songs internationally, and a cover of John Lennon's 'Jealous Guy', which became Roxy Music's one and only number 1 hit (in the UK and Australia) in February 1981. It was the first of these aforementioned tracks that essentially mapped the direction Roxy Music would take during the later years of the 1970s. Released in September 1975, a year before the emergence of punk, 'Love Is the Drug' demonstrated a shift in direction for Roxy Music to a more dance-orientated style that the band was to refine on the albums *Manifesto* and *Flesh and Blood*, released respectively in 1979 and 1980. Following a two-year period of inactivity, Roxy Music having disbanded after the tour to promote the 1975 album *Siren*, the material featured on *Manifesto* and *Flesh and Blood* registered some new musical directions for the band, with the latter album in particular being quite removed from the much of their earlier work. *Manifesto* was an album that retained elements of previous Roxy Music albums but also absorbed contemporary influences of the time, notably new wave and dance music. The second single taken from Manifesto, a remixed version of the song 'Dance Away', deftly targeted the dance audience, as had its predecessor 'Love Is the Drug' several years before with both songs becoming major trans-Atlantic hits for Roxy Music. It was on *Flesh and Blood*, however, that Roxy Music's biggest foray into the dance music field was achieved, the album drawing together influences from disco and the emerging strains of synth-pop. *Flesh and Blood* provided Roxy Music with their first number 1 album since 1973's *Stranded*, but the reactions of the music press to the band's new direction were quite mixed, with negative reviews appearing in publications such as *Rolling Stone*, whose praise for the band's earlier work had been critical to the success they had achieved during the early 1970s. The final Roxy Music album, *Avalon*, released in May 1982 again saw the band embracing a more contemporary pop aesthetic although at the same time a number of tracks on the album, including the title track, had a more ambient feel than work featured on their previous two albums. Contrasted with their debut album, released ten years earlier, however, *Avalon* demonstrated the extent to which *Roxy Music* had abandoned the more avant-garde elements of their earlier music to nurture a sound that fitted seamlessly with the highly polished pop that was beginning to appear during the early 1980s from bands such as Culture Club, Duran Duran and Spandau Ballet (the latter two bands acknowledging a debt to early seventies–era Roxy Music and David Bowie later in their careers). Given the success of *Avalon*, which became Roxy Music's third number 1 album in the UK, and its compatibility with the British popular music soundscape of the early 1980s, it is probable that the band could have continued through the 1980s and into the 1990s. However, following a tour to promote *Avalon*, Roxy Music again disbanded, only reuniting again in 2001 to celebrate the band's thirtieth anniversary. The band toured and performed at festivals for the next ten years before their final dissolution in 2011. By this time, Roxy Music too had earned the status of a heritage music act (Bennett, 2009), and live performances were largely drawn from their rich back catalogue, including much of what had by then come to be regarded as the band's 'classic material' from the early 1970s. Although work on a new Roxy Music album was apparently underway, this came to an end when the band broke up, and as yet there are no plans to complete and release the album.

By far the most seamless transition for a progressive pop artist from the pre-punk to the post-punk 1970s was seen in the case of David Bowie. By the mid-1970s Bowie had abandoned his Ziggy Stardust alias and also transgressed beyond the post-Ziggy raggedness of his *Diamond Dogs* (1974) album to a new white soul sound punctuated by his 1975 album *Young Americans*. However, Bowie's early fascination with Iggy Pop, who was to become a role model for punk, and his own tenure as Ziggy Stardust when numerous future punks had witnessed the spectacle of Bowie's epochal appearances on *Top of the Pops*, had done much to endear the artist to the punk generation. If Bowie had been a quintessentially British artist during the first half of the 1970s, based in London and a key figure in the city's music scene, throughout the latter half of the decade, Bowie existed in state of self-imposed exile, living first in the United States and then relocating to West Berlin, where he was to produce some of his most influential work (Trynka, 2011). Although Bowie's work up to and including *Diamond Dogs* had illustrated an eclecticism in his music that was largely unrivalled at this point, it was with *Young Americans* that the artist's penchant for taking musical risks came into sharp relief. Bowie's most 'un-British' album at that point, *Young Americans* abandons the rock foundations of his earlier 1970s music and pursues instead the artist's even earlier fixation with American soul music. The follow-up album *Station to Station* (1976) demonstrated a further evolution in Bowie's music as the soul and funk elements he had perfected on *Young Americans* were blended with the electronic styles of German bands, such as Kraftwerk and Neu! *Young Americans* or *Station to Station* did not bear much resemblance to punk, nor did they have much in common, stylistically speaking, with the forms of rock music that punk was opposed to. Indeed, in the case of *Station to Station*, it has been suggested that this album came to be highly influential on the post-punk music scene in Britain as artists such as Gary Numan and Magazine came into the frame.

It was perhaps in the next phase of Bowie's career, however, that his reputation as a highly innovative, and adaptable, progressive pop artist was consolidated. Following completion of work on *Station to Station* and with an escalating drug problem, Bowie took the decision to leave Los Angeles, relocating first to Switzerland and then to West Berlin. Between 1977 and 1979 he released three albums, *Low* (1977), '*Heroes*' (1977) and *Lodger* (1979). Collectively these albums came to be regarded as the 'Berlin Trilogy', although in truth only '*Heroes*' was recorded exclusively in Berlin (at Hansa Studio by the Wall) while parts of *Low* were recorded in France and *Lodger* was recorded in Montreux and New York. Nevertheless, the aura of West Berlin as a city known for its art and culture, including a wealth of underground and alternative scenes, and located behind the Iron Curtain brought an added air of mystique to Bowie's work at the end of the 1970s, his image and music becoming stark and minimalist following the flamboyance of the early 1970s and the apparently self-destructive path Bowie had been set on during the middle of the decade. Although Bowie's career and artistic credibility were to survive intact until his death in January 2016, the reception of his later work was noticeably varied, beginning in early 1977 with the release of *Low*. Although this album is now regarded as one of Bowie's most influential works, at the time of its release, audiences and critics were confused by an album that seemed to be a radical departure from anything Bowie had previously released. While the album would climb to number 2 in the UK album charts, many of those listening to *Low* for the first time found it difficult to accept the eclecticism of the music, particularly the album's B side, which contained a series of instrumental tracks that were soundscapes rather than songs. This had much to do with Bowie's developing collaborations with Brian Eno, who would ultimately contribute to all three 'Berlin' albums. Eno at this time was refining a style of minimalist music that would later be termed 'ambient', and the influence of Eno's musical departures at this point is clearly in evidence on *Low*.

The follow-up album '*Heroes*' yielded in its title track one Bowie's most enduring songs. Released in September 1977, the song appeared in various different language versions, a feature which led to its becoming a significant international hit for Bowie. 'Heroes' was also distinctive due to the recording technique used to record Bowie's vocals. Referred to as the 'multi-latch' technique, this involved positioning several microphones at various positions in the studio. When the intensity of Bowie's voice increased during the recording of the vocal track, the noise gates (devices used to shut off an instrument or microphone below a certain volume) on the microphones opened up one by one, giving the song an added dimension of depth. A further signature sound on the track is the melody contributed by King Crimson guitarist Robert Fripp, who was able to control the pitch of the feedback produced by his guitar through sitting in different parts of recording booth. Interestingly, although 'Heroes' is now considered a masterpiece, and a song that demonstrates Bowie's ability to both read and pre-empt developing trends in popular music, at the time of its release, 'Heroes' was one of Bowie's poorest performing singles in the UK. Failing to reach the top 20, the song peaked at number 24. Just as the Beatles had surprised their fans in early 1967 with the release of double A side 'Penny Lane/Strawberry Fields Forever' (a pairing that broke the Beatle's uninterrupted string of UK number 1 hits that had begun with 'From Me to You' in 1962), so it would seem that with 'Heroes', Bowie may have moved too far and too fast even for an artist whose success had hinged on his capacity for consistent musical and stylistic evolution. As it transpired, however, by the beginning of the 1980s, Bowie's penchant for progressive pop music reassumed its critical resonance with the cultural zeitgeist as his most unusual single to date 'Ashes to Ashes' gave him his first UK number 1 since the re-release of 'Space Oddity' in 1975. *Scary Monsters (And Super Creeps)*, the album from which 'Ashes to Ashes' was drawn, also became Bowie's first number 1 album in the UK since *Diamond Dogs* (1974). By this time, Bowie's legacy was beginning to manifest in the number of new artists he had influenced, among them Steve Strange of British synthpop band Visage, who was closely associated with the New Romantic movement of the early 1980s (see Bennett, 2015). Strange was also heavily associated with the 'Blitz Kids', a group of young people who frequented London's Blitz club-night in London's Covent Garden. Strange and other members of the Blitz Kids were invited by Bowie to appear in the ethereal video that accompanied 'Ashes to Ashes'. Featuring the then new and novel solarized colour effect, the video features Bowie wearing a Pierrot clown costume along with Blitz scene members in similarly striking costumes being followed by a bulldozer as they walk along a deserted beach. Considered to be one of the most innovative pop videos ever made, it consolidated Bowie's transition from the 1970s to the new age of pop video that coincided with the beginning of the 1980s and the launch of MTV. The impact of video on the trajectory of British progressive pop in the 1980s is considered later in this chapter.

Three minutes of 'prog'

During the late 1970s the AOR-pop crossover element of the British music charts was to receive another, somewhat unanticipated influx of songs in the form of a sudden spike of British progressive rock acts releasing commercially successful, and in some instances top 10, singles. Although on balance this amounted to a relatively small number of artists overall, the fact that some of these artists had had no chart presence in Britain at all up to that point in the 1970s made even this small increase in chart activity striking, particularly given the disdain being directed towards them at the time by punk and much of the British music press. While the reasons for this sudden and unprecedented spate of chart activity on the part of progressive rock bands are not entirely clear, one possible explanation is that as they came increasingly under attack from punk and the British music press, many progressive rock bands took heed from their progressive pop counterparts and sought a more crossover audience for their music. Either way, this development offers further evidence that the painting of 1977 as a punk year zero in British popular music is to a fair degree myopic and somewhat reductionist in its reading of the trajectory of music and musical taste at this point in the 1970s. The possibility of a progressive rock band crossing over to a pop audience in the UK had been briefly tested in 1973 when an edited version of the Genesis song 'I Know What I Like (In Your Wardrobe)' from the album *Selling England By the Pound* had climbed to number 21 in the British singles charts. Although only a relatively minor hit for Genesis, the song proved the point that progressive rock could appeal to a more mainstream audience (other left-field UK hits that year with a progressive rock feel included the instrumentals 'Sylvia' and 'Hocus Pocus' by Dutch band Focus). The period between late 1976 and 1978 saw a larger number of the more staunchly album-oriented British progressive rock bands appearing in the UK singles charts, in many cases for the very first time in careers which in some instances dated back to the late 1960s. This began in December 1976 when Jethro Tull returned to the UK charts after a period of six years and scored a top 30 hit with 'Ring out Solstice Bells'. According to Jethro Tull frontman, Ian Anderson, in writing the track, he was deliberately aiming for a song that would have chart appeal. As it happened the song peaked at number 28 in the British charts. However, this was a high-enough position to secure Jethro Tull an appearance on *Top of the Pops* (*TOTP*). The band's image as rustic characters with a vaguely historical look about them (having taken the name Jethro Tull from a seventeenth-century English agricultural pioneer) and Ian Anderson's flute brandishing antics surprised many viewers and cut an interesting contrast with other artists appearing on the *TOTP* during that period, including Showaddywaddy, Johnny Mathis and Tina Charles.

More surprising still was the debut appearance on *TOTP* the following year of Emerson, Lake and Palmer (ELP), one of the most reviled of the British progressive rock bands in punk circles given their perceived self-indulgence, including going on the road with three juggernauts full of equipment, each trailer being emblazoned on its roof with the name of an individual band member. With their blend of progressive rock and classical music, ELP perhaps more than any other progressive rock band consolidated the discourse of 'prog' as a music homologically interwoven with the elitism and intellectual snobbery of a middle-class student audience (see, for example, Willis, 1978), whose disdain of chart music was measured through their embrace of the 'high-end' AOR music endorsed by musical tastemakers such as Bob Harris and his late-night AOR music offering the *Old Grey Whistle Test* (see Chapter 2). And yet, at precisely the same time in 1977 that the Sex Pistol's 'God Save the Queen' was banned from British radio and television due to its anti-monarchist sentiment on the very eve of Queen Elizabeth's sliver jubilee (see Laing, 1985), ELP took a rock version of American contemporary composer Aaron Copland's 'Fanfare for the Common Man' to number 2 in the UK charts. Just as Laing (1985) points out that by no means all those who bought the Sex Pistols records were punks, in all likelihood most of those who bought 'Fanfare for the Common Man' were not ELP fans nor indeed fans of progressive rock per se. Uninterested in the genre distinctions (and divisions) being rehearsed by the music press, pop fans were drawn to the novelty of ELP's reworking of Copeland's composition in the same way that they had been drawn to Queen's reworking of opera in 'Bohemian Rhapsody' two and a half years earlier. A further point of commonality with 'Bohemian Rhapsody' was ELP's decision to make a promotional video for 'Fanfare for the Common Man' rather than appearing in the *TOTP* studio. Still in its infancy at this point, video could add instant novelty and appeal to a pop single. In this particular case, the grandiose scale of the music was matched by the visual spectacle of the video which, like the 'Bohemian Rhapsody' video, assumed an intertextual quality that contributed to the aura and spectacle of ELP as they reached out to a chart audience. As a setting for the video, the snowbound Winter Olympic Stadium in Montreal was chosen. Ostensibly packaging up the musical and visual bombast of progressive rock in ways that had by then become a customary spectacle, there is arguably another way of reading the scene depicted in the 'Fanfare for the Common Man' video. Thus, the choice of setting for the video could also be seen as a pushback against the negativity the band had endured from punk due to its alleged self-indulgence. By then a prime example of a stadium rock act, Emerson, Lake and Palmer are portrayed in the video performing in a stadium-sized venue devoid of people and in freezing-cold conditions. The possible sentiment being implied through such imagery is that the band's music speaks for itself irrespective of the size, or even presence, of an audience.

Two months later, Yes, another progressive rock band which had attracted the contempt of punk, scored a number 7 hit with 'Wondrous Stories', a song taken from their first album in three years, *Going for the One*. This album saw Yes reunited with keyboard player Rick Wakeman again after a period of around two years. Wakeman had left Yes after their 1974 tour to promote the double album *Tales from Topographic Oceans* on the grounds that he was uncomfortable with the new direction that the band seemed to be heading in. Following a further foray into lengthier conceptual pieces with 'The Gates of Delirium' from their 1974 album *Relayer*, featuring Swiss keyboard player Patrick Moraz, *Going for the One* marked a return for Yes to the shorter, self-contained songs featured on earlier albums such as *The Yes Album* and *Fragile*, with 'Wondrous Stories' being an illustrative example of the band's ability to write shorter, more accessible and radio-friendly material. This pattern of progressive- rock-band-turned-singles-artist continued in February 1978 when Genesis, reduced to a trio following the departure of original vocalist Peter Gabriel in 1975 and subsequently lead guitarist Steve Hackett in 1977, had a worldwide hit with the song 'Follow You Follow Me'. In the case of Genesis, the success of this one particular song was to have a transforming influence on the band's overall musical direction. Between 1980 and 1991 the three remaining members of Genesis, Phil Collins (drums and vocals), Mike Rutherford (guitars and bass) and Tony Banks (keyboards), enjoyed significant commercial success as the only one of the original British progressive rock bands to make a successful and sustained transition from AOR to mainstream pop. Also in February 1978, guitarist Gordon Giltrap, an artist not typically documented in accounts of progressive rock, academic or otherwise, but associated with the genre nevertheless, reached number 21 in the UK charts with his instrumental track 'Heartsong'. The track gained increasing popularity when it was adopted as the theme tune for the popular BBC tourism programme *Holiday*. Finally, in August 1978, Renaissance, one of the very few progressive rock bands at that time to be fronted by a female lead vocalist, Annie Haslam, had a top 10 hit with 'Northern Lights'. In the case of both Giltrap and Renaissance, this was to be their only foray into the charts but consolidates a wave of chart success for progressive rock that remains relatively distinctive to this period in the late 1970s and serves to challenge the historical perception of this as a time when the British hit parade was dominated by punk and new wave music.

Evolving to survive

Earlier in this chapter it was noted how David Bowie's 'Ashes to Ashes' video marked a critical turning point for British progressive pop as the currency of music as a medium began to rest increasingly on both its aural *and* its visual representation. Many of those artists who had contributed to the progressive pop era of the 1970s experienced difficulty in making the transition to the video age. And yet, even as video became the all-embracing medium for pop in the 1980s, a clutch of British artists who had emerged or found creative renewel at the very end of the 1970s preserved the spirit of British progressive pop in the new decade. The year 1977 saw the re-emergence of singer Peter Gabriel, whose song 'Salisbury Hill' reached 13 in the UK singles charts. An established artist in the progressive rock genre, Gabriel was the original lead singer and one of the founding members of Genesis, leaving the band in 1975 after the tour to promote the band's double album *The Lamb Lies Down on Broadway*. 'Salisbury Hill' was written by Gabriel following a spiritual experience on Salisbury Hill in the county of Somerset in southwest England. With its overarching theme of letting-go, the song has been associated with Gabriel's departure from Genesis in order to have more creative freedom to experiment with new musical styles and directions. Based on a repeated riff played on a double-tracked[2] acoustic guitar, 'Salisbury Hill' has a folky feel to it, but at the same time, it harks back to Gabriel's progressive rock days with its unusual 7/4 time signature and the synthesizer work of Larry Fast, which brings a melancholy tone to the song reminiscent of early Genesis tracks such as 'The Fountain of Salmacis' from the band's 1971 album *Nursery Cryme*. The album from which 'Salisbury Hill' is taken, the first of four eponymously titled albums that Gabriel would release between 1977 and 1982, similarly displayed Gabriel's progressive rock roots but importantly also demonstrated a rapidly emerging pop sensibility that would come to fruition on his third album released in 1980 and containing the hit single 'Games without Frontiers'. Gabriel, like Bowie, both understood and was able to productively engage with the new musical currents of the early 1980s and the evolving technologies that were opening up new opportunities for musical composition and production. As Genesis, with new vocalist Phil Collins, managed a seamless transition from progressive rock to pop during the early 1980s, Gabriel's own progressive rock roots manifested in a strikingly different way as the artist experimented with electronic and sampled sounds, drawing on musical influences beyond Western rock and pop. Tracks such as 'Shock the Monkey' and 'I Have the Touch' from Gabriel's fourth album, untitled but often referred to as 'Security' (1982), were difficult to categorize in terms of genre, a trend that was also manifesting among other contemporary artists of the day such as new wave band Japan, whose track 'Ghosts' (1982) has been described as one of the most unlikely hits in the history of UK chart music due to its highly abstract compositional and sonic qualities. Gabriel is also credited as a pop video innovator, the video for his 1986 song 'Sledgehammer' featuring claymation, pixilation and stop motion animation techniques.

    Earlier in this book, it was suggested that the term 'progressive pop' is something of a ghost terminology, manifesting at different points in popular music history, contingent on specific moments of creative innovation, technological production and the operational logic of the music industry. During the early 1970s, it has been argued, progressive pop in Britain demarcated a particular era of musical activity that straddled the AOR and pop markets. By the early 1980s, the AOR-pop divide was being challenged. Many of those artists whose work had upheld the AOR label in the UK, such as Led Zeppelin, Yes and ELP, had disbanded, while others such as Genesis had transformed into mainstream pop artists. At the same time, the focus on the album as a creative work distinct from chart releases was beginning to fade as an increasing number of singles were drawn from a given album, as exemplified by Michael Jackson's *Thriller* (1982), from which seven of the album's nine songs were released as singles. Progressive pop in the 1980s thus assumed different resonances, continuing to work across the albums and singles markets but also increasingly working in the realm of popular music video and utilizing the new medium as an additional vehicle for the expression of creativity. A new British progressive pop artist who appeared tailor-made for the video age was Kate Bush. Bush had first come to public attention in the UK in February 1978 when she appeared on *TOTP* with her debut single 'Wuthering Heights', a track that went to number 1 for four weeks and remains Bush's most well-known song. Bush cited Genesis as one of her key early influences, and later went on to collaborate with Peter Gabriel. In many respects, Bush's strong presence in both the album and singles charts at the end of the 1970s and into the 1980s offers strong parallels with the progressive pop artists of the early 1970s. What set her apart, however, was the highly performative aspect of her song delivery – a facet of Bush's craft that was evident from her very first television performances, where her unusual and highly distinctive voice was matched with a well-honed ability for dance and mime. Such carefully choreographed qualities of Bush's performances blended well with the pop video format. During the 1980s, videos produced to accompany Bush's songs saw her in a range of contexts ranging from a ballet-style dance sequence ('Running up That Hill', 1985) to assuming the role of a young boy whose father, played by Canadian acting stalwart Donald Sutherland, is a scientist working on a secret invention to control the weather ('Cloudbusting', 1985). Speaking about the transition to video production that he and Kevin Godley made following their departure from 10cc at the end of 1976, in the documentary *I'm Not in Love*, Lol Creme notes how he and Godley quickly came to view video as creative canvass, much as they had viewed music in the 1970s.[3] It is clear that British progressive pop artists in the 1980s such as Kate Bush, Peter Gabriel and David Bowie viewed video in much the same way, that is to say as an additional creative resource that they could use to explore and articulate the meanings and messages they wished to convey through their music.

Conclusion

By the end of the 1970s, it was clear that the conditions that had allowed British progressive pop to flourish earlier in the decade were being significantly compromised due to the emergence of punk and its influence on the British music industry. Although this did not lead to a sudden displacement of progressive pop, its main exponents were nevertheless forced to reckon with a new set of expectations, including shorter and more musically straightforward songs in keeping with the ethos of punk and its successor, new wave. As this chapter has demonstrated, progressive pop's transition was somewhat uneven. For example, ELO released arguably their most quintessentially progressive pop album, *Out of the Blue* during 1977, a year that is often held to be the 'year of punk' in the popular imagination. In the same year, Queen executed a radical about face with an album that confronted punk antagonism head-on, while David Bowie's *Low* and '*Heroes*' albums appeared to sidestep punk, completely anticipating instead the new wave, electronic and ambient styles that form a bridge between the late 1970s and early 1980s. The extent to which punk alone was a driver for musical shifts among progressive pop artists is difficult to ascertain. Upon the release of Queen's *News of the World* album, interviews with members of Queen revealed that Freddie Mercury had grown temporarily frustrated with the long hours the band were spending in the studio and the band overall felt that a fresh approach was needed. Similarly, 10cc's shift in musical direction from 1977 onwards was largely prompted by the departure of Kevin Godley and Lol Creme from the band in late 1976 rather than by a felt need to adapt musically due to the emergence of punk. Nevertheless, punk's presence was keenly felt by the British music industry such that by 1978 a new trend towards simpler, shorter and more direct songs was evident in the nation's popular music to the extent that survival often meant adaptation to the musical tastes of a new generation of fans. At this point, popular music video was also becoming an increasingly important medium in popular music. As such, by the end of the 1970s, a 'new wave' of British progressive pop spearheaded by the likes of David Bowie, Peter Gabriel and Kate Bush took on-board the new musical currents while also embracing pop video as a new creative medium. These artists and others, including Japan, Ultravox and Visage, would continue to explore and develop progressive trends in British popular music.

Notes

1 On the episode of British television programme *Classic Albums* (see Bennett and Baker, 2010) dedicated to *Never Mind the Bollocks*, this aspect of the album's recording is dealt with in an interestingly circumspect fashion as if attempting to retrospectively uphold the aura of the album as a tribute to punk's shunning of musical ability and back-to-basics ethos.
2 Double tracking refers to a technique whereby a musical passage played by an instrument or sung by a voice is recorded twice, producing an out-of-phase effect that thickens the sound of the original single track. The effect was first made popular when used in the early recordings of the Beatles (see Martin, 1979).
3 *I'm Not in Love – The Story of 10cc* (BBC Documentary, 2015).

References

Altham, K. (1973) 'Genesis: The Genesis Bag', *New Musical Express*, 10 February edition. https://www-rocksbackpages-com.libraryproxy.griffith.edu.au/Library/Article/genesis-the-genesis-bag (accessed on 25 May 2019).
Anderton, C. (2010) 'A Many-Headed Beast: Progressive Rock as European Meta-Genre', *Popular Music*, 29 (3): 417–35.
Anderton, C. (2011) 'Music Festival Sponsorship: Between Commerce and Carnival', *Arts Marketing: An International Journal*, 1 (2): 145–58.
Assmann, A. (2011) *Cultural Memory and Western Civilization: Functions, Media, Archives*, Cambridge: Cambridge University Press.
Auslander, P. (2006) *Performing Glam Rock: Gender and Theatricality in Popular Music*, Ann Arbor, MI: University of Michigan Press.
Baker, A. (2012) *Virtual Radio Ga Ga, Youths and Net-Radio: Exploring Subcultural Models of Audiences*, New York, NY: Hampton Press.
Bal, M., Crewe, J. and Spitzer, L. (eds) (1999) *Acts of Memory: Cultural Recall in the Present*, Hanover, NH: University Press of New England.
Barthes, R. (1990) 'The Grain of the Voice', in S. Frith and A. Goodwin (eds) *On Record: Rock, Pop and the Written Word*, London: Routledge.
Bennett, A. (1999) 'Subcultures or Neo-Tribes? Rethinking the Relationship between Youth, Style and Musical Taste', *Sociology*, 33 (3): 599–617.
Bennett, A. (2001) *Cultures of Popular Music*, Buckingham: Open University Press.
Bennett, A. (ed.) (2004) *Remembering Woodstock*, Aldershot, Ashgate.
Bennett, A. (2007) 'The Forgotten Decade: Rethinking the Popular Music of the 1970s', *Popular Music History*, 2 (1): 5–24.
Bennett, A. (2009) '"Heritage Rock": Rock Music, Re-Presentation and Heritage Discourse', *Poetics*, 37 (5–6): 474–89.
Bennett, A. (2010) 'Missing Links: Britpop Traces, 1970–1980', in A. Bennett and J. Stratton (eds) *Britpop and the English Music Tradition*, Aldershot: Ashgate.
Bennett, A. (2013) *Music, Style and Aging: Growing Old Disgracefully?* Philadelphia: Temple University Press.
Bennett, A. (2015) 'Fade to Grey: The Forgotten History of the British New Romantic Movement', in C. Feldman-Barrett (ed.) *Lost Histories of Youth Culture*, New York: Peter Lang.
Bennett, A. (2017) 'Wrapped in Stardust: Glam-Rock and the Rise of David Bowie as Pop Entrepreneur', *Continuum: Journal of Media & Cultural Studies*, 31 (4): 574–82.

Bennett, A. and Baker, S. (2010) 'Classic Albums: The Re-presentation of the Rock Album on British Television', in I. Inglis (ed.) *Popular Music on British Television*, Aldershot: Ashgate.

Bennett, A. and Stratton, J. (eds) (2010) *Britpop and the English Music Tradition*, Aldershot: Ashgate.

Bennett, A. and Rogers, I. (2016) *Popular Music Scenes and Cultural Memory*, Basingstoke: Palgrave.

Brackett, J. (2008) 'Examining Rhythmic and Metric Practices in Led ZeFppelin's Musical Style', *Popular Music*, 27 (1): 53–76.

Brontë, E. (1847) *Wuthering Heights*, London: Thomas Cautley Newby.

Cagle, V.M. (1995) *Reconstructing Pop/Subculture: Art, Rock and Andy Warhol*, London: Sage.

Caterson, S. (2006) 'A Western State of Mind', *Quadrant*, 50 (6): 77–80.

Chambers, I. (1985) *Urban Rhythms: Pop Music and Popular Culture*, London: Macmillan.

Charlesworth, C. (1983) 'The Original Soundtrack: 10cc Brought a New Breadth of Vision to Rock', *The History of Rock*, (8) 96: 1913–15.

Charone, B. (1983) 'Pilgrimage: The Twin Guitar Odyssey of Wishbone Ash', *History of Rock*, 8 (87): 1736–7.

Chase, J. and Healey, M. (1995) 'The Spatial Externality Effects of Football Matches and Rock Concerts: The Case of Portman Road Stadium, Ipswich, Suffolk', *Applied Geography*, 15 (1): 18–34.

Clecak, P. (1983) *America's Quest for the Ideal Self: Dissent and fulfilment in the 60s and 70s*, Oxford: Oxford University Press.

Clerk, C. (2006) *The Saga of Hawkwind*, London: Omnibus Press.

Cohen, Sara, Knifton, R., Leonard, M. and Roberts, L. (eds) (2015) *Sites of Popular Music Heritage*, Routledge: London.

Cohen, Stanley (1987) *Folk Devils and Moral Panics: The Creation of the Mods and Rockers*, 3rd edn. Oxford: Basil Blackwell.

De Nora, T. (2000) *Music in Everyday Life*. Cambridge, Cambridge University Press.

Denski, S. and Scholle, D. (1992) 'Metal Men and Glamour Boys: Gender Performance in Heavy Metal', in S. Craig (ed.) *Men, Masculinity and the Media*, Newbury Park: Sage.

Devlin, J. P. (2018) *From Analogue to Digital Radio: Competition and Cooperation in the UK Radio Industry*, Basingstoke: Palgrave.

Doherty, H. (1977) '10cc: A Repeat Performance', *Melody Maker*, December.

Doherty, H. (2011) *40 Years of Queen*, New York, NY: St. Martin's Press.

Dyer, R. (1990) 'In Defense of Disco', in S. Frith and A. Goodwin (eds) *On Record: Rock, Pop and the Written Word*, London: Routledge.

Eyerman, R. and Jamison, A. (1998) *Music and Social Movements: Mobilizing Traditions in the Twentieth Century*, Cambridge: Cambridge University Press.

Fast, S. (2001) *In the Houses of the Holy: Led Zeppelin and the Power of Rock Music*, Oxford University Press, Oxford.

Friedlander, P. (1996) *Rock and Roll: A Social History*, Boulder, Colorado: Westview.

Frith, S. (1981) 'The Magic That Can Set You Free: The Ideology of Folk and the Myth of Rock', *Popular Music*, 1: 159–68.

Frith, S. (1983) *Sound Effects: Youth, Leisure and the Politics of Rock*, London: Constable.

Frith, S. (1987) 'Towards an Aesthetic of Popular Music', in R. Leppert and S. McClary (eds) *Music and Society: The Politics of Composition, Performance and Reception*, Cambridge: Cambridge University Press.

Frith, S. (1988) *Music for Pleasure: Essays in the Sociology of Pop*, Oxford: Polity Press.

Frith, S. (1996) *Performing Rites: On the Value of Popular Music*, Oxford: Oxford University Press.

Frith, S. (1997) 'Formalism, Realism and Leisure: The Case of Punk', in K. Gelder and S. Thornton (eds) *The Subcultures Reader*, London: Routledge.

Frith, S. (2002) 'Look! Hear! The Uneasy Relationship of Music and Television', *Popular Music*, 21 (3): 277–90.

Frith, S. and Horne, H. (1987) *Art into Pop*, London: Methuen.

Frith, S. and McRobbie, A. (1990) 'Rock and Sexuality', in S. Frith and A. Goodwin (eds) *On Record: Rock, Pop and the Written Word*, London: Routledge.

Fryer, P. (1986) 'Punk and the New Wave of British Rock: Working Class Heroes and Art School Attitudes', *Popular Music & Society*, 10 (4): 1–15.

Fryer, P. (1997) '"Everybody's on Top of the Pops": Popular Music on British Television 1960–1985', *Popular Music & Society*, 21 (3): 153–71.

Fuller, G. (1983) 'For Your Pleasure: Out of the Blue Came Roxy Music', *History of Rock*, 8 (91): 1804–11.

Furedi, F. (2004) *Therapy Culture: Cultivating Vulnerability in an Uncertain Age*, London: Routledge.

Fyfe, A. (2003) *When the Levee Breaks: The Making of Led Zeppelin IV*, Chicago, Ill: Chicago Review Press.

Garner, K. (1993) *In Session Tonight*, London: BBC Books.

Gittins, I. (2007) *Top of the Pops: Mishaps, Miming and Music–True Adventures of TV's No. 1 Pop Show*, London: BBC Books.

Green, B. (2016) '"I Always Remember That Moment": Peak Music Experiences as Epiphanies', *Sociology*, 50 (2): 333–48.

Grossberg, L. (1994) 'Is Anybody Listening? Does Anybody Care? On Talking about "The State of Rock"', in A. Ross and T. Rose (eds) *Microphone Fiends: Youth Music and Youth Culture*, London: Routledge.

Guesdon, J. M. and Margotin, P. (2013) *All the Songs: The Story behind Every Beatles Release*, New York, NY: Black Dog and Leventhal.

Gunn, J. and Jenkins, J. (1992) *Queen: As It Began*, London: Pan Books.

Hall, S. and Jefferson, T. (eds) (1976) *Resistance through Rituals: Youth Subcultures in Post-War Britain*, London: Hutchinson.

Hardy, P. (1973) 'Wizzard: *Wizzard Brew* / Electric Light Orchestra: *ELO 2* (Harvest)', *Let It Rock*, June edition. https://www-rocksbackpages-com.libraryproxy.griffith.edu.au/Library/Article/wizzard-iwizzard-brewielectric-light-orchestra-ielo-2i-harvest (accessed on 25 May 2019).

Harron, M. (1990) 'McRock: Pop as a Commodity', in S. Frith (ed.) *Facing the Music: Essays on Pop, Rock and Culture*, 2nd edn. London: Mandarin.

Hawkings, R. (2014) '"Sheilas and Pooftas": Hyper-Hetromasculinity in 1970s, Australian Popular Music Cultures', *Limina: A Journal of Historical and Cultural Studies*, 20 (4): 1–14.

Hebdige, D. (1979) *Subculture: The Meaning of Style*, London: Routledge.

Hebdige, D. (1987) *Cut 'n' Mix: Culture, Identity and Caribbean Music*, London: Routledge.

Hebdige, D. (1988) *Hiding in the Light: On Images and Things*, London: Routledge.

Hegarty, P. and Halliwell, M. (2011) *Beyond and Before: Progressive Rock since the 1960s*, New York: Continuum.

Herman, G. (1983) 'Music and Movement: The Move, Mainline Pop and Stage Outrage', *History of Rock*, 5 (60): 1182–5.

Hill, D. (1986) *Designer Boys and Material Girls: Manufacturing the '80s Pop Dream*, London: Blandford Press.

Hill, S. (2016) *San Francisco and the Long 60s*, New York, NY: Bloomsbury.

Hodkinson, M. (1995) *Queen: The Early Years*, London: Omnibus Press.

Holm-Hudson, K. (ed.) (2002) *Progressive Rock Reconsidered*, New York: Routledge.

Howard, D.N. (2004) *Sonic Alchemy: Visionary Music Producers and the Maverick Recordings*, Milwaukee, WI: Hal Leonard.

Ingham, J. (1975) '10cc and Ready to Roar', *Hit Parader*, Retrieved 6 September 2018, from: http://www.rocksbackpages.com.libraryproxy.griffith.edu.au/Library/Article/10cc-and-ready-to-roar (08 June 2019).

Janssen, S., Kuipers, G. and Verboord, M. (2008) 'Cultural Globalization and Arts Journalism: The International Orientation of Arts Journalism in American, Dutch, French and German Newspapers', *Sociological Review*, 73 (5): 719–40.

Jewell, D. (1983) 'Mike Oldfield: His "Tubular Bells" Rang Cash Registers Worldwide', *History of Rock*, 8 (96): 1916–17.

Johnson, P. (1964) 'The Menace of Beatlism', *The New Statesman*, 28 February: 326–7.

Jones, C.W. (2008) *The Rock Canon: Canonical Values in the Reception of Rock Albums*, Aldershot: Ashgate,.

Jones, L. (2018) *Bohemian Rhapsody: The Definitive Biography of Freddie Mercury*, London: Hodder and Stoughton.

Jones, S. (1988) *Black Culture, White Youth: The Reggae Tradition from JA to UK*, London: Macmillan.

Kaplan, E.A. (1987) *Rocking Around the Clock: Music Television, Postmodernism and Consumer Culture*, London: Methuen.
Kassabian, A. (2013) *Ubiquitous Listening: Affect, Attention, and Distributed Subjectivity*, Los Angeles and Berkeley, CA. University of California Press.
Kotarba, J. (2002) 'Rock 'n' Roll Music as a Timepiece', *Symbolic Interaction*, 25 (3): 397–404.
Kutulas, J. (2010) 'That's the Way I've Always Heard It Should Be': Baby Boomers, 1970s Singer-Songwriters, and Romantic Relationships', *Journal of American History*, 97 (3) 682–702.
Laing, D. (1985) *One Chord Wonders: Power and Meaning in Punk Rock*, Milton Keynes: Open University Press.
Laing, D. (1994) 'Scrutiny to Subcultures: Notes on Literary Criticism and Popular Music', *Popular Music*, 13 (2): 179–90.
Lena, J. C. and Peterson, R.A. (2008) 'Classification as Culture: Types and Trajectories of Music Genres', *American Sociological Review*, 73 (5): 697–718.
Lewis, G.H. (1992) 'Who Do You Love? The Dimensions of Musical Taste', in J. Lull (ed.) *Popular Music and Communication*, 2nd edn. London: Sage.
Leys, C. (1983) *Politics in Britain: An Introduction*, London: Verso.
Lipsitz, G. (1994) 'We Know What Time It Is: Race, Class and Youth Culture in the Nineties' in A. Ross and T. Rose (eds) *Microphone Fiends: Youth Music and Youth Culture*, London: Routledge.
Logan, N. and Woffinden, B. (eds) (1977) *The NME Book of Rock 2*, London: Wyndham.
Macan, E. (1997) *Rocking the Classics: English Progressive Rock and the Counterculture*, Oxford: Oxford University Press.
Martin, B. (1998) *Listening to the Future: The Time of Progressive Rock*, Chicago: Open Court.
Martin, G. with Hornsby, J. (1979) *All You Need Is Ears*, London: Macmillan.
Marwick, A. (2005) 'The Cultural Revolution of the Long Sixties: Voices of Reaction, Protest, and Permeation', *The International History Review*, 27 (4): 780–806.
Massey, H. (2015) *The Great British Recording Studios*, Milwaukee, WI: Hal Leonard Books.
McKay, G. (2000) *Glastonbury: A Very English Fair*, London: Victor Gollancz.
McLeod, K. (2016) *We Are the Champions: The Politics of Sport and Popular Music*, London: Routledge.
McRobbie, A. and Garber, J. (1976) 'Girls and Subcultures: An Exploration', in S. Hall and T. Jefferson (eds) *Resistance Through Rituals: Youth Subcultures in Post-War Britain*, London: Hutchinson.
Mercer, K. (1991) 'Monster Metaphors: Notes on Michael Jackson's Thriller', in C. Gledhill (ed.) *Stardom: Industry of Desire*, London: Routledge.
Middleton, R. (1990) *Studying Popular Music*, Milton Keynes: Open University Press.
Mills, P. (2010) 'Stone Fox Chase: *The Old Grey Whistle Test* and the Rise of High Pop Television', in I. Inglis (ed.) *Popular Music and Television in Britain*, Farnham: Ashgate.

Moore, A.F. (1993) *Rock: The Primary Text – Developing a Musicology of Rock*, Buckingham: Open University Press.

Morley, D. (1983) 'Rod: Never a Dull Moment from the Flying Stewart', *History of Rock*, 8 (87): 1722–7.

Murdock, G. and McCron, R. (1976) 'Youth and Class: The Career of a Confusion', in G. Mungham and G. Pearson (eds) *Working-Class Youth Culture*, London: Routledge and Kegan Paul.

Nathanson, P. (1991) *Over the Rainbow: The Wizard of Oz as a Secular Myth of America*. Albany, NY: State University of New York Press.

Nelson, E. and Nikolov, K. (2003) 'UK Inflation in the 1970s and 1980s: The Role of Output Gap Mismeasurement', *Journal of Economics and Business*, 55 (4): 353–70.

Nowak, R. (2015) *Consuming Music in the Digital Age: Technologies, Roles and Everyday Life*, Basingstoke: Palgrave.

Nowak, R. and Bennett, A. (2014) 'Analyzing Everyday Sound Environments: The Space, Time and Corporality of Musical Listening', *Cultural Sociology*, 8 (4): 426–42.

O'Grady, Terence J. (1979) 'Rubber Soul and the Dance Tradition', *Ethnomusicology*, 23 (1): 87–94.

Orwell, G. (1945) *Animal Farm*, London: Secker and Warburg.

Ostopowich, M. (2003) *Greenpeace*. Mankato, MN: Weigl Publishers Inc.

Palmer, T. (1977) *All You Need Is Love: The Story of Popular Music*, London: Futura.

Pattie, D. (2016) 'Taking the Studio by Strategy', in S. Albiez and D. Pattie (eds) *Brian Eno: Oblique Music*, London: Bloomsbury.

Peterson, R.A. and Kern, R.M. (1996) 'Changing Highbrow Taste: From Snob to Omnivore', *American Sociological Review*, 61 (5): 900–7.

Pidgeon, J. (1973) '10cc: *10cc* (UK)', *Let It Rock*, September edition. https://www-rocksbackpages-com.libraryproxy.griffith.edu.au/Library/Article/10cc-i10cci-uk (accessed on 08 June 2019).

Platoff, J. (2005) 'John Lennon, "Revolution," and the Politics of Musical Reception', *The Journal of Musicology*, 22 (2): 241–67.

Plasketes, G. M. and Plasketes, J.C. (1987) 'From Woodstock Nation to Pepsi Generation: Reflections on Rock Culture and the State of Music, 1969-Present', *Popular Music and Society*, 2 (2): 25–52.

Ramsden, J. (1996) *The Winds of Change: Macmillan to Heath, 1957–1975*. London: Longman.

Reich, C. A. (1971) *The Greening of America*, Middlesex, England, Allen Lane.

Reich, J. (2008) '"The World's Most Perfectly Developed Man": Charles Atlas, Physical Culture and the Inscription of American Masculinity', *Men and Masculinities*, 12 (4): 444–61.

Regev, M. (1994) 'Producing Artistic Value: The Case of Rock Music', *Sociological Quarterly*, 35: 85–102.

Reynolds, S. (2011) *Retromania: Pop Culture's Addiction to Its Own Past*, Basingstoke: Macmillan.

Richards, A.J. (1997) *Miners on Strike*, Oxford: Berg.

Romer, C.D. (1990) 'The Great Crash and the Onset of the Great Depression', *The Quarterly Journal of Economics*, 105 (3): 597–624.

Rossi, F., Parfitt, R. with Wall, M. (2004) *XS All Eras: The Status Quo Autobiography*, London: Sidgwick and Jackson.

Roszak, T. (1969) *The Making of a Counter Culture: Reflections on the Technocratic Society and Its Youthful Opposition*, London: Faber and Faber.

Rothenbuhler, E. W. and McCourt, T. (1992) 'Commercial Radio and Popular Music: Processes of Selection and Factors of Influence', in J. Lull (ed.) *Popular Music and Communication*, Newbury Park CA: Sage.

Rutherford, M. (2014) *The Living Years*, London: Constable.

Savage, J. (1992) *England's Dreaming: Sex Pistols and Punk Rock*, London: Faber and Faber.

Schmutz, V. (2005) 'Retrospective Cultural Consecration in Popular Music', *American Behavioral Scientist*, 48 (11): 1510–23.

Schowalter, D. F. (2000) 'Remembering the Dangers of Rock and Roll: Toward a Historical Narrative of the Rock Festival', *Critical Studies in Media Communication*, 17 (1): 86–102.

Shearman, C. (1983) 'ELO: Pop Classics from the Electric Light Orchestra', *History of Rock*, 88 (8): 1746–9.

Shuker, R. (2001) *Understanding Popular Music*, 2nd edn. London: Routledge.

Shumway, D. (1992) 'Rock and Roll as a Cultural Practice', in A. DeCurtis (ed.) *Present Tense: Rock and Roll and Culture*, Durham, North Carolina, Duke University Press.

Simmons, C. (2009) 'Dear Radio Broadcaster: Fan Mail as a Form of Perceived Interactivity', *Journal of Broadcasting & Electronic Media*, 53 (3): 444–59.

Simpson, J. (2002) *Top of the Pops: 1964–2002*. London: BBC Worldwide Ltd.

Sinclair, D. (1983a) 'Sheer Chart Attack: The Mercurial Rise of Queen', *History of Rock*, 8 (91): 1812–17.

Sinclair, D. (1983b) 'All the Young Dudes – Mott the Hoople: Raw Rock and Seventies Sleaze', *History of Rock*, 8 (91): 1818–20.

Spence, S. (2016) *When the Screaming Stops: The Dark History of the Bay City Rollers*, London: Omnibus Press.

Spicer, M. (2018) 'The Electric Light Orchestra and the Anxiety of the Beatles Influence', in L. Burns and S. Lacasse (ed.) *The Pop Palimpsest: Intertextuality in Recorded Popular Music*, Ann Arbor, MI: University of Michigan Press.

Stone, C. (2009) 'The British Pop Music Festival Phenomenon', in Ali-Knight, J., Robertson, M., Fyall, A. and Ladkin, A. (eds) *International Perspectives of Festivals and Events: Paradigms of Analysis*, San Diego, CA: Academic Press.

Stratton, J. (1983) 'What Is "Popular Music"?', *Sociological Review*, 31 (2): 293–309.

Stratton, J. (1986) 'Why Doesn't Anybody Write Anything about Glam Rock', *Australian Journal of Cultural Studies*, 4 (1): 15–38.

Stump, P. (1997) *The Music's All That Matters: A History of Progressive Rock*, London: Quartet Books.

Swenson, J. (1974) 'Genesis: No "Pale" Imitation', *Crawdaddy!*, March edition. Retrieved 18 May 2019, from: https://www-rocksbackpages-com.libraryproxy.griffith.edu.au/Library/Article/genesis-no-pale-imitation.

Tamm, E. (1995) *Brian Eno, His Music and the Vertical Colour of Sound*, New York, NY: Da Capo Press.

Taylor, I. and Wall, D. (1976) 'Beyond the Skinheads: Comments on the Emergence and Significance of the Glamrock Cult', in G. Mungham and G. Pearson (eds) *Working Class Youth Culture*, London: Routledge and Kegan Paul.

Théberge, P. (2001) '"Plugged In": Technology and Popular Music', in S. Frith, W. Straw and J. Street (ed.) *The Cambridge Companion to Rock and Pop*, Cambridge: Cambridge University Press.

Thomas, D. (1999) 'Their Britannic Majesties Request', *Mojo*, 69, August: 72–88.

Thompson, D. (2017) *The Cost of Living in Dreams: The 10cc Story*, Revised edn. Published by Dave Thompson.

Thuber, J. (1939) *The Secret Life of Walter Mitty/The New Yorker*, 18 March.

Tincknell, E. (2010) 'A Sunken Dream: Music and the Gendering of Nostalgia in Life on Mars', in I. Inglis (ed.) *Popular Music and Television in Britain*, Farhham: Ashgate.

Tobler, J. (1978) *Guitar Heroes*, Singapore: Marshall Cavendish.

Toynbee, J. (1993) 'Policing Bohemia, Pinning Up Grunge: The Music Press and Generic Change in British Pop and Rock', *Popular Music*, 12 (3): 289–300.

Tremlett, G. (1976) *The 10cc Story*, London: Futura.

Trynka, P. (2011) *Starman – David Bowie: The Definitive Biography*, London: Sphere.

van Dijck, J. (2006) 'Record and Hold: Popular Music Between Personal and Collective Memory', *Critical Studies in Media Communication*, 23 (5): 357–74.

Vickers, G. (2010) *Rock Music Landmarks of London: 66 Locations Where Rock's Heroes and Heroines Lived, Loved Played and Died*, 2nd edn. London: Omnibus Press.

Waksman, S. (1996) 'Every Inch of My Love: Led Zeppelin and the Problem of Cock Rock', *Journal of Popular Music Studies*, 8: 5–25.

Waksman, S. (2009) This Ain't the Summer of Love: Conflict and Crossover in Heavy Metal and Punk. Berkeley, CA: University of California Press.

Warner, M. (2011) *No Go the Bogeyman: Scaring, Lulling, and Making Mock*, London: Vintage Books.

Watkinson, M. and Anderson, P. (2007) *Crazy Diamond: Syd Barrett and the Dawn of Pink Floyd*, London: Omnibus Press.

Weisbard, E. and Marks, C. (eds) (1995) *'Roxy Music': Spin Alternative Guide*, New York, NY: Vintage Books.

Wells, A. (1987) 'The British Invasion of American Popular Music: What Is It and Who Pays?', *Popular Music & Society*, 11 (2): 65–78.
White, C. (1994) *The Life and Times of Little Richard*, New York, NY: Da Capo Press.
Whiteley, S. and Sklower, J. (eds) (2014) *Countercultures and Popular Music*, Farnham: Ashgate.
Wiggins, N. (1983) 'Again and Again: The Timeless Boogie of Status Quo', *History of Rock*, 8 (87): 1730–5.
Willis, P. (1978) *Profane Culture*, London: Routledge and Kegan Paul.
Wilson, B. with B. Greenman (2016) *I am Brian Wilson*, London: Coronet.
Witts, R. (2012) 'Needle Time: The BBC, the Musicians' Union, Popular Music, and the Reform of Radio in the 1960s', *Popular Music History*, 7 (3): 241–62.
Young, J. and Lang, M. (1979) *Woodstock Festival Remembered*, New York, NY: Ballantine Books.
Zagorski-Thomas, S. (2014) *The Musicology of Record Production*, Cambridge: Cambridge University Press.

Index

Abbey Road (The Beatles) 17, 52, 58
Aha Norwegian band 30
Aladdin Sane (Bowie) 59, 75, 112–13
album bands 22–4
album-oriented-rock (AOR) 4, 13, 22, 25, 28, 30, 41, 44–53, 61, 65, 67–9, 75–6, 79, 87, 91, 99, 105, 122, 125–6, 130, 137–9, 142
'All Men Are Hungry' (*Timeless Flight*) 111
'All the Young Dudes' (Mott the Hoople) 64
Altham, Keith 72
ambient music 49, 60–1, 136
Anderson, Ian 138
Anderton, C. 55 n.4
Animal Farm (Orwell) 125
Animals (Pink Floyd) 104, 125
'Another Brick in the Wall, Part 2' (*The Wall*) 44, 125
'Another One Bites the Dust' (*The Game*) 128
Appleton, Michael 50, 93–4
Arden, Don 40
'Art for Art's Sake' (*How Dare You!*) 109
'Ashes to Ashes' (*Scary Monsters (And Super Creeps)*) 137, 140
Atlas, Charles 62
Atom Heart Mother (Pink Floyd) 42, 59
Auslander, P. 39, 55 n.1
Avalon (Roxy Music) 134
avant-garde music 20, 24, 32, 51, 131, 133

Bach, Johan Sebastian 19
back-to-basics approach 17, 38, 121, 123
Baker, Roy Thomas 54, 64, 97–8
ballad 8, 54, 93, 95, 98, 108
'Banana Rock' (The Wombles) 108
Banks, Tony 42, 72, 140
Barrett, Syd 36, 42
Barthes, R. 110
Bay City Rollers pop band 41, 69, 103
BBC 88
   Junior Choice (radio programme) 86

OGWT (*see Old Grey Whistle Test (OGWT)* television show)
Pick of the Pops 86–7
Solid Gold Sixty 87
Today (television programme) 122
Top Gear (radio programme) 45
TOTP. (*see Top of the Pops (TOTP)* television show)
The Beach Boys rock band 16, 22, 62, 94
The Beatles rock band 1, 3, 5, 11, 15–19, 22–3, 26, 31–2, 35, 42, 48–53, 57, 61, 66, 79, 81, 94, 124, 136
   Abbey Road 17, 52, 58
   compilation albums of 57
   pop promos for 92
   Revolver 18–19, 23
   Rubber Soul 17–18
   Sgt. Pepper's Lonely Hearts Club Band 17–19, 22–3, 50, 54, 130
   White Album 23
Bell Records record label 41
Bennett, A. 5, 82–3, 86
Berlin Trilogy, Bowie's 60–1, 135–6, 143
Berry, Chuck 66–7, 71
Bevan, Bev 3, 130
Black Sabbath rock band 43, 50
Blitz Kids 137
Blue for You (Status Quo) 91
'The Bogus Man' (*For Your Pleasure*) 68, 110–11
Bohemian Rhapsody (Queen) film 97
'Bohemian Rhapsody' (*A Night at the Opera*) song 3, 21, 24, 29, 31, 65, 85, 87–8, 92–9, 126, 128, 139
Bolan, Marc 39, 57, 92
Bolder, Trevor 1
boogie rock 37–8, 90
Bowie, David 1, 5–6, 15–16, 21, 27, 29–31, 33, 39–41, 47–9, 64, 68, 73–4, 76, 84–5, 87, 90–2, 105, 107, 113–18, 120, 125, 133–7, 143–4
   Aladdin Sane 59, 75, 112–13

Index

Berlin Trilogy 60–1, 135–6, 143
Diamond Dogs 75, 134, 137
Hunky Dory 55 n.6, 59, 112
The Rise and Fall of Ziggy Stardust and the Spiders from Mars 1, 22, 48–9, 88, 90–1, 112–13
Scary Monsters (And Super Creeps) 137
Station to Station 135
Young Americans 57, 135
Ziggy Stardust 2, 59, 85, 90, 105, 112–14, 125, 134–5
'Brand New Day' (*The Original Soundtrack*) 108
The British art school 15–16
British music press 14, 27, 46, 52, 57, 60, 63, 72–3, 82, 104–6, 121, 126–7, 132, 137
British popular music 1, 3, 6, 11, 13–17, 19, 22–3, 32–3, 41, 58, 73–4, 79, 84, 99, 102–3, 107, 114, 121–2, 125, 131–2, 138. *See also* popular music
    artists 21, 28–30, 32, 76, 103
    back-to-basics approach 17, 38, 121, 123
    in early 1970s 27, 29, 35–41, 47, 54, 79, 104
    gender politics 114–17
    political voice (*see* political rock/voice)
Britpop 5
Bulsara, Farrokh. *See* Mercury, Freddie
Burgess, Paul 132
'Burn Baby Burn' (Hudson-Ford) 101
Burrell, Raymond 'Boz' 36
Bush, Kate 126, 142–4
'Bye Bye Baby' (Bay City Rollers) 103
Byrne, David 110

canon, musical 25–6, 55 n.4, 82–3
Cassidy, David 69, 75
Charisma Records 77 n.5
chart music 20, 36, 45, 61, 63, 65, 70, 99, 141
chart-orientated artists 36, 38, 40–1
Chicory Tip pop group 38
The Clash punk band 112
Classic Albums (television programme) 144 n.1
classical music/rock 17, 19, 22–3, 42, 46–7, 51, 66, 73, 79, 116, 123, 129, 134
Clecak, P. 23

Cockney Rebel. *See* Steve Harley and Cockney Rebel rock band
Collective Consciousness Society (CCS) 44
Collins, Phil 140–1
Commercialism 106
Concerto for a Rainy Day (ELO) 129
Consequences (Godley and Creme) 55 n.5, 108, 131, 133
conventional pop 42, 49, 54, 60, 82, 90
Cook, Paul 124
Cooper, Alice 47
Copland, Aaron 139
counterculture, 1960s 11, 15, 23, 25–6, 35, 37, 103–4, 106, 111
Coverdale, David 117
'Crazy Little Thing Called Love' (*The Game*) 128
Creme, Lol 4, 16, 36, 52, 55 n.5, 58, 62, 64, 94–7, 108, 120 n.1, 131–3, 143
    Consequences 108, 131, 133
    Freeze Frame 133
    L 133
Crimson, King 37, 42, 136
'cultural information,' music 82
cultural memory 12–13, 51, 89, 99
Culture Club pop band 133–4

'Dancing with the Moonlit Knight' (Genesis) 105
Dark Side of the Moon (Pink Floyd) 43–4, 59, 125
A Day at the Races (Queen) 127
Deacon, John 2, 93, 128
'The Dean and I' (*10cc*) 63
Deceptive Bends (10cc) 100 n.2, 132
Deep Purple rock band 28, 36, 43, 50, 66, 71
Diamond Dogs (Bowie) 75, 135, 137
digital music technology 85–6
disco 39, 104, 128, 130, 134
Discovery (ELO) 130
'Doing Alright' (*Queen*) 64
'Donna' (*10cc*) 51–2, 62–4
double speed technique 63
double tracking technique 144 n.2
'Drive-in Saturday' (*Aladdin Sane*) 59, 113–14
Duran Duran band 133–4
Dylan, Bob 83, 112

Eagles rock band 80
The Electric Light Orchestra (ELO) rock band 1, 3, 5–6, 21, 30–1, 33, 40–1, 48, 51, 55 n.5, 57, 66–7, 74, 76, 84–5, 87, 118, 121, 123, 126, 131, 142–3
   classic line-up 77 n.4
   Concerto for a Rainy Day 129
   Discovery 130
   ELO 2 67
   Face the Music 55 n.5, 85
   Out of the Blue 22, 51, 129–30, 143
   Showdown 51
   Time 130
electronic techniques/technology 19, 49, 58, 61, 71, 91–2
electro-pop styles 38–9, 130
Emerson, Lake and Palmer (ELP) progressive rock band 42, 45, 121, 126, 138–9
EMI record label 40, 50, 96–7, 122
Eno, Brian 2, 16, 49, 60, 67–8, 115–16, 133, 136
entrepreneur, pop-rock 73, 105
environmental politics 101
'establishment music' 123
'Eve of Destruction' (McGuire) 112
Everett, Kenny 97
'Evil Woman' (*Face the Music*) 51, 85

Faces rock band 19, 37
Face the Music (ELO) 55 n.5, 85
'Fanfare for the Common Man' (Copland) 139
fans, music 13, 35, 45–6, 48, 53, 70, 75, 79–80, 82, 86, 89–90, 97, 99, 125, 139
Fast, Larry 141
Ferry, Bryan 2, 16, 74–5, 92, 110, 115
'Five O'clock in the Morning' (Godley and Creme) 108
'Five Years' (*The Rise and Fall of Ziggy Stardust and the Spiders from Mars*) 113
flanging effect 19, 33 n.2
Flesh and Blood (Roxy Music) 133–4
Fogarty, John 37
'Follow You Follow Me' (Genesis) 140
Ford, John 101

For Your Pleasure (Roxy Music) 2, 22, 67–8, 75, 110
'The Fountain of Salmacis' (*Nursery Cryme*) 141
Fragile (Yes) 140
Frame, Roddy 91
Freeman, Alan 'Fluff' 45, 48, 87
Free rock band 36
Freeze Frame (Godley and Creme) 133
Frey, Glen 80
Frith, Simon 16, 23, 80, 83, 89, 106, 116–17
Fuller, G. 92

Gabriel, Peter 126, 140–4
The Game (Queen) 128
Garber, J. 69–70
'The Gates of Delirium' (*Relayer*) 140
gender politics 114–17
Genesis progressive rock band 13, 21, 42–3, 45, 72–3, 121, 126, 140, 142
   Invisible Touch 77 n.5
   The Lamb Lies Down on Broadway 104, 130, 141
   Nursery Cryme 141
   Selling England by the Pound 104–5, 138
'Ghosts' (Japan) 141
Giltrap, Gordon 126, 140
glam rock style 9 n.1, 13–14, 22, 38–41, 48, 90, 114
Godley, Kevin 4, 16, 52, 55 n.5, 58, 94–7, 108, 120 n.1, 131–3, 142–3
   Consequences 108, 131, 133
   Freeze Frame 133
   L 133
'God Save the Queen' (The Sex Pistols) 107, 124, 127, 139
Going for the One (Yes) 139–40
'Golden Brown' (The Stranglers) 124
'Good Company' (*A Night at the Opera*) 111
'Good Morning Judge' (*Deceptive Bends*) 132
Gouldman, Graham 3–4, 52, 58, 94–7, 100 n.2, 109, 120 n.1, 131–3
Graham, Bill 106
The Grain of the Voice (Barthes) 110
'500 Greatest Albums,' *Rolling Stone*'s 82
Green, B. 82

Greenpeace organization (nongovernment) 101
Grossberg, L. 12
Grundy, Bill 122–3

'Hammer to Fall' (*The Works*) 111
hard rock 1, 30–1, 33 n.3, 36–7, 43, 50, 64–5, 71, 88, 116
Hardy, Phil 67
Harley, Steve 5, 9 n.2, 111–12
Harris, Bob 27–8, 46, 50, 55 n.5, 125, 139
Harrison, George 5, 18, 58, 133
Harvest record label, EMI's 35, 40
Haslam, Annie 140
Hayward, Justin 20
'Heartsong' (Giltrap) 140
heavy metal bands 30, 43, 48, 55 n.3, 71, 83, 124
hegemonic masculinity 116, 120
Hendrix, Jimi 31, 64
'Here Comes the Sun' (*Abbey Road*) 5, 58
heritage rock 46–7, 131
Heroes (Bowie) 60, 135–6, 143
'Heroes' (Bowie) 60, 125, 136
'Hey Rock and Roll' (Showaddywaddy) 108
'high-brow' music 18, 44, 98, 107
'high glam' artists 39–41, 114
hippie counterculture 23, 25, 71–2
Horne, H. 16, 106
Hot Space (Queen) 128
How Dare You! (10cc) 4, 108–10, 131
Howe, Steve 55 n.2
Hudson-Ford rock band 101
Hudson, Richard 101
The Human League electro-pop band 130
The 101ers pub rock band 123
Hunky Dory (Bowie) 55 n.6, 59, 112

'I Am the Walrus' (The Beatles) 3, 67
'Iceberg' (*How Dare You!*) 109–10
'I'd Like to Teach the World to Sing' (The New Seekers) 103
'I Know What I Like (In Your Wardrobe)' (*Selling England By the Pound*) 138
I Love the '70s (television series) 12
'I'm Not in Love' (*The Original Soundtrack*) 21, 24, 87, 94–6, 99, 131
I'm Not in Love: The Story of 10cc (10cc) documentary 131–2, 143

'In Every Dream Home a Heartache' (Roxy Music) 68, 110
Ingham, John 97
Innuendo (Queen) 129
'Innuendo' (*Innuendo*) 128
'intellectual' style of music 26–7, 44, 84, 107
Invisible Touch (Genesis) 77 n.5
'Is This the World We Created?' (*The Works*) 111
'Itchycoo Park' (Small Faces) 19, 33 n.2
'I Wanna Rule the World' (*How Dare You!*) 109, 131

Jackson, Michael 30, 142
The Jam new wave band 123–4
Japan new wave band 141, 144
Jazz (Queen) 128
'The Jean Genie' (*Aladdin Sane*) 76, 88
Jethro Tull progressive rock band 42, 45, 138
Jet record label 40
John, Elton 91
John Fogarty (Fogarty) 37
Junior Choice (radio programme) 86

Kassabian, A. 80
'Killer Queen' (*Sheer Heart Attack*) 50, 66, 76, 117
King Crimson rock band 2
King, Jonathon 3
The Kinks rock band 18, 112
Kirke, Simon 36
Korner, Alexis 44
Kubrick, Stanley 113
Kutulas, J. 25

L (Godley and Creme) 133
Laing, D. 73, 123, 139
The Lamb Lies Down on Broadway (Genesis) 104, 130, 141
Lang, Michael 106
Led Zeppelin rock band 13, 28, 31, 36–7, 44, 46, 50, 57, 64, 71, 121, 142
  Led Zeppelin IV 37
  The Song Remains the Same 46, 67
Lennon, John 16, 24, 51, 57–8, 83, 85
Lewis, G. H. 72
'Life on Mars' (*Hunky Dory*) 59, 93

Life on Mars (television crime drama) 58–9
Lift Off with Ayshea (television show) 12, 45, 74
Little Richard 114
Live and Let Live (10cc) 132
Lodger (Bowie) 60, 135
Logan, N. 88
'London Calling' (The Clash) 112
'long sixties' 11, 15–20
'Love Is the Drug' (*Siren*) 85, 133–4
Low (Bowie) 60–1, 135–6, 143
LP (Long Player) record 22
Lynne, Jeff 3, 51, 55 n.5, 66, 129–30

Made in Heaven (Queen) 129
Magic Years: Volume 1 documentary 93, 98
mainstream pop 26, 28, 30, 32, 46, 51, 58, 61, 66, 70, 76, 87–8, 104–5
'Make Me Smile (Come Up and *See* Me)' (Steve Harley and Cockney Rebel) 4, 9 n.2, 76
Manifesto (Roxy Music) 40, 133
Martin, George 18, 52
Massey, H. 21
'Masters of War' (Dylan) 112
Matlock, Glen 123
May, Brian 2, 31, 58, 64–5, 98, 127–8
McCartney, Paul 17, 58, 120 n.1
McCourt, T. 86
McCron, R. 70
McGuire, Barry 112
McKay, Andy 16, 115
McRobbie, Angela 69–70, 116–17
Meanwhile (10cc) 120 n.1
Melody Maker (newspaper) 25
Mercury, Freddie 2, 16, 65, 93–5, 97–8, 116–17, 126–9, 143
The Moody Blues rock band 20, 42, 66–7
Moroder, Giorgio 39
Motörhead rock band 124
Mott the Hoople rock band 64
The Move rock band 3
'Mr Blue Sky' (*Out of the Blue*) 129
Mud glam rock band 22, 38–9, 103
multi-latch technique 136
multitrack recording 20–1, 61–2
Murdoch, G. 70
music journalism 14, 24–8, 76, 106

Neanderthal Man (Hotlegs) 4
Never Mind the Bollocks (The Sex Pistols) 124, 144 n.1
New Musical Express (newspaper) 25, 46, 72, 121
New Romantic movement 137
The New Seekers pop group 103
News of the World (Queen) 127–9, 143
New Wave of British Heavy Metal (NWOBHM) label 124
A Night at the Opera (Queen) 22, 65, 111, 127, 129
'The Night Comes Down' (Queen) 65
Nightingale, Annie 125
'Nights in White Satin' (The Moody Blues) 20, 67
999 rock band 123
Noone, Peter 112
No Pussyfooting (Eno) 61, 77 n.1
'nostalgic innovation' 79
Nowak, R. 86
Numan, Gary 130, 135
Nursery Cryme (Genesis) 141

O'Grady, Terence J. 18
Oh Boy! (television show) 89
'Oh You Pretty Things' (*Hunky Dory*) 112
Oldfield, Mike 59–60, 63
Old Grey Whistle Test (*OGWT*) television show 28, 45–50, 65, 91, 93, 125, 139
The Old Grey Whistle Test Story documentary 46
Omnibus (television show) 46
The Original Soundtrack (10cc) 4, 94–5, 97, 108
Orwell, George 125
out-of-phase effect 19, 144 n.2
Out of the Blue (ELO) 22, 51, 129–30, 143
overtures 41–4

Page, Jimmy 37
Parker, Alan 43
Peel, John 45, 48
Pick of the Pops (radio programme) 86–7
Pidgeon, John 63
Pink Floyd: Live at Pompeii film 46
Pink Floyd progressive rock band 13, 28, 36, 42–3, 46, 121, 124

Animals 104, 125
Atom Heart Mother 42, 59
Dark Side of the Moon 43–4, 59, 125
pop promos 92
Wish You Were Here 125
Pink Floyd: The Wall film 43–4, 125
Plant, Robert 117, 124
Plasketes, G. M. 81
Plasketes, J. C. 81
playback technologies 81
political rock/voice 23, 26, 35, 100, 101–7
   (post)apocalypse 112–14
   awakenings 114–17
   recession, Britain 102
   sensibilities among youth 117–19
   social disease 107–12
Polydor label 40
Pop, Iggy 135
pop music 24–8, 36, 45, 123
'pop promos' 92
popular music 1, 18, 26–7, 29–30, 33, 46, 73, 102, 114, 119–21, 143–4. *See also* British popular music
   artists 1, 16, 25–6, 32, 49
   in early 1970s 20, 27, 45, 100, 103, 112
   as everyday soundtrack 80–5
   pop video 30
   reconstructing 12–15
post-modern pop 32
Potger, Keith 103
'Power to All Our Friends' (Richard) 103
pre-digital era 86, 89
pre-punk 1970s 17, 28, 112, 134
Presley, Elvis 40, 62, 81, 128
Price, Bill 124
Procul Harem rock band 19, 42, 124
progressive pop 6, 27–32, 48, 53, 59, 75–7, 84, 88, 94, 99–100, 102, 105, 107, 114, 118–20, 125–6, 129, 133, 137, 142–4
   artists 36, 51–4, 70, 74, 79–81, 87, 107, 119, 122, 126, 129
   crossover appeal of 69–75
   in early 1970s 11–12, 15, 17, 24, 57, 140
progressive rock 41–4, 48, 51, 55 n.4, 60, 70–1, 76, 87–8, 104, 126, 129, 137
   bands 35–6, 42–5, 137–8
   classical influences 73

protest songs 112. *See also* political rock/voice
The Psychomodo (Steve Harley and Cockney Rebel) 4, 75
'Psychomodo' (*The Psychomodo*) 111
public address (PA) system 43
pub rock 38, 123
punk, musical genre 1, 14, 17, 26–7, 30, 38, 80–1, 83, 100, 105, 118, 120–7, 129, 132, 135, 138–9, 143

Quatro, Suzie 55 n.1
Queen rock band 1–3, 5–6, 14, 16, 21, 27, 29–31, 33, 40–1, 47–50, 58, 61, 64, 73–6, 79, 84–5, 87, 91, 107, 111, 116–24, 126–8, 131
   Bohemian Rhapsody film 97
   A Day at the Races 127
   The Game 128
   Hot Space 128
   Innuendo 129
   Jazz 128
   line-ups of 2
   Made in Heaven 129
   News of the World 127–9, 143
   A Night at the Opera 22, 65, 111, 127, 129
   Queen 50, 64–5
   Queen II 50, 54, 64–5, 75, 88, 93
   Sheer Heart Attack 65–6, 75, 127
   The Works 111

radio 1, 19, 29, 36, 43–5, 48, 72, 85–8, 97, 99, 139
Ralphs, Mick 36
RCA record label 40–1, 55 n.6, 59
recording artists 16, 21, 85
recording studio 16–18, 21–2, 24, 60–1, 65, 107
record labels. *See specific record label*
Reed, Lou 40
reggae, musical genre 14, 132
Relayer (Yes) 140
Renaissance rock band 126, 140
'Revolution' (The Beatles) 23–4, 103
Revolver (The Beatles) 18–19, 23
Richard, Cliff 103
Richards, Keith 16

The Rise and Fall of Ziggy Stardust and the Spiders from Mars (Bowie) 1, 22, 49, 112–13
rock-and-roll 66–7, 71, 81, 121
rock artists 1, 14, 26–7, 29, 38, 43, 47, 57, 60, 64, 91, 106, 122, 126
rock festivals 26, 37, 43, 53, 96, 106, 116, 134
rock journalism 25–6, 33, 46
Rock, Mick 93, 114
rock music 23–8, 38, 43, 46–7, 106, 117–18, 120, 124, 135
Rogers, I. 82–3
Rogers, Paul 36
'Rollermania' (Bay City Rollers) 103
Rolling Stone (Magazine) 25, 37, 46, 82–3, 134
The Rolling Stones rock band 15, 18, 23, 26
'Roll Over Beethoven' (Berry) 66–7, 85
Ronson, Mick 1, 31, 115
Rothenbuhler, E. W. 86
rotoscoping technique 31
Roxy Music rock band 1–2, 5–6, 15, 27, 29–31, 33, 39–41, 47–9, 53, 58, 60, 65, 74, 76, 85, 87, 91–2, 106–7, 110, 115–17, 120, 124, 130, 133
   Avalon 134
   Flesh and Blood 133–4
   Manifesto 40
   Roxy Music 2, 134
   Siren 133
   Stranded 75, 134
   For Your Pleasure 2, 22, 67–8, 75, 110
'Rubber Bullets' (*10cc*) 62–3, 76, 88
Rubber Soul (The Beatles) 17–18
Rubettes pop group 22, 38, 103
Rutherford, Mike 43, 72, 140

'The Sacro-Iliac' (*Sheet Music*) 108
'Salisbury Hill' (Gabriel) 141
'Sand in My Face' (*10cc*) 62
Saturday Rock Show (radio programme) 45, 87
Scary Monsters (And Super Creeps) (Bowie) 137
Schmutz, V. 82
'Security' (Gabriel) 141
Selling England by the Pound (Genesis) 104–5, 138

'serious music' 25, 46, 48, 87, 91, 107
'The Seven Seas of Rhye' (*Queen*) 50, 53–4, 64, 74, 85, 88, 116
The Sex Pistols punk band 122–6
   Never Mind the Bollocks 124, 144 n.1
Sgt. Pepper's Lonely Hearts Club Band (The Beatles) 17–19, 22–3, 50, 54, 130
'Sgt. Pepper's Lonely Hearts Club Band' (The Beatles) 3
Sham 69
   punk band 123
'Shang-a-lang' (Bay City Rollers) 103
Shang-a-Lang (television show) 12, 45
'Sheer Heart Attack' (*News of the World*) 127
Sheer Heart Attack (Queen) 65–6, 75, 127
Sheet Music (10cc) 4, 22, 75, 94, 107–8, 131
'Shine a Little Love' (*Discovery*) 130
Showaddywaddy pop group 41, 103, 138
Showdown (ELO) 51
Shumway, D. 104
Simmons, C. 86
Siren (Roxy Music) 133
sixteen-track tape recorders 21, 62
Slade rock band 27, 39
'Sledgehammer' (Gabriel) 142
'Sleeping on the Sidewalk' (*News of the World*) 127
Small Faces rock band. *See* Faces rock band
Smile rock band 2
Smokie soft-rock band 103
soft metal bands 30
Solid Gold Sixty (radio programme) 87
The Song Remains the Same (Led Zeppelin) 46, 67
'Space Oddity' (Bowie) 24, 85, 90, 137
'Speed Kills' (*10cc*) 63
Spicer, M. 17
stadium rock 27, 33 n.3, 43
Staffell, Tim 2, 65
Stardust, Alvin 22, 38–40
'Starman' (*The Rise and Fall of Ziggy Stardust and the Spiders from Mars*) 48, 88, 90–1, 113
'Start' (The Jam) 124
state-of-the-art recording 18, 88
Station to Station (Bowie) 135
Status Quo rock band 27, 90–1

Blue for You 91
  hit songs of 37
Steve Harley and Cockney Rebel rock band 1, 4–6, 30–1, 33, 40–1, 47–8, 53, 58, 68–9, 74, 76, 85, 91, 111
  hit singles of 4
  The Psychomodo 4, 75
  Timeless Flight 111
Stewart, Eric 3–4, 52, 58, 94–6, 99, 107, 120 n.1, 131–2
Stewart, Rod 37
Stranded (Roxy Music) 75, 134
Strange, Steve 137
The Stranglers punk band 123–4
Stratton, J. 38
Strawberry Studios 4, 62, 88, 95–6
Strawbs rock band 101
'Street Fighting Man' (Rolling Stones) 23, 103, 107
Strummer, Joe 123
studio technology 11, 21, 24, 32, 52, 60–1, 79, 94, 107
Summer, Donna 39
'Supersonic Rocket Ship' (The Kinks) 112
Sutherland, Donald 142
The Sweet glam rock band 39–41, 75, 77 n.3
Swenson, John 72–3
symphonies 41–4

Take on Me (Aha) 30–1
Tales from Topographic Oceans (Yes) 104, 130, 139
Taylor, I. 43, 73–4, 115
Taylor, Roger 2, 58, 98–9, 127–8
technological expansion 33 n.1, 86
  amplification technology 66–7
  electronic technology 19, 49, 58, 61, 71, 91–2
  playback technologies 81
  recording technology 20–2, 42
  studio technology 11, 21, 24, 32, 52, 60–1, 79, 94, 107
  VCS3 electronic synthesizer 2, 91
teenyboppers 69–75
10cc rock band 1, 3–5, 16, 24, 27, 29–31, 33, 41, 48, 51–3, 61–3, 65, 69, 74, 76, 84–5, 87, 118, 120–1, 123, 131, 143

10cc 4, 63–4, 94
Deceptive Bends 100 n.2, 132
How Dare You! 4, 108–10, 131
  line-ups of 132–3
Live and Let Live 132
Meanwhile 120 n.1
The Original Soundtrack 4, 94–5, 97, 108
Sheet Music 4, 22, 75, 94, 107–8, 131
'10538 Overture' (ELO) 3, 51, 66, 85
Théberge, P. 17
'therapy culture' 109
'The Things We Do for Love' (*Deceptive Bends*) 27, 132
Thomas, Chris 124
Thomas, David 105
Thompson, Dave 133
Thriller (Jackson) 30, 142
Thuber, James 110
Time (ELO) 130
Timeless Flight (Steve Harley and Cockney Rebel) 111
Today (television programme) 122
Top Gear (radio show), BBC's 45
Top of the Pops (*TOTP*) television show 1, 40, 44–5, 48–9, 53–4, 74, 81, 85, 87, 88–94, 101, 104, 113, 115–17, 135, 138, 142
'A Town Called Malice' (The Jam) 124
Townshend, Pete 16, 31
track bouncing 18, 33 n.1, 62
Trynka, P. 39, 117
Tubular Bells (Oldfield) 59–60, 63
2001: A Space Odyssey (Kubrick) 113

'ubiquitous' music 80, 83, 85
UK Records music label, King's 3, 94
'Under Pressure' (*Hot Space*) 128
'Une Nuit a Paris' (*The Original Soundtrack*) 95, 97–8, 131
up-tempo rock style 20

VCS3 electronic synthesizer 2, 91
The Velvet Underground rock band 114
Vicious, Sid 126–7
'Virginia Plain' (Roxy Music) 48, 76, 91–2
Virgin Records 77 n.5
vocal tracks 95–6, 98, 110, 120 n.1, 136

Wakeman, Rick 24, 42, 139
Wall, D. 43, 73–4, 115
'The Wall Street Shuffle' (*Sheet Music*) 107–8
White Album (The Beatles) 23
white label 50, 55 n.7
A Whiter Shade of Pale (Procul Harem) 19
The Who rock band 15, 18, 26, 37, 64
Willis, P. 71–2
Wish You Were Here (Pink Floyd) 125
Wizzard glam rock band 9 n.1, 39
Woffinden, B. 88
The Wombles pop group 108
'Wondrous Stories' (*Going for the One*) 140
Woodmansey, Mick 'Woody' 1
Wood, Roy 3, 9 n.1, 39, 51, 66
The Works (Queen) 111
'Wuthering Heights' (Bush) 126

The Yardbirds rock band 3
Yes progressive rock band 13, 28, 42, 45, 121, 126, 142
  Fragile 140
  Going for the One 139–40
  Relayer 140
  Tales from Topographic Oceans 104, 130, 139
  The Yes 140
'Yesterday' (McCartney) 17
Young Americans (Bowie) 57, 135
youth culture 12, 26, 33, 37, 70–2, 74, 81, 103, 112, 115, 118

Ziggy Stardust 2, 59, 85, 90, 105, 112–14, 125, 134–5

Lightning Source UK Ltd.
Milton Keynes UK
UKHW020105060122
396701UK00005B/138